Educational Linguistics/TESOL,
Graduate School of Education
University of Pennsylvania
3700 Walnut Street/Cl
Philadelphia, PA 19104

ORIGINS OF THE YIDDISH LANGUAGE

LANGUAGE AND COMMUNICATION*
An Interdisciplinary Journal
Editor: Roy Harris, University of Oxford

The primary aim of the journal is to fill the need for a publication forum devoted to the discussion of topics and issues in communication which are of interdisciplinary significance. It will publish contributions from researchers in all fields relevant to the study of verbal and non-verbal communication.

Emphasis will be placed on the implication of current research for establishing common theoretical frameworks within which findings from different areas of study may be accommodated and interrelated.

By focusing on the many ways in which language is integrated with other forms of communicational activity and interaction behaviour it is intended to explore ways of developing a science of communication which is not restricted by existing disciplinary boundaries.

* Free specimen copy available on request.

LANGUAGE AND COMMUNICATION LIBRARY
Series Editor: Roy Harris, University of Oxford

ORIGINS OF THE YIDDISH LANGUAGE

Winter Studies in Yiddish Volume 1

Papers from the First Annual Oxford Winter Symposium in Yiddish
Language and Literature, 15–17 December 1985

Editor: Dovid Katz

Wolf Corob Fellow in Yiddish Language and Literature, Oxford Centre for Postgraduate
Hebrew Studies and Leslie Paisner Fellow at St. Antony's College, Oxford, U.K.

Published in cooperation with the Oxford Centre for Postgraduate
Hebrew Studies

Pergamon Press
OXFORD · NEW YORK · BEIJING · FRANKFURT
SÃO PAULO · SYDNEY · TOKYO · TORONTO

U.K.	Pergamon Press, Headington Hill Hall, Oxford OX3 0BW, England
U.S.A.	Pergamon Press, Maxwell House, Fairview Park, Elmsford, New York 10523, U.S.A.
PEOPLE'S REPUBLIC OF CHINA	Pergamon Press, Room 4037, Qianmen Hotel, Beijing, People's Republic of China
FEDERAL REPUBLIC OF GERMANY	Pergamon Press, Hammerweg 6, D-6242 Kronberg, Federal Republic of Germany
BRAZIL	Pergamon Editora, Rua Eça de Queiros, 346, CEP 04011, Paraiso, São Paulo, Brazil
AUSTRALIA	Pergamon Press Australia, P.O. Box 544, Potts Point, N.S.W. 2011, Australia
JAPAN	Pergamon Press, 8th Floor, Matsuoka Central Building, 1-7-1 Nishishinjuku, Shinjuku-ku, Tokyo 160, Japan
CANADA	Pergamon Press Canada, Suite No. 271, 253 College Street, Toronto, Ontario, Canada M5T 1R5

First edition 1987

British Library Cataloguing in Publication Data

Oxford Winter Symposium in Yiddish Language
and Literature (*1st : 1985*)
Origins of the Yiddish language : papers
from the First Annual Oxford Winter
Symposium in Yiddish Language and
Literature, 16–17 December 1985. —
(Language and communication library).
1. Yiddish language — History
I. Title   II. Katz, Dovid   III. Series
437'.947   PJ5113

ISBN 0 08 034156 X

Published as a supplement to *Language and Communication,* An
Interdisciplinary Journal

Printed in Great Britain by A. Wheaton & Co., Ltd., Exeter

LANGUAGE & COMMUNICATION
an interdisciplinary journal

CONTENTS

ORIGINS OF THE YIDDISH LANGUAGE

Language & Communication, Vol. 7, Supplement, pp. 1–5, 1987.
Printed in Great Britain.

0271-5309/87 $3.00 + .00
Pergamon Journals Ltd.

PREFACE

ON THE FIRST WINTER SYMPOSIUM

Yiddish linguistics is a small field focusing upon a minority language. Nevertheless, as a subject of human enquiry the discipline has a proud and intellectually complex history spanning nearly five centuries. Fascination with a language stretching at its geolinguistic peak over a huge portion of Europe, one that comprises the familiar Germanic with the exotic Semitic, is first documented in the works of early sixteenth century Christian scholars of Hebrew and Aramaic in Germany. By the early seventeenth century, Johann Buxtorf the Elder (1609: 639–669) produced a highly sophisticated survey of the language, that was surpassed only in the eighteenth by Chrysander's (1750a, 1750b) studies and Friedrich's (1784) lexicographical and dialectological compendium. Alongside this academic interest, inspired at the outset by the spirit of European Humanism, a host of extraneously motivated works on the language were published, among others, by missionaries, anti-Semites and writers of business people's manuals (see Katz 1986).

The rise of the 'Science of Judaism' movement amongst German-Jewish scholars in the early nineteenth century led its leaders to research Yiddish linguistics tangentially (Zunz 1832: 428–442) but their socially conditioned biases against the language precluded followups. In the arena of general linguistics, the ascent of the comparative method encouraged the incorporation of Yiddish into the orbit of both Germanic linguistics (Saineanu 1889 and Landau 1896) and Hebrew philology (Lebensohn 1874) by the late nineteenth century. In the twentieth, Yiddish linguistics came into its own by redefinition as a research discipline in and of itself, rather than a satellite of another, by its modern founder, Ber Borokhov (1913a; 1913b). His works posthumously inspired the golden era of Yiddish linguistics in interwar Eastern Europe. Its crowning achievement was the establishment of the Yivo Institute in Vilna in 1925 (See Shtif 1925 and Weinreich 1925).

The annihilation of most of Yiddish speaking European Jewry and its scholars by the Nazis and their collaborators, and the resulting irrecoverable loss of a vast quantity of unpublished work, are tragedies of immense proportions. Nevertheless, Yiddish linguistics as a university field of professional research was able to reemerge and to blossom anew, in good measure due to the lifework of Max and Uriel Weinreich, who both escaped the Nazis thanks to the coinciding of the Fifth International Congress of Linguists in Brussels, 28 August–2 September 1939, with the German invasion of Poland. Max Weinreich, a delegate from Vilna, read a paper on the origins of the Yiddish language at that Congress (Weinreich 1939), to which he had brought his teenage son Uriel. Max Weinreich at City College, and Uriel Weinreich at Columbia University, both in New York, succeeded in bringing Yiddish linguistics into the postwar mainstream of Western academia. Their broadly conceived approach incorporates research in linguistic theory benefitting from the fertile testing ground provided by Yiddish as well as study of the history and structure of Yiddish and its interaction with its Germanic, Semitic and Slavonic cognates. The emergence of Oxford as a centre of Yiddish Studies, with an emphasis upon linguistics, would not have been conceivable were it not for the Weinreichs' legacy.

Two factors are particularly conspicuous in the development of Yiddish Studies at Oxford. First is the Bodleian Library's vast Yiddish collection, deriving chiefly from its acquisition in 1829 of the Oppenheimer Collection which has long attracted Yiddish researchers to Oxford (see Judd 1983: 12–13). Second, and in a sense the key catalyzing force, is the work of the Oxford Centre for Postgraduate Hebrew Studies, an associate institute of the University, founded in 1972 by Dr David Patterson to provide for the expansion and enhancement of Jewish Studies at Oxford University. From the very outset, Yiddish Studies were incorporated into the Centre's agenda. The early and consistent assistance of Mr Ron May, formerly Senior Assistant Librarian of the Department of Oriental Books in the Bodleian Library, Professor Chone Shmeruk and Professor Chava Turniansky, both of the Yiddish Department of Hebrew University, Jerusalem, and of Professor Marvin Herzog of the Linguistics Department at Columbia University, New York, is gratefully acknowledged.

In a closely coordinated array of activities collectively subsumed by its *Oxford Programme in Yiddish,* the Centre organizes courses, conferences and publications in the field of Yiddish language and literature, while providing doctoral supervision for the University's graduate research students who have come to Oxford from America, Israel, Great Britain and Europe to work on theses in the field. At the Centre's initiative, degree options in Yiddish Literature have been introduced into the BA in the University's Faculty of Medieval and Modern Languages and the MPhil and MSt in Modern Jewish Studies in its Faculty of Oriental Studies. Two international conferences were organized jointly with Hebrew University and Columbia University in 1979 and 1983. Since 1982, the Centre has offered the *Oxford Summer Programme in Yiddish Language and Literature,* an intensive one month summer course at which some three hundred students from twenty-two countries have studied Yiddish language, literature and linguistics in a rigorous academic framework. While many individuals and institutions have helped to facilitate these and other advances, the overriding factor in their successful establishment has been the dedicated support and wise counsel of Dr Patterson, the University's Cowley Lecturer in Postbiblical Hebrew, and Professor S. S. Prawer, its Taylor Professor of German Language and Literature.

In the years since Uriel Weinreich's untimely death in 1967, the wider intellectual interest in Yiddish linguistics which he did so much to foster has continued to grow. Research is pursued by scholars in the fields of General Linguistics, German, Hebrew and Aramaic, and Slavonic, as well as those in the adjacent disciplines of folklore, history and comparative literature. The number of specialists in Yiddish linguistics per se has multiplied severalfold in the course of the last decade.

The need for both an annual meeting and the swift publication of its work is felt more acutely with each passing year. By establishing the yearly *Oxford Winter Symposium in Yiddish Language and Literature,* the Centre hopes to inspire new research by providing an annual forum of international scope that is sharply focused upon a single coherent issue, while facilitating the publication of its papers on a regular basis in the *Winter Studies in Yiddish* series, of which this is the inaugural volume.

The first Winter Symposium was opened on Sunday evening, 15 December 1985 by Dr Patterson, who read a telegram of greetings from the dean of Yiddish linguists, Professor Solomon A. Birnbaum, just over a week before Professor Birnbaum's ninety-fourth birthday. A welcoming speech was delivered by Dr Geza Vermes, Reader in Jewish Studies at the University of Oxford and Professorial Fellow at Wolfson College, Oxford.

The organizers are proud that the volume begins with the two papers sent by Professor Birnbaum to the Winter Symposium. Both deal with crucially important methodological strategies that have been sadly neglected. The first outlines the paleographic method which he pioneered for dating Old Yiddish manuscripts. The second sketches the strategies for discovering etymologies, or more precisely, for avoiding self delusion via false etymology. By debunking all of the heretofore proposed etymologies for the target item—thought to be one of the oldest in the language—without proposing a new one, Professor Birnbaum delivers the powerful and timely message that etymological searches must be conceived in a spirit of professional restraint and within the structural context of amply attested phonological and morphological change in analogous noncontroversial items. The systematic and cautious extrapolation from the known to the unknown underlies both of Professor Birnbaum's papers.

The organizers are equally proud that two young scholars, Christopher Hutton and Dov-Ber Kerler, both doctoral candidates in the University of Oxford, make their academic débuts in this volume. Mr Hutton's paper studies the double and triple negative in older Yiddish texts, drawing inferences on the reconstruction of the oldest stages of the language. Mr Kerler succeeds in abstracting theories on the origins of Yiddish from the work of interwar Soviet Yiddish linguists, whose conspicuous concerns were oriented toward normativist issues.

It is known from the history of ideas that new bursts of intellectual energy in a field of human enquiry are from time to time characterized by a number of independently generated analogous results. The first Winter Symposium will perhaps best be remembered in the history of Yiddish linguistics for relocating the presumed origins of Yiddish to the Danube Basin while rejecting the traditionally accepted Rhineland. This stampede was presaged as long ago as the 1920s by the lonely voice of Matisyohu Mieses (1924: 269–318). In recent years it was launched by Robert King's (1979: 7) question, "Where is Loter?" By the first Winter Symposium the notion of a rather more easterly origin of the language is supported in varying degrees and via diverse research strategies in the papers of Faber, Jofen, Katz, King and Wexler. At the same time, the Rhineland theory itself yields new modification in Fuks's paper.

To ensure rapid publication, a deadline requiring Winter Symposium participants to submit final versions of their papers within three weeks of the Symposium was strictly enforced. It is regretted, but not unexpected, that not all participants were able to meet this requirement and it is hoped that papers not included will appear elsewhere in due course. The reader is invited to peruse the schedule of papers actually read before the Winter Symposium. It appears on p. 143.

The scholars whose work appears on these pages come to Yiddish linguistics with varying academic backgrounds and styles. Apart from requiring adherence to the bibliographic format adopted, editing has been kept to a minimum. One important exception concerns the nomenclature of Yiddish dialectology. The confusing term "Central Yiddish", used ambiguously both for the dialect whose heartland is Congress Poland (Prilutski 1920: 79) and for the parts of Hungary and Czechoslovakia intermediate between Western and Eastern Yiddish (Birnbaum 1979: 95) is deleted throughout. This dialect, popularly known as "Polish" is consistently referred to as *Mideastern Yiddish,* contrasting with the two other principal varieties of Eastern Yiddish—*Southeastern Yiddish* (popularly "Ukrainian") and *Northeastern Yiddish* (popularly "Lithuanian") which are nonambiguous and are retained untouched (see Katz 1983: 1020–1021).

Where linguistic accuracy in the narrow sense is not at stake, Yiddish names, concepts and bibliographic citations are transcribed, as is traditional in the field, according to the system of the Yivo Institute for Jewish Research, with some modification. The system is based upon approximations of English orthographic values for phonemic units of Standard Yiddish, which is closest to Northeastern Yiddish in its phonemic inventory. Its salient features are [c]→*ts,* [č]→*tsh,* [j]→*y,* [ǰ]→*dzsh,* [š]→*sh,* [x]→*kh,* [ž]→*zh,* [ɛ]/[ə]/[ɪ]→*e,* [ɔ]→*o.* An exception is made in the case of Professor Birnbaum's paper, where his own transcriptions are retained at his request.

While fully adequate for the transcription of modern (= Eastern) Yiddish names and bibliographic references, where a closer phonetic transcription of one or another of the dialects would serve only to complicate matters unnecessarily, the Yivo system was not designed to cope with the rather different phonemic system of older forms of Western Yiddish. The present volume introduces a modified version adapted to Western Yiddish works written and published on Western Yiddish speech territory. Its key features are as follows. Vowels 24 (Mideastern [aj] ‖ Southeastern and Northeastern [ej]), and 44 (Mideastern and Southeastern [ɔj] ‖ Northeastern [ej]), merged as unitary [ā] in the West, are transcribed *aa.* Vowels 42 (Mideastern and Southeastern[ɔj] ‖ Northeastern [ej]), and 54 (Mideastern [ɔu]/[ō]/[ɔ] ‖ Southeastern [ɔu]/[u] ‖ Northeastern [ɔj]/[uj]), generally merged as unitary [ɔu] in the West, are transcribed *ou.*

The Winter Symposium's exceptional organization is principally due to the talents of Ms Jean Nightingale, the Oxford Centre's Administrative Secretary, who serves as Administrative Director of the Oxford Programme in Yiddish. Warm thanks are also due to Christopher Hutton and Dov-Ber Kerler who spared neither time nor energy to ensure the success of the project from the day it was conceived. John and Elsie Roberts, steward and housekeeper of Yarnton Manor, the Oxford Centre's early seventeenth century estate, arranged for a hearty welcoming supper. The hospitality of St Cross College in organizing a wine party at the Winter Symposium's conclusion is thankfully acknowledged.

The appearance of the volume is due to both the vision and the efficiency of Pergamon Press. The organizers are particularly grateful to Dr Ivan F. Klimeš, Associate Publisher and Director of Pergamon Press, and to Ms Sammye Haigh, Managing Editor for Social Sciences and Ms Jane Buekett, Journals Production Controller, for their invaluable advice and assistance at each stage of the project. Ms Marion Aptroot (Wolfson College, Oxford), Ms Devra Asher (St Cross College, Oxford) and Mr David Schneider (Exeter College, Oxford), kindly gave of their time to assist in proofing. Sincere thanks are due to Roy Harris, Professor of General Linguistics in the University of Oxford, to Mr Robert Maxwell, publisher of Pergamon Press, and to Ms Elizabeth Maxwell, for making this book possible.

REFERENCES

BEN-ZEEYV, Y.-L. 1874 *Seyfer talmud leshoyn ivri.* Vilna, Romm.

BESCH, W., KNOOP, U., PUTSCHKE, W. and WIEGAND, H. (eds) 1983 *Dialektologie. Ein Handbuch zur deutschen und allgemeinen Dialektforschung* [= *Handbduch zur Sprach- und Kommunikationswissenschaft, 1*]. Walter de Gruyter, Berlin, New York.

BIRNBAUM, S. A. 1979 *Yiddish. A Survey and a Grammar.* Manchester University Press, Manchester & University of Toronto Press, Toronto.

BOROKHOV, B. 1913a Di ufgabn fun der yidisher filologye. In Niger, S. (ed.), 1913, pp. 1–22.

BOROKHOV, B. 1913b Di biblyotek funem yidishn filolog. Fir hundert yor yidishe shprakh-forshung. In Niger, S. (ed.), pp. 1–68.

BUXTORF, J. 1609 *Thesaurus grammaticus linguae sanctae Hebraeae.* Conrad Waldkirch, Basel.

CHRYSANDER, W. C. J. 1750a *Jüdisch-Teutsche Grammatick.* J. C. Meisner, Leipzig, Wolfenbüttel.

CHRYSANDER, W. C. J. 1750b *Unterricht vom Nutzen des Juden-Teutschen.* J. C. Meisner, Wolfenbüttel.

FRIEDRICH, C. W. 1784 *Unterricht in der Judensprache, und Schrift. zum Gebrauch für Gelehrte und Ungelehrte.* C. G. Ragoczy, Prenzlau.

GELBER, M. H. (ed.) 1986 *Identity and Ethos. A Festschrift for Sol Liptzin on the Occasion of his 85th Birthday.* Peter Lang, New York, Berne, Frankfurt am Main.

JUDD, R. 1983 *Report of the Oxford Centre for Postgraduate Hebrew Studies, Eleventh Academic Year 1982-1983.* Oxford Centre for Postgraduate Hebrew Studies, Oxford.

KATZ, D. Dialektologie des Jiddischen. In Besch, W. *et al.* (eds.) 1983, pp. 1018-1041.

KATZ, D. 1986 On Yiddish, in Yiddish and for Yiddish: five hundred years of Yiddish scholarship. In Gelber, 1986, pp. 23–36.

KING, R. D. 1979 New perspectives on the history of Yiddish. The evidence of the German component. Paper placed before the International Conference on Research in Yiddish Language and Literature at the Oxford Centre for Postgraduate Hebrew Studies, 6–9 August.

LANDAU, A. 1896 Das Deminutivum der galizisch-jüdischen Mundart. Ein Capitel aus der jüdisch-deutschen Grammatik. *Deutsche Mundarten* **1**, 46–58.

LEBENSOHN, A. 1874 [= Avrom Dov-Ber Mikhaliskher] Hakoyheyn ben Khayim, " Yisroyn leodom". Subtextual commentary in Ben-Zeeyv, Y.-L., 1874.

MIESES, M. 1924 *Die jiddische Sprache. Eine historische Grammatik des Idioms der integralen Juden Ost- und Mitteleuropas.* Benjamin Harz, Berlin, Vienna.

NIGER, S. (ed.) 1913 *Der pinkes. Yorbukh far der geshikhte fun der yidisher literatur un shprakh, far folklor, kritik un biblyografye.* B. A. Kletskin, Vilna.

PRILUTSKI, N. 1920 *Tsum yidishn vokalizm. Etyudn* [= his *Yidishe dyalektologishe forshungen. Materyaln far a visnshaftlekher gramatik un far an etimologish verterbukh fun der yidisher shprakh 4 = Noyakh Prilutskis ksovim* 10]. Warsaw.

SAINEANU, L. 1889 *Studiu Dialectologic asupra Graiului Evreo-German.* Eduard Wiegand, Bucharest.

SHTIF, N. 1925 Vegn a yidishn akademishn institut. *De organizatsye fun der yidisher visnshaft,* Vilna, 3–34.

WEINREICH, M. 1925 Vilner tezisn vegn yidishn visnshaftlekhn institut. *Di organizatsye fun der yidisher visnshaft,* Vilna, 35–39.

WEINREICH, M. 1939 A tentative scheme for the history of Yiddish. *Vme Congrès International des Linguistes. Bruxelles, 28 août-2 septembre 1939. Résumés des Communications,* Brussels, pp. 49–51.

ZUNZ, L. 1832 *Die gottesdienstlichen Vorträge der Juden, historisch entwickelt. Ein Beitrag zur Alterthumskunde und biblischen Kritik, zur Literatur- und Religionsgeschichte.* A. Asher, Berlin.

Dovid Katz
Oxford, January 1986

Language & Communication, Vol. 7, Supplement, pp. 7–14, 1987.
Printed in Great Britain.

0271-5309/87 $3.00+ .00
Pergamon Journals Ltd.

TWO METHODS

SOLOMON A. BIRNBAUM

Toronto

I. Paleography: Manuscripts in Old Yiddish

The great libraries of Europe and America contain a considerable number of Old Yiddish manuscripts. These are valuable sources for research into the linguistics and phonology of Old Yiddish, literature in Old Yiddish, Ashkenazic biography, the history of Ashkenazic settlements, history of the halacha and paleography of the Ashkenazic type of the Hebrew script. Regrettably, only few have been published so that most of the material remains a hidden treasure.

In many cases a manuscript is of value to research only if it is known when and where it was penned; it is also sometimes necessary to know as much as possible about the scribe himself. In some manuscripts there is a colophon, a formal ending whch contains this information, or at least part of it. But this is rare: either the scribe provided no colophon, or the end of the manuscript is missing. Hence the editor or the cataloguer has to determine the date and provenance of the manuscript. He can draw conclusions from a number of facts: the kind of writing material, the kind of paper used, watermarks (if any), the writing instrument, the ink, internal evidence. Conclusions based on these facts will only in rare cases lead to sufficiently precise dates. That, however, can be achieved by the paleographical method. In order to make use of it, the editor or cataloguer of a manuscript written in the Hebrew alphabet must know not only the language very well but the script, too.

Manuscripts written in the Square style will not be difficult to read but cursive or mashait writing presents, in general, various degrees of difficulty—and these are the styles in which very many, probably the great majority, of the manuscripts are written. Mashait is an old term which I have revived, in order to replace the nonsensical term "Rabbinic writing". I have, however, narrowed its meaning to make it more precise. It is a formal book hand developed from Cursive (see Birnbaum 1971: 189, 311). The old sense was "Non-Square", i.e., it included both cursive *and* mashait. However, in the case of the Ashkenazic script there is, to the practiced eye, at no period any great difficulty in reading cursive or mashait.

The Ashkenazic type is only one among many kinds of very varied form. Some differ so much from Ashkenazic as to be at first unrecognizable as being Hebrew scripts. The difference is not simply that between Ashkenazic and Sephardic, as one might imagine on the basis of the present ignorant and ridiculous usage by which all non-Ashkenazim, including Baghdadim, Bukharim, Temanim, etc., etc., are included in a single entity termed Sephardim. This misconception has made it possible to encounter a Jew whose ancestors, far from having seen Spain, never left Asia, yet who thinks he is a Sephardi!

As far as determining dates is concerned, Yiddish has a certain advantage when compared to Hebrew. Hebrew manuscripts are mostly written in Square or mashait style—rarely in cursive. Yiddish manuscripts, on the other hand, are mostly cursive, occasionally mashait, but never Square.

Now, Square script changes very, very slowly over time, so that the determination of even a very approximate date is usually extremely difficult. But the pace of cursive development is fairly quick, so that one can often arrive at rather precise results.

Let me give an illustration of how a manuscript was actually dated by the paleographical method.

About forty years ago I ordered photostats of folios 129v–130r of the Paris MS Héb. 589. These pages contain a little epic poem (incipit *Iüdišer štam*), part of which I intended to publish (see now Birnbaum 1979: 157f). The catalogue estimated the date as "XVI siècle". One should realise that the authors of catalogues, or scholars who had worked on manuscripts in their research, had gained a certain amount of experience in matters paleographical, but had not had systematic paleographical training and were not paleographers. In fact, no catalogue of Hebrew manuscripts has had the assistance of a paleographer. No disrespect is intended, but the expertise of these cataloguers and scholars was in the contents of the manuscripts rather than the forms of their script.

In other contexts it might well be satisfactory to date a manuscript within a century, but in this case more precision was needed, and an exact examination of the script was necessary.

The natural method is to compare the form of each letter with its form as it appears in dated manuscripts. Those whose forms are closest to the forms in our manuscript provide us with its date.

I had at that time a considerable collection of photostats and photos of specimens of dated manuscripts (and inscriptions), as well as alphabet tables, which I had myself drawn from manuscripts and photostats. Having sufficient experience, I did not have to examine every letter of the alphabet but was able to simplify the process by examining only certain characteristic letters (see Fig. 1: a page of the manuscript, and Fig. 2: my sketch of relevant letters and the documented lifespans of their forms).

On looking through my dated material, I noted down for each form of letter close to the Paris manuscript, the first and last years in which it had appeared. I was able to use this method because the forms of the various letters do not change all at the same time, but each letter goes its own individual way. Thus each letter has its own particular span of time and there are considerable differences in the length of these periods. It is therefore reasonable to state that such a manuscript as ours was penned during the time span which all the letters have in common. This was the period between the latest year when a certain form came into existence, and the earliest year when a certain form had disappeared.

In our case, examining the forms of final *pe* and *ayin,* I found these years to be 1551 and 1596. This is a span of less than two generations. It would, therefore, not be too risky to think that the middle of this period would not be far from the time our manuscript was penned. The middle year, 1574, we may for the sake of convenience, call the paleographical date.

Many years later I learned that there *is* a date in the manuscript; the cataloguer obviously did not notice it. And that year is 5339 i.e. 1579. The paleographical date and the real one were identical. This degree of precision is of course fortuitous, but to have arrived at the correct quarter of a century is not.

Another illustration. Earlier, in 1934, I made a dating experiment. Sitting in the British Museum Library with a manuscript in Old Yiddish (Add. 19972) written in the mashait

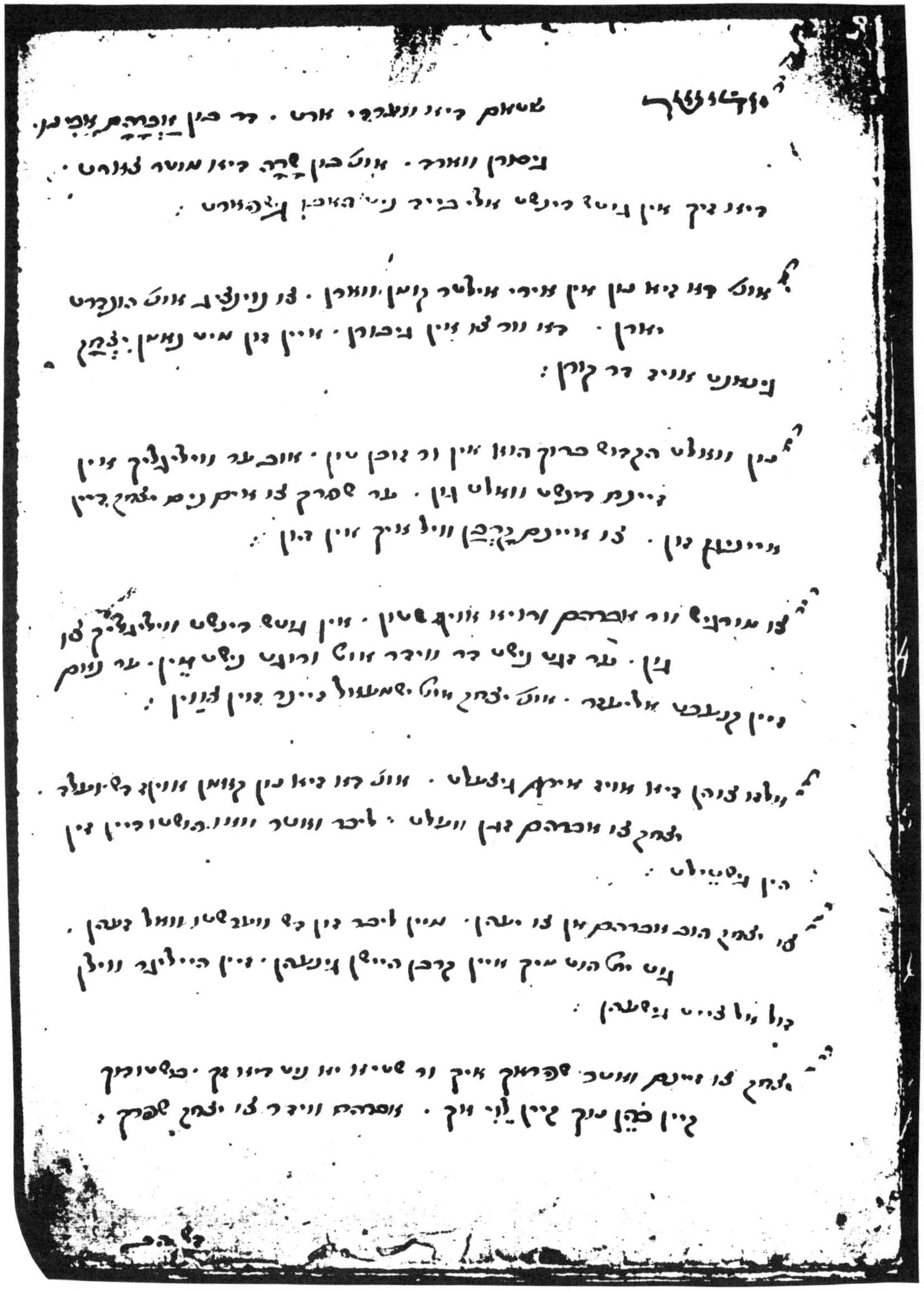

Fig. 1. A page of Paris MS Héb. 589.

1421 – 1608

1421 – 1750

1499 –

1428 – 1596

1344 – 1674
1515 –

1532 – 1662

1551 – 1698

1421 – 1700

Fig. 2. Select Yiddish letter forms and their documented lifespans.

style, I did not know its date but did know that it was, in fact, dated. I should, therefore, be able, to test the paleographical method. I examined each letter of the alphabet and arrived at a dating between near the end of the fourteenth century and the first quarter of the fifteenth. This resulted in a paleographical date of 1410. I then looked up the colophon: the year was 5153, i.e. 1393. The difference between the paleographical and the real date was, accordingly, only seventeen years—a perfectly satisfactory result.

Later in the same year, I made a further test and determined the paleographical date of British Library manuscript Add. 26919, written in Ashkenazic cursive, as 1553. On then referring to the colophon, I found the date to be 5309, i.e. 1549 (details of both experiments are to be found in Birnbaum 1971: 343–345).

The paleographical method is both natural and reliable if the eyes of the researchers—and preferably also their hands—are familiar with form, for paleography is concerned only with form: the form of writing, letters or other symbols. Anything else connected with writing, such as writing materials, their form (scrolls, codices), type of books, binding, etc., is beyond the purview of paleography.

It is most regrettable that today no one seems to specialize in research in Hebrew script during the three millennia of its existence. My own paleographical work has been only a beginning.

REFERENCES

BIRNBAUM, S. A. 1971 *The Hebrew Scripts*. E. J. Brill, Leiden. *Part two: The Plates*. London, 1954–1957.
BIRNBAUM, S. A. 1979 *Yiddish. A Survey and a Grammar*. University of Toronto Press, Toronto and Manchester University Press, Manchester.

II. Etymology: davənən

An unusually large number of etymologies have been proposed for Yiddish *davənən* 'pray (the established Jewish prayers)', a word used many times a day, every day of the year.

(1) *dafnən* from the Hebrew *daf*, which has the figurative meaning 'leaf of a book (= two pages)'. Because one turns the pages of a prayer book?

(2) Lithuanian *davana*, Lettish *dovana* 'gift' "because *mínxə/minḥá* which is the name of a prayer, originally meant in Hebrew 'gift'". How could the name of one prayer—and that, quantitatively speaking, the least important one—become the term for praying in general? And who in the last two thousand years would have thought of the original meaning 'offering' when he spoke, heard, wrote or read the name *tplt mnḥh* 'afternoon prayer?'.

(3) The English *dawn*. Because morning is the time of prayer? But normally the Jewish morning prayer is not said at dawn, and there are important prayers at other times of the day. The proposer evidently did not know the pronunciation of the word and took the *w* as the German *w*.

(4) *Latin devovere*. Because in prayer one devotes oneself to God?

(5) Latin *divinus*. Because prayer is a Godly affair?

(6) Arabic *dîwân* 'collection of poems'. Because a "prayer" consists of a collection of

hymns, poems and prayers? It is rather surprising that, as far as I know, nobody has proposed the Arabic word from which *dîwân* is derived—*dawwana* 'record, set down, write'.

(7) Hebrew *d-ovinu/dˀbynw* 'of our father' because each of the three daily prayers was, according to a midrash, instituted by one of "our Fathers", i.e. the Patriarchs.

These etymologies are so bizarre, absurd and phonologically impossible that it is superfluous to refute them.

(8) The Arabic *daʿwa* is supposed to have come into Yiddish from Turkish Jews. This implies the existence of Turkish speaking Jews in former centuries, or at least of Jews who were so strongly influenced by their Islamic environment that they adopted a religious term. However, there seem to be no historical sources which mention Turkish speaking Jews. In the various lands which became the Ottoman Empire the Jews spoke Yevanic from late antiquity onwards, Arvic from Islamic times onwards and Jidezmu (*Jidyó, Jidic, Jidish*) from the end of the fifteenth century onwards, with the arrival of the Sephardic refugees. Nor seems anything to be known of a Jewish influx into the East Ashkenazic area from the south, apart from that of the Karaites. They came in small numbers and kept themselves apart from the Rabbanites. They did not speak "Turkish" i.e. Osmanli, but a Turkic language of their own (Karai). In a glossary (see Kowalski 1927) only the Hebrew word *tefila* appears for 'prayer'. So the *daʿwa* etymology via the "Turkish Jews" cannot be accepted. Further, the Turkish word *dava* (< Arabic *daʿwa*) does not mean 'prayer' at all. It signifies 'lawsuit, charge, doctrine'; in the form *davet* it means 'invitation'.

Leaving Turkish, we now turn to the possibility of the word coming direct from Arabic. What channel could there have been to cause a word from Arabic speaking regions to penetrate into northeastern Europe? Also, the specific Arabic word for 'prayer' is not *daʿwa* but *ṣalât* (cf. Talmudic *ṣly* 'pray'), while 'prayer' is but one meaning of *daʿwa,* and that a secondary one. the word normally signifies 'case, action, suit, lawsuit, invitation'. It is not used for the official prayers.

Another obstacle to *daʿwa* is the presence of an ayin, which is a consonant. Hence *daʿwa* would have had to come into Yiddish via a non-Semitic Islamic language, in which the original ayin of the Arabic had already disappeared. Such a language could have been Turkish or Persian. That it was not Turkish we have just seen. For Persian the same reasons hold good. Here *daʾva* does not mean 'prayer' at all, but 'quarrel, dispute, litigation, lawsuit' while the form *daʾvet* signifies 'invitation, call, convivial meeting'. Again, there is the same geographical difficulty as with Arabic and Turkish, namely the great distance between the Persian speaking area and that of Yiddish. We cannot, on the strength of this very partial phonetic similarity between *daʾva* and *davənən,* reasonably postulate the existence of some Oriental Jews who brought the word to the Eastern Ashkenazim. One would also expect that had there been such an influence, it would have left more traces in Yiddish. But there are none.

(9) The most recent etymology proposed was that by my late friend M. Kosover (1964: 365–362 [=Yiddish pagination 166–169]). Nobody, as far as I know, has opposed or discussed it and D. L. Gold (1983:8) has recently accepted it.

Kosover's note can be summarised as follows. In the Paris MS. Héb. 586 of the early fifteenth century we find many times *dr ḥzn dwynṭ,* i.e. *der xazən dɔint* 'the "cantor" prays'. In the case of the "cantor" the term *dɔinən* is used, to differentiate it from the praying of the congregation, when the word *ôrən* is employed. The source of *dɔinən* is

the MHG verb *dœnen* 'sing, play, sound'. Now, in the regions of Minsk and Vitebsk in Byalo-Russia, Yiddish has *dɔinən* instead of *davənən* exactly as in the Paris MS. This identity proves that we have here the source of the subdialectal form and thus have discovered the etymology of *davənən*. The development of *dɔinən* to *davənən* was effected by "diftongyn-cjrikgang".

Let us now examine his discussion. I have written *dɔinən* in order to present his reading. However, there was never such a word in early Yiddish. He simply pronounced the letters he saw as if the word were written according to the present day spelling system. But it is obvious that it must be pronounced according to the system of early Yiddish. There the sequence *wy* is the sign for the *Umlaut* of /o/ or /u/. Therefore *dwynṭ* is to be pronounced as one of these four: /dönt, dȫnt, dünt, dǖnt/. Our word is, of course, the second: *dȫnt,* the equivalent of MHG *dœnt* and the translation is simply 'sings, chants', or, to use the identical English word, 'intones' (some English translations of the liturgy use this term).

We now turn to a phonological examination of this etymology. The first problem is to explain how the /ɔi/ of *dɔinən* became the /av/ of *davənən*. Kosover created the problem because he proceeded from the unspoken assumption—self-evident to him—that the /ɔi/ of the northern dialect is the original Yiddish form, this dialect representing the "real" Yiddish, as it were. He then equated the pair *dɔinən/davənən* with pairs like *mɔiər/movər* 'wall', *bɔiən/bovən* 'build', *zɔiər/zovər* 'sour' and concluded from this parallelism that *davənən* is derived from *dɔinən*.

There are three principal objections to this equation. Firstly, the two forms compared belong to two very different dialects, /ɔi/ to the northern, /ɔv/ to the southern. They therefore are normally not comparable. Secondly, in our case it is not a question of /ɔi/ and /ɔv/ at all but of /ɔi/ and /av/. Kosover could have chosen a certain northern dialect which actually has the /av/ form but presumably did not know of it. Thirdly, he correctly gives MHG *dœnen* as the source of *dɔinən* but does not explain how this development came about, probably not seeing any problem here. However, there is one. The Yiddish representative of MHG <œ> (= /ȫ/) is not /ɔi/ but /ȫ/ which later was unrounded and finally diphthongized, e.g. MHG *schœne* 'clear, bright, shining, beautiful'—Yiddish *śö:n > śe:n > śɛin > śain* 'beautiful'. Our word is therefore to be read as *dȫnt.* If it still existed in Yiddish it would be **dainən, dɛinən* (or perhaps *tɛinən*), not *davənən*.

Another phonological problem: If *dɔinən* were the original form, how could the /v/ in *davənən* be explained? I cannot see any phonetic likelihood for such a development. We would have to assume a *creatio e nihilo.*

Further: if *dɔinən* were the original form, its MHG equivalent would be *dûnen*, not *dœnen,* in the same way as northern *hɔiz* corresponds to MHG *hûs* 'house'. However, there is no word *"dûnen"* in MHG. In short, there never was a word *dɔinən* in early Yiddish, and the real word, *dȫnən,* could not have developed into *davənən*.

A semantic examination leads to the same result. Kosover tacitly assumes the equation 'sing, play, sound' (the meanings of MHG *dœnen*) = 'to pray', or rather, the development of 'sing, play, sound' > 'sing prayers' > 'pray'. Although the contents of the "cantor's" singing are prayers, this does not give us the right to establish that transfer of meaning. The "cantor" prays, of course, like everybody else in the congregation, but the term *dȫnən* is concerned only with the way in which he does it—in contrast to the others, he renders the prayers aloud and in a musical form. Such a transfer could not have occurred here.

Certain prayers are not sung by him but are prayed silently as they are by everyone else. The scribe of MS Heb. 586 could not have written that the "cantor" $d\bar{o}nt$ such a silent prayer because one cannot sing silently. He would have used the term $\bar{o}rən$, the same as for the other members of the congregation. Thus it is clear that $d\bar{o}nən$ means 'sing, intone', whatever the contents, whether sacred or profane, prayer or song. It is true that the most strange psychological reasons can bring about very surprising semantic developments. However, in the present case there is no evidence to support a transfer of meaning, and we need not search for psychological or other reasons to explain a nonexistent transfer of meaning. The semantic examination alone, even without our phonological discussion, would cause us to reject Kosover's etymology.

The term does not exist in Western Yiddish. Hence its source must be looked for in the east. Our first thought is, of course, Slavonic. Here we actually find a form that is phonetically identical with our stem, dav. It is the stem dav of the Slavonic verb $davat$ 'give'. We would have to assume that the bridge from 'giving' to 'praying' had already been built in Slavonic and the Jews had adopted the secondary meaning. But this theory would lead us nowhere because the Slavonic dictionaries report no such sense. Thus the phonetic identity is purely fortuitous.

Since we went as far as to search the far away Islamic area for the origin of our word, we might also look at the pre-Islamic period, the Byzantine one. In the Byzantine Empire the Jews had for centuries been speaking Yevanic (the Jewish parallel of Greek). However, since there is not one word in the Greek dictionaries that has the slightest touch of similarity to $dav,$ a Yevanic etymology seems to be out of the question.

The problem of $davənən$ is still waiting to be solved.

REFERENCES

GOLD, D. L. 1983 More on the Etymology of Yiddish *doynen/davnen/davenen*. *Comments on Etymology*, **12,** 9–10, 3–9.

KOSOVER, M. 1964 Doynen = davnen; toytsn = tetshn; shalt = tsholnt. In *For Max Weinrich on his Seventieth Birthday. Studies in Jewish Language, Literature, and Society*. pp. 368–355 (Yiddish pagination, 163–176). Mouton, The Hague.

KOWALSKI, T. 1927 *Karaimische Texte im Dialekte von Troki*. Cracow.

Language & Communication, Vol. 7, Supplement, pp. 15–22, 1987.
Printed in Great Britain.

0271-5309/87 $3.00 + .00
Pergamon Journals Ltd.

A TANGLED WEB:
WHOLE HEBREW AND ASHKENAZIC ORIGINS

ALICE FABER

University of Florida at Gainesville

It is clear that studies of Ashkenazic Whole Hebrew—the language of Jewish religious texts—have the potential to add materially to our understanding of the development of Ashkenazic Jewry; it is for that very reason that investigations into Hebrew reading traditions—and not only those of Ashkenazic Jews—like those of Gumperz and Idelsohn are so intriguing. But, it is virtually never obvious how to interpret any particular datum about liturgical Hebrew. Only after a datum has been placed in context with other data, both actual and conceivable, concerning Ashkenazic Jewry and its culture can more general, higher order conclusions safely be advanced.

As is clear from recent linguistic studies (e.g. Weinrich 1980, Faber and King 1984, Katz 1985 and this volume, and Wexler this volume), the traditional historical picture of Ashkenazic development is in need of revision. At the very least, it is necessary to distinguish between the ancestry of Ashkenazic Jews, to the extent that it is uniform, and the sources of their culture, including their languages. It must further be recognized that the cultural heritage of Ashkenaz consists of more than the rituals and texts emanating from the documented early medieval Jewish communities of the Rhine Valley, central though these may be in the Ashkenazic Jewish consciousness.

At the core of any discussion of Ashkenazic origins lies one simple demographic dilemma: The Polish Jewish population grew rapidly in the early modern period, from at most *c.* 50,000 in 1500 to *c.* 500,000 in 1648, a ten-fold increase (Dubnow 1916: 66n). As suggested in Faber and King (1984: 395–396, 409, w. lit.), there were simply not enough Jews in supra-Pyrennean Western Europe prior to the Crusades and the Black Death to account for this rapid increase, especially given the hostile conditions under which the various expulsions from Western Europe took place (see, e.g. Dinur 1969: 30). As a consequence of this blatant discrepancy, alternative sources for the demographic bulk of Ashkenazic Jewry have been proposed. These range from the relatively implausible Khazar hypothesis, propounded most recently by Koestler (1976) (for discussion, see Faber and King 1984: 411-412), to the more plausible suggestion of migrants from the southeast (Babylon and Persia [M. Weinreich 1980: 377; cf. Katz 1985: 100, who ascribes to Aramaic speaking migrants a definitive role in the formation of Yiddish] or Byzantium [Baron III: 206]). Conspicuously absent is any suggestion of a semi-autochthonous Bavarian community (cf. Faber and King 1984); nor, outside of the Khazar hypothesis, is the possibility of large scale conversion to Judaism entertained, despite the evidence for conversion to Judaism in Imperial Rome prior to Hadrian (Gager 1985: 42, 59ff, 77, 86–7) and Roman and Christian bans on Jewish proselytization (Parkes 1934: 63). A qualitatively different sort of solution to the problem is proposed by Weinryb (1976: 115); he both suggests revised population estimates (a maximum of only 170,000 in 1648, compared with Dubnow's *c.*

500,000) and provides possible explanations why the Jewish population in Poland might have increased at a greater rate than the non-Jewish population.

I would like to raise at this point the possibility that the confused picture just presented is a consequence of something more than the vagaries of historical preservation. Absent either internal or external records of Jewish settlement, difficulties of toponymic interpretation notwithstanding (e.g., Golb 1976: 96ff), only speculation of the sort I have just sketched is possible. An alternative approach is to assume that systematic factors of a sort not hitherto discussed in the context of Jewish settlement in Europe led *inevitably* to systematic underreporting of Jewish population in greater Bavaria in the early medieval period.

While the distribution of Jewish settlement under the Late Empire is often conceived of in terms of the Roman *limes* (Baron III: 207ff), it is generally overlooked that actual documentary evidence for Jewish settlement outside of Rome is available only for the period after which, to quote Baron (II: 87), "Roman Catholicism . . . became the heir of Imperial Rome", and "Roman Imperialism readily lent itself to being translated into Christian Imperialism" (Baron II: 152; Parkes 1934: 317): the earliest evidence for Jewish settlement in Cologne is found in correspondence to Jewish leaders of the city from the Emperor Constantine, under whose rule Catholicism became the religion of the Empire (Baron III: 489). As is well known, the Jewish communities of the Rhineland are well documented into the beginning of the second millennium. As the Roman *limes* receded, these communities were situated within Gallic and then Frankish territory; the Franks were the only one of the Germanic tribes to convert directly to Roman Catholicism (Wallace-Hadrill 1962: 69). All other German tribes, without exception, converted to Arian rather than Roman Christianity (Wallace-Hadrill 1962: 23); subsequently, of course, the Arian 'heresy', first promulgated by an Alexandrian Presbyter named Arius early in the fourth century, was eradicated, or, at least, forced underground. Because history is written by winners (see, similarly, Gager 1985: 265-6), histories of early medieval Europe, based as they are on earlier attempts to demonstrate the ineluctability of the Roman Catholic rise to domination (Clebsch 1979: 3; MacMullen 1984: 6), often pass over the Arian period, either due to its perceived irrelevance or because documentation of the transition to Catholicism was destroyed. In any case, Bavarian history, for example, seems to begin later than does Rhenish history, and, when it begins, it is primarily Catholic.

It must further be understood that both Christianization and Catholicization were gradual processes, proceeding independently of doctrinal niceties (MacMullen 1984: 5). Wallace-Hadrill (1976: 15) refers to Germanic gravegoods "that leave one wondering what on earth the pious kindred understood by Christianity" (see also Wallace-Hadrill 1962: 87). In discussion of Syria of this period, Gager (1985: 265) distinguishes among heretics, the Orthodox, Christian Judaisers, Jews, and Gentile sympathizers with Judaism. There is no reason to expect that any less diversity was found in Europe. Further, as noted by MacMullen (1984: 85), at the turn of the fifth century, more than half of the Empire was still non-Christian.

While, on one level, the conflict between Catholic and Arian Christianity was a doctrinal one, revolving around the latter group's rejection of the Nicene creed, the actual, practical distinction was more of a political one. The Germanic tribes' acceptance of Arian rather than Catholic Christianity allowed them to maintain a measure of distinctness from Rome (Wallace-Hadrill 1962: 25; Burns 1984; 159–161), despite their assimilation to the trappings

of the Empire. Aside from the ethnopolitical distinction, Arians and Catholics differed in their attitudes toward doctrinal non-conformity: Arians generally were more tolerant of variations in Christian doctrine than were Catholics (Wallace-Hadrill 1962: 29; Burns 1984: 159). This greater Arian tolerance was manifested also in greater tolerance of Jews (Falco 1964: 55; cf. Parkes [1934: 210] on the actual tolerance shown Jews by the Catholic Pope Gregory I, as compared with his derogatory exegetical statements regarding Biblical Jews); it was only after the conversion of the Spanish Visigothic King Reccared from Arian to Catholic Christianity in 589, for example, that systematic anti-Jewish policies were adopted in Spain.

A further issue to be addressed is that of the perceived similarities between Arians and Jews. Arians, as well as other so-called heretics, were sometimes labeled Jews by their opponents (Baron II: 188; Parkes 1934: 300), but it is not clear whether there was anything to this accusation other than invective (Baron III: 178). Furthermore, the recently Arianized Lombard invaders of Rome (Wallace-Hadrill 1962: 54) classified Jews with other Roman population elements, not with themselves (Baron III: 25).

As a consequence of the Arians' greater tolerance, it seems reasonable to expect less juridical mention of Jews in Arian-controlled territory than in Catholic-controlled territory, assuming, as we, in fact, cannot, comparable representation in the overall population; Arians would have been less likely to impose legislative limits on Jews and less likely to note that a party to a contract was Jewish. Because of the ultimate Catholic political domination of Europe, documentation of any sort regarding Catholic territory is more extensive than is documentation regarding Arian territory. So, the two factors—not necessarily independent of each other—coincide: the greater Catholic concern with noting and restricting non-conformity, including Judaism, and the ultimate domination of Catholicism. As a consequence, it is probably unrealistic to expect to be able to document a Jewish presence in areas under Arian control, as census data are necessarily limited by the extent to which local authorities, for whatever reason, cared enough to count.

One might want to argue against the approach I have suggested on the basis of the internal documentation for the primacy of the Rhineland Jewish communities. Such an argument, would, however, be fallacious; it is based on the false presupposition that Jewish communal self-definition in a particular time and place is independent of how that community is viewed from without. It cannot be coincidence that Jewish communities are more religiously focused in precisely those areas where the theological predilections of the majority communities in which they are embedded place them most on the defensive. Certainly, to the extent that this is a relevant consideration, one would expect Jewish commmunities coexisting with Catholicism to be more active religiously than those coexisting with Arianism.

The sociohistorical model just outlined provides a context within which to analyze linguistic data from Yiddish and Ashkenazic Hebrew. While comparison of, for example, the Old French contributions to Yiddish (see, most recently, Katz 1985: 87) with those of Old Czech (Weinreich 1980: 544ff) may prove instructive, I will limit myself here to discussion of three facets of Whole Hebrew pronunciation in Europe: sibilant pronunciation, realization of "soft" BEGED-KEFET, and the number of distinct vowel qualities utilized. In all three cases, the facts are well known, and I will be contributing little, if anything, to low level analysis of the phenomena. My interest lies, rather, in the extent to which they can be or have been explained with reference to phenomena in coterritorial languages, including Yiddish, and, derivatively, in the extent to which they accord with various demographic hypotheses concerning Ashkenazic Jewry.

Early Rhineland documents in which Hebrew is used to transliterate Old French names and terms do not use the letter *samekh* at all, using *shin/sin* to transliterate all sibilants. This orthographic convention, coupled with Yekutiel of Prague's thirteenth century reference to Ashkenazim who did not differentiate *shin* from *sin,* has been taken (e.g. by Gumperz 1942 and Eldar 1978) to mean that Rhineland liturgical Hebrew had only a single sibilant. This conclusion is particularly attractive to Gumperz, as he wishes to relate the maintenance of but a single sibilant in early Ashkenazic Whole Hebrew to the phenomenon of SABESDIKER LOSN, that is, neutralization of the /s/ ~ /š/ contrast (U. Weinreich 1952), in Northeastern Yiddish, thus implicitly strengthening the presumed demographic and cultural links between Rhineland and Eastern European Jewry.

Unfortunately, however, as I have argued elsewhere (Faber 1982), neither the Rhineland nor the Lithuanian facts admit so simple an explanation. Lack of *samekh* in Hebrew renderings of Old French items means simply that *samekh* represented a sound, LAMINAL [s̪] (in which the blade of the tongue approaches the alveolum), that did not exist in Old French, prior to the deaffrication of /c̪/ (<Latin *k). Old French inherited APICAL /s/ (in which the tongue tip approaches the alveolum; Joos 1952, Fought 1979) was perceived as more similar to Hebrew apical /š/ (*shin*) than to laminal /s̪/ (*samekh*), and, thus, *shin* rather than *samekh* was used to represent it. Furthermore, the Lithuanian Yiddish neutralization of sibilant contrasts has more plausible sources than the putative influence of liturgical language on the phonology of an "everyday" language, contrary to normal expectation. Bin-Nun (1973: 367) suggests that Lithuanian Yiddish represents the descendant of a Middle High German dialect in which the changes that, in most High German dialects, transformed the contrast of apical /s/-laminal /c̪/ to one of hushing /š/ ~ hissing /s/ occurred in a different order, so that reflexes of both became apical /s/ (according to Bin-Nun [1973: 366], the single sibilant was distinct both from Standard Yiddish /s̪/ and /š/). In addition, as suggested by U. Weinreich (1963: 354), the Northeastern Yiddish sibilant system may have been influenced by Polish MAZURZENIE, comparable lack of sibilant-shibilant contrast, which developed in some Polish dialects around the turn of the thirteenth century (Stieber 1968: 67-68), perhaps, coincidentally, shortly after the earliest notices of Jewish settlement in Poland (Przemyśl: eleventh century [Gieysztor, *et al.,* 1968: 73]; Wroclaw: late twelfth century [Weinryb 1976: 24]; and Cracow: 1304 [Baron X: 41]). As noted in Faber (1982: 91–92), the influence of Polish mazurzenie could easily have counteracted tendencies to restandardize a sibilant-shibilant contrast in a Proto-Northeastern Yiddish dialect which, in accord with Bin-Nun's model, had earlier neutralized the contrast.

As a consequence of the independent explanations I have advanced for attested sibilant values in early Rhineland Whole Hebrew and in Lithuanian Yiddish (and, by extension, in Lithuanian Whole Hebrew), no support for a historical-demographic link between the two communities is generated. This essentially negative result is only worrisome in light of an *a priori* insistence on such a link.

While the phenomenon of BEGED-KEFET, or, in general linguistic terms, POSTVOCALIC SPIRANTIZATION, is clearly defined, it is not altogether well understood. I will follow in my discussion here the exposition in Faber (1986). Postvocalic spirantization arose in the bilingual Hebrew-Aramaic community of the Second Temple period, as a response to the continued presence in Aramaic of phonemic /ð/ and /θ/, which had long since merged with *z and *š in Hebrew. By the beginning of the Christian Era, *w had merged with [v] (<*b), creating a phonemic contrast between /b/ and /v/, albeit with some complicated morphophonemic interactions. Similarly, Malone (1969: 538) notes non-canonical forms

involving post-vocalic [t], suggesting the possibility of a /t/ ~ /θ/ phonemic contrast; Morag (1972: 53) suggests a comparable incipient phonemic contrast in Biblical Aramaic. The phonemic status of the other stop-spirant alternations is less clear; it is certainly not inconceivable that /k/–/x/, /p/–/f/, /g/–/ɣ/ and /d/–/ð/ were all distinct phonemes, again, as already noted, participating in complicated morphophonemic alternations.

The ultimate realization of this alternation in Ashkenazic Whole Hebrew differs from the prototype just described in two crucial ways: (1) the spirant variant of /t/ is /s/ rather than /θ/, and (2) /d/ and /g/ cease to spirantize. An examination of the manuscript evidence raises the possibility (although it is by no means a certainty) that these two deviations from what can be assumed to be original Hebrew norms originated in geographically distinct areas.

Probable non-spirantization of /d/ and /g/ is reflected in the *Maḥzor Vitry* (mid twelfth century, northern France); *bet, peh, tav* and *kaf* appear both with and without *dagesh*, while no such contrast is evident for *dalet* and *gimel* (Eldar 1975: 207; cf. M. Weinreich [1980: 383], who sees in Swabian *yus* 'ten' < Hebrew **yod* evidence for early [ð] rather than as the expected reflex of an intermediate **yut* by the Old High German consonant shift).

Similarly, the thirteenth century Latin transcript of the Paris disputation on the Talmud (Paris Lat. 16558), discussed by Gumperz' (1953) and Merchavia (1965), reflects a dual realization of *bet, peh* and *kaf,* but not of *gimel.* Despite Gumperz' (1953: 10) claim to the contrary, Merchavia (1965: 249) sees no evidence for a dual realization of *dalet;* the enlarged ⟨Z⟩ observed by Gumperz turns out not to be at all systematic. ⟨z⟩ and ⟨d⟩ are both used for post-vocalic *dalet,* although the latter predominates. And the distinction between ⟨t⟩ and ⟨th⟩ in the manuscript does not correlate with the normative Hebrew distribution of /t/ and /θ/. The value of the Latin transcriptions is, however, diminished by the fact that the Latin, not surprisingly, is most faithful to Hebrew norms in those cases in which Latin provides a simple spelling for the spirant alternant: /x f v/ ⟨ch f v⟩, but not /ð ɣ θ/. Nonetheless, it is probably safe to assume that neither the disputation manuscript nor the Maḥzor Vitry reflects /s/ as the post-vocalic variant of /t/.

The two manuscripts just described contrast with those treated by Eldar (1978) in his study of what he calls pre-Ashkenazic (that is, pre-thirteenth century) Hebrew manuscripts. In these manuscripts, spirant variants of both *dalet* and *tav* are regularly indicated (Eldar 1978: 104). There is little evidence available concerning the phonetic realization of postvocalic *dalet,* although some evidence suggests /z/ (Eldar 1978: 107). In contrast, that the postvocalic variant of /t/ was /s/ is certain, given the not infrequent substitutions of *shin* and *samekh* for *tav.* Unfortunately, Eldar does not comment directly on the postvocalic realization of *gimel.*

Given the relative cross linguistic frequency of /ð/ > /d/ and /ɣ/ > /g/, I will concentrate now on the source of /s/ as a postvocalic variant of /t/. The effect of /s/ replacing /θ/ as the postvocalic reflex of /t/ is that the general statement of Hebrew spirantization of voiceless stops exactly mirrors the clause of the Old High German consonant shift affecting postvocalic voiceless consonants (outside of clusters). This change, in its most general form, occurred in Bavarian, Alemannic, and Rhine and East Franconian German, beginning in preliterary times, that is, by the seventh century (Braune 1925: 72; Bach 1965: 105). Unlike Hebrew spirantization, the Old High German shift did not leave morphophonemic traces that might have led speakers to posit a synchronic rule. So, if the Ashkenazic Whole Hebrew spirantization pattern is to be attributed to the Old High German shift, a substantial body

of Whole Hebrew users must have been located in one of the aforementioned High German dialect areas by that time.

Now it will be recalled that Eldar's (1978) pre-Ashkenazic manuscripts are from the Rhineland, most of which is in dialect areas in which the Old High German shift operated to completion. There is, thus, a temptation to associate the Whole Hebrew pronunciation tradition which was apparently influenced by the Old High German shift with the historically attested Rhineland communities. But, this is not a logically necessary association, given that the German component of Yiddish itself is predominantly Bavarian (Faber and King 1984: 398–399; cf. Katz 1985: 87). Whether one treats the liturgical pronunciation as something that evolved in tandem with the religious and cultural traditions of the Rhineland or independently of them depends in large measure on one's (possibly romanticized) preconceptions about the centrality of religious observance in the Jewish past.

Finally, I would like to discuss briefly the growth of the Tiberian reading tradition in thirteenth and fourteenth century Ashkenaz (M. Weinreich 1980: 369ff). In this "imported" system, two new vowel contrasts, *tsere-segol* and *patach-kamatz,* are realized. As Max Weinreich notes, superimposition of the new vowel system on the earlier five vowel system, reflected in both Whole and Merged Hebrew, involved two aspects: adoption of the Tiberian orthography, and adoption of the pronunciation reflected in that orthography. Paradoxically, the means by which this Tiberian tradition was transmitted throughout Ashkenaz was via Babylonian scholars. Weinreich (1980: 377) refers to a small but influential influx of Babylonian scholars as bearers of a "Babylonian renaissance", but, if Katz's (1985) model of the development of Yiddish is correct, the number of Aramaic speaking immigrants to Southeastern Europe, presumably from Babylonia, was not as small as Weinreich supposes. Furthermore, Lowenstamm's suggestion (1985) that phonological alternations within Merged Hebrew can best be explained on the basis of an underlying seven vowel system provides an additional basis for supposing that such an influx provided a non-trivial segment of the ultimate Ashkenazic population.

In any case, the question that interests me here is not how and why the pronunciation according with the Tiberian vocalization was adopted, but, rather, the contrast with BEGED-KEFET. As I have already argued, the distribution and nature of stop-spirant alternants in Ashkenazic Whole Hebrew resulted from the influence of the Old High German consonant shift and allied changes in an era far earlier that that in which the Tiberian vocalization system was adopted. Even though the Tiberian system provides orthographic differentiation for *dalet* and *gimel* in environments exactly mirroring those conditioning, for example, the /p/ ~ /f/ alternation, there was apparently no attempt to modify Hebrew pronunciation accordingly, reinstituting postvocalic variants of *dalet* and *gimel.* The most plausible explanation for this differential influence of the Tiberian orthography is that, in the case of the vowels Proto Yiddish utilized vowels matching the target realizations of the Tiberian symbols. In contrast, German no longer had available voiced fricatives that could serve as analogs to the Tiberian postvocalic *dalet* and *gimel.*

The linguistic evidence regarding Whole Hebrew can be summarized as follows: no special link between France and Lithuania can be posited on the basis of apparent non-normative treatment of sibilants. The treatment of spirantization suggests that there was a community of Whole Hebrew users in High German speech areas at the time of the Old High German consonant shift. Their tradition was modified but not supplanted following the late importation of the Tiberian vocalization system and allied pronunciation norms to South-eastern Germany. If Katz (1985) is correct about Yiddish being a fusion of Bavarian and

East Central German with the Aramaic presumably spoken by those immigrants who brought with them the Tiberian tradition, we are forced to contend with the possibility that there were indeed largely undocumented—and, I would contend, undocumentable—Jewish populations in greater Bavaria prior to the "Babylonian renaissance"; otherwise, the congruence between Ashkenazic Whole Hebrew pronunciation norms and the Tiberian orthography would be complete.

REFERENCES

BACH, A. 1965 *Geschichte der deutschen Sprache,* 8th ed. Queller und Meyer. Heidelberg.

BARON, S. W. 1952 *A Social and Religious History of the Jews,* 16 Vols. Columbia University Press, New York.

BIN-NUN, Y. 1973 *Jiddisch und die deutschen Mundarten.* Max Niemeyer, Tübingen.

BRAUNE, W. 1925 *Althochdeutsche Grammatik,* 4th ed. Max Niemeyer, Halle.

BURNS, T. 1984 *A History of the Ostrogoths.* Indiana University Press, Bloomington.

CLEBSCH, W. A. 1979 *Christianity in European History.* Oxford University Press, New York.

DINUR, B. 1969 *Israel in the Diaspora.* Jewish Publication Society, Philadelphia.

DUBNOW, S. 1916 *History of the Jews in Russia and Poland.* Jewish Publication Society, Philadelphia.

ELDAR, I. 1975 The vocalization of the Haggada in Mahzor Vitry (Ms. Sassoon 535). *Leshonenu* **39,** 192–216.

ELDAR, I. 1978 *The Hebrew Language Tradition in Medieval Ashkenaz (ca. 950-1350 CE),* Vol. I: *Phonology and Vocalization.* (Publications of the Hebrew University Language Traditions Project, IV). Kiryath Sepher, Jerusalem.

FABER, A. 1982 Early Medieval Hebrew sibilants in the Rhineland, South Central and Eastern Europe. *Hebrew Annual Review,* **6,** 81–96.

FABER, A. 1986 On the origin and development of Hebrew spirantization. *Mediterranean Language Review* **2,** 117–138.

FABER, A. and KING, R. D. 1984 Yiddish and the settlement history of Ashkenazic Jewry. *Mankind Quarterly* **24,** 393–425.

FALCO, G. 1964 *The Holy Roman Empire: A Historic Profile of the Middle Ages.* Kent, K. V. (trans.). Allen and Unwin, London.

FISHMAN, J. A. (ed.) 1985 *Readings in the Sociology of Jewish Languages.* Brill, Leiden.

FOUGHT, J. 1979 The Medieval sibilants of the *Eulalia-Ludwigslied* manuscript and their development in early Old French, *Language* **55,** 842–858.

GAGER, J. J. 1985 *The Origins of Anti-Semitism: Attitudes Toward Judaism in Pagan and Christian Antiquity.* Oxford University Press, Oxford.

GIEYSZTOR, A. *et al.* 1968 *History of Poland.* Cekalska, K. *et al.* (trans.). Warsaw.

GOLB, N. 1976 *History and Culture of the Jews of Rouen in the Middle Ages.* Dvir, Tel Aviv.

GUMPERZ, Y. 1942 The *Shin* and its metamorphoses. *Tarbiz* **13,** 107–115.

GUMPERZ, Y. 1953 *Pronunciations of Our Language.* Jerusalem.

JOOS, M. 1952 The Medieval sibilants. *Language* **28,** 222–231.

KATZ, D. 1985 Hebrew, Aramaic and the Rise of Yiddish. In Fishman, 1985, 85–103.

KOESTLER, A. 1976 *The Thirteenth Tribe.* Random House, New York.

LOWENSTAMM, J. 1985 Absolute neutralization in Yiddish: synchronic and diachronic consequences. Paper placed before the First Annual Oxford Winter Symposium in Yiddish Language and Literature, 15–17 December.

MACMULLEN, R. 1984 *Christianizing the Roman Empire (A.D. 100–400).* Yale University, New Haven.

MALONE, J. L. 1969 Rules of synchronic analogy: a proposal based on evidence from three Semitic languages. *Foundations of Language* **5,** 534–559.

MERCHAVIA, H. 1965 On the transliteration of Hebrew words in a 13th century Latin manuscript. *Leshonenu* **29,** 103–114, 247–274, **30,** 41–53.

MORAG, S. 1972 *The Vocalization Systems of Arabic, Hebrew and Aramaic.* Mouton, The Hague.

PARKES, J. 1934 *The Conflict of the Church and the Synagogue.* Soncino, London.

STIEBER, Z. 1968 *The Phonological Development of Polish,* Schwarz, E. S. (trans.). Department of Slavic Languages and Literatures, Ann Arbor, MI.

WALLACE-HADRILL, J. M. 1962 *The Barbarian West: The Early Middle Ages.* Torchbooks, New York.

WALACE-HADRILL, J. M. 1976 Early Medieval history. *Early Medieval History,* New York, 1–18.

WEINREICH, M. 1980 *History of the Yiddish Language.* Noble, S. (trans.). Univeristy of Chicago, Chicago.

WEINREICH, U. 1952 Sabesdiker Losn in Yiddish: a problem of linguistic affinity. *Word* **8,** 260–267.

WEINREICH, U. 1963 Four riddles of bilingual dialectology. In *American Contributions to the 5th International Conference of Slavicists,* pp. 335–359, Mouton. The Hague.

WEINRYB, B. D. 1976 *The Jews of Poland: A Social and Economic History of the Jewish Community of Poland from 1100 to 1800.* Jewish Publication Society, Philadelphia.

Language & Communication, Vol. 7, Supplement, pp. 23–25, 1987.
Printed in Great Britain.

0271-5309/87 $3.00 + .00
Pergamon Journals Ltd.

THE ROMANCE ELEMENTS IN OLD YIDDISH

LEO FUKS

University of Amsterdam

The determination of the origins of the Romance elements in Old Yiddish may elucidate the birth and early development of Yiddish itself.

It has hitherto been accepted that the rudiments of Jewish Romance vernacular, which derived from a Jewish language which Max Weinreich (1973, I: 48, 99 ff, 334–353) called *Zarphatic* must be the source of the Romance elements in Old Yiddish (see Birnbaum 1979: 64, 66–67; U. Weinreich 1972: 795–796). According to this theory, Jews from northern France emigrated to the cities which were situated on the rivers Rhine and Moselle in the ninth and tenth centuries of the common era. The forebears of these new Jewish settlers had left the same cities some five centuries earlier, during the break up of the Roman Empire in the West under the onslaught of the Germanic tribes. The Jewish immigrants adopted the German idiom which was spoken in their new dwelling places and shaped it into a Jewish language, retaining elements of their former Zarphatic language which were preserved in the later phases of the Yiddish language.

Since Max Weinreich made his investigations, the results of which were laid down in his *Geshikhte fun der yidisher shprakh,* new light has been shed on the early history of the German cities which were the cradle of Old Yiddish. Weinreich refers to works published between the two World Wars. But after 1945 new archaeological finds and systematic studies have changed the outlook on the origins and development of the former Roman cities in the region of the Rhine and the Moselle. These new insights are of great importance, too, for a better knowledge of the conditions in which the Jews lived in the area and for the development of the language they spoke.

In our days it is common knowledge that the break up of the Roman Empire in the West did not transpire suddenly, at least not on the Continent. Even after the waves of invading Germanic tribes from Eastern Europe and beyond, Roman administration, organization, culture and language survived after the fourth century. As the Germanic tribes shunned city life and preferred to dwell in the country, the Roman cities remained centres of trade, crafts and administration for the centuries to come. The more so, because advancing Christianity took over the Roman cities and their administration for its own purposes.

From the fifth century onwards, until the consolidation of the Karolingian empire in the ninth century, the former Roman cities were islands of Roman language and culture in a sea of Germanic rural life. The inhabitants of the cities consisted of Gallo-Romans who spoke Vulgo Latin and Jews who spoke more or less the same language. As the cities had originated as civilian quarters near to the Roman garrisons, most of the inhabitants were merchants, craftsmen and administrators. Slowly, as Roman power crumbled, the

bishops of the Christian church took over wordly power in the cities, retaining the traditional Roman laws and administrative structure as well as the Latin language.

The last written vestiges of Jewish habitation in the Roman cities on the Rhine and Moselle date from the fourth century, especially from Cologne and Trier (Ristow 1963: 39ff). In the following century the area was invaded by Burgunds and Franks and from 486 Cologne and its environment were incorporated into the realm of the Merovingian Franks. The Jews were now under nominal jurisdiction of the Merovingian Kings who tried to curb their traditional rights in favour of the Christian church (Ristow 1963: 44–45). But the role of the Jewish merchants was too important to make the new legislation more than a courteous bow to the Church. The Jews possessed the connections with the Eastern parts of the Mediterranean area, whence the much valued luxury goods, including silk, brocades, spices, incense, jewels, and silver and gold for the minting of money. The Jews, like most of the more well to do inhabitants of the cities owned estates outside the cities where wine and all kinds of vegetables were grown. Recent research in the early history of German cities has revealed an unbroken continuity of the old Roman cities until far into Merovingian times (Ennen 1972: 27ff).

Archaeological finds and systematic topographical research have proven that the topographical layout of the old Roman cities only changed very slowly. Formerly, the city consisted of the garrison with the administrative centre and temples, with the living quarters of the civilians at the side. In many cities the bishops took over the main Roman buildings and converted them into churches and made use also of the other official buildings. The civilian quarters where the Jews lived, too, remained as they were. Only when the cities lost parts of their population, did the old Roman part of town fall into ruins and become quarries for new parts of the cities to be erected in Karolingian times and later (Planitz 1954: 24–34). The study of tombstones excavated at Mayence and Ratisbon reveals that the process of Germanization of the inhabitants of the towns reached its conclusion only in the Karolingian reign, between 800 and 900. Until that time, Gallo-Roman names appeared on the tombstones, to be replaced by Germanic ones about 900 (Planitz 1954: 31).

These new facts about the development of the former Roman cities in the area which Max Weinreich called LOTER, compel us to consider the impact of these data on the origins and development of Old Yiddish, with special emphasis on its Romance elements. In this light the theory of the flight of the Jews from the Roman cities in the area of the Rhine and the Moselle in the fourth century has to be revised. There are no indications whatsoever that the Jews had fled before the Germanic tribes while the other Roman inhabitants of the cities stayed. As I have suggested before (Fuks 1965: 5), the Jews remained in the Roman cities of Loter, lived there in peace under the Merovingian kings and slowly changed their Romance vernacular into a Germanic one, much like the other inhabitants of those cities. The long continuity of Roman speech and lifestyle in the cities was enhanced by the Christian Church with its Latin liturgy and educational system. Latin was the only written language in the Germanic realms for centuries thereafter. And this situation also characterized the Jews who kept their Judeo-Latin until it slowly gave way to Germanic speech.

The theory of the remigration of Jews to the cities on the Rhine and Moselle after five hundred years, due to persecutions in other parts of the Karolingian Empire, cannot be proven. On the contrary, the importance of Jewish merchants had increased after the Islamic conquest of the greater part of the Eastern Mediterranean area and Spain in the seventh and eighth centuries. The Jews were the only people who had access to both inimical camps.

They were, therefore, much favoured by the Karolingian rulers, causing grave discontent amongst important churchmen. The expulsion of Jews from German cities, such as Mayence, only took place in the eleventh century (Baron 1957, IV: 66–67, 85n, 171–172).

Assuming that the Judeo-Latin speaking Jews in the cities of Loter remained undisturbed from Roman times until the eleventh century, we may conclude that the Romance elements in Old Yiddish did not derive from Zarphatic, the Northern French Jewish idiom, but from Judeo-Latin. That would, among other things, explain why the verb *bentshn* has retained the likeness to Latin *benedicere* instead of to French *bénir* (Birnbaum 1979: 67).

The undisturbed continuity of Jewish life in the area may also explain the complete absence of Jewish written sources in the period until the eleventh century. Silence in history and linguistics may be interpreted in many ways. It may account for well-being as well as for the opposite, although times of persecution in Jewish history have always yielded written evidence in the form of lamentations and chronicles. Moreover, the early centuries of the European Middle Ages were remarkably silent ones anyway. Written evidence is extremely scarce, partly due to the fact that Latin was the only written language in those days. The various spoken languages had not yet reached the state of writing. It was only in the wake of the Karolingian Renaissance that the European vernaculars came of age, and one among them was the Old Yiddish language.

REFERENCES

BARON, S. W. 1957 *A Social and Religious History of the Jews,* Vol. IV. New York.

BIRNBAUM, S. A. 1979 *Yiddish. A Survey and a Grammar.* Manchester University Press, Manchester & University of Toronto Press, Toronto.

ENNEN, E. 1972 *Die europäische Stadt des Mittelalters.* Göttingen.

FUKS, L. 1965 *Das altjiddische Epos Melokim-Buk,* Vol. I. Assen.

PLANITZ, H. 1954 *Die deutsche Stadt im Mittelalter. Von der Römerzeit bis zu den Zunftkämpfen.* Graz, Köln.

RISTOW, G. 1963 Zur Frühgeschichte der rheinischen Juden. Von der Spätantike bis zu den Kreuzzügen. In *Monumenta Judaica. 2000 Jahre Geschichte und Kultur der Juden am Rhein. Handbuch.* Köln.

WEINREICH, M. 1973 Geshikhte fun der yidisher sprakh. Bagrifn, faktn, metodn, IV Vols. Yivo Institute for Jewish Research, New York.

WEINREICH, U. 1972 Yiddish language. *Encyclopaedia Judaica* **16,** 789–798.

Language & Communication, Vol. 7, Supplement, pp. 27–37, 1987.
Printed in Great Britain.

0271-5309/87 $3.00 + .00
Pergamon Journals Ltd.

NEGATION IN YIDDISH AND
HISTORICAL RECONSTRUCTION*

CHRISTOPHER HUTTON

Oxford Centre for Postgraduate Hebrew Studies and Wolfson College, Oxford

Modern Yiddish linguistics has concentrated on three main areas of inquiry: dialectology, historical linguistics and language planning. Although major studies of Yiddish syntax have been produced, no extensive non-normative study of Yiddish has been written in the postwar period. Given the bias of both dialectology and historical linguistics towards phonology and away from syntax, it is not surprising that Landau's (1901: 23) observation about the lack of a general historical grammar of Yiddish against which to set the language of individual texts is still largely valid, though a number of detailed studies of individual premodern texts have been made (e.g. Herzog 1965; Lockwood 1975; Goldwasser 1982).

The factors that militate against the study of historical morphology and syntax are not difficult to discern. In general linguistics we have the belief that syntactic structures are somehow less concrete than phonological ones (especially within the Neogrammarian tradition), though this view has been criticized (Watkins 1964: 1035). For the historical linguist concerned with Yiddish, the regularity of the correspondences between the stressed vowel systems of the dialects (Katz 1980: 9, 1983: 1018) seemed to invite comparative reconstruction in phonology rather than in any other sphere. A third factor that may have contributed to the relative neglect of historical morphology and syntax was a doubt about the status of Old Yiddish and Early Middle Yiddish literary documents as reflections of the history of the spoken language. Tavyov (1914: 142) expresses scepticism about the value of written documents as guides to the history of spoken Yiddish and the debate between Marchand (1959) and M. Weinreich (1960) about the status of the *Cambridge Codex* of 1382 (published by Fuks 1957, E. Katz 1963 and Hakkarainen 1967 among others) shows the complex interaction of linguistic interpretation and historical and ideological presupposition. For Marchand, the ability to identify the text closely with a particular German dialect area, i.e. Hessen (Marchand 1959: 388) argues against considering the text as any kind of early Yiddish, whereas for Weinreich, the fusion characteristics of the text (i.e. German dialect fusion, Weinreich 1960: 114) are held to show that the text is something other than German in Hebrew letters. Neither of these conclusions follows necessarily from the respective versions of the linguistic facts, but the discussion can serve as an illustration of the complexity of the problems involved in the evaluation of Old Yiddish and Early Middle Yiddish texts (see M. Weinreich 1973, II: 383–396 for discussion of the periodization of Yiddish).

The methodological and philosophical problems associated with older Yiddish texts should

*I would like to thank Dovid Katz for generously allowing me access to his library and for constant encouragement and advice, and Dov-Ber Kerler for help in obtaining materials and for many useful discussions. Responsibility for all errors of fact and interpretation is of course my own.

not however dissuade us from a close study of them. It would be perfectly legitimate to construct a history of the written language conceived of as an entity in principle distinct from the spoken language. An awareness of genre and social function, of variation within individual texts and in successive editions of the same text might also shed some light on developments in the spoken language. It is clear that older Yiddish texts cannot be discounted in our tracing of the linguistic history of Jews in Europe, given that any text in Hebrew characters was obviously directed towards a Jewish audience (though possibly a socially restricted one) and thus the language of the texts cannot have been wholly foreign to at least a section of the community (Lockwood 1975: 1).

In this paper negation will be used to illustrate the history and reconstruction of Yiddish morphology and syntax. Negation lends itself to historical research because of its frequency of occurrence (making it in this sense analagous to phonological features) and because, unlike word order (the usual object of syntactic reconstruction, see Hymes 1955, Watkins 1964), it has independent morphological realizations, as well as relevance to descriptive units of utterance length. It might be argued that the negative system cannot be reconstructed given its inherent instability. Negative morphemes are often unstressed and thus liable to drastic phonological reduction. Furthermore, negative morphemes are often ambiguous in scope, a factor that seems to account at least in part for the prevalence of so called 'double negatives' in many different languages. Ambiguity of scope can be illustrated by a Yiddish sentence such as *er hot nisht gevolt geyn* 'he didn't want to go', where we can see *nisht* as negating the proposition expressed by the whole sentence, or as negating *gevolt* or *geyn* and so on. The ambiguities around the force and scope of negative particles can also be seen in subordinate clauses such as the following: *ikh hob moyre der tish zol nit faln* 'I'm afraid the table will fall', literally 'shouldn't fall' (see Lötzsch 1974: 456). Thus it might be argued that a feature such as double or multiple negation might arise spontaneously in any language at any time and therefore that its history cannot be traced. Against this argument we should stress the clarity of many of the relevant isoglosses in Yiddish and German dialectology, the stability of a particle such as *kein* in German from about the 14th century when it acquired its exclusively negative meaning, and the demonstration by Pensel (1981) that comparative statistical studies of different texts from different regions and different periods can yield important generalizations about the geographical and historical characteristics of various negative structures in German.

In this paper three aspects of negation in Yiddish will be considered: double and multiple negation, the origin of the Eastern Yiddish structure *nisht keyn* as in *ikh hob nisht keyn tsayt* 'I have no time' and the origin of the Eastern Yiddish form *gornisht* 'nothing' (West Yiddish *niks/nisht* 'nothing').

The working definition of multiple negation that will be adopted here will be as follows: multiple negation is the presence of two or more particles in the same clause where both are capable of occurring independently with negative force. There are many sentences which under this definition would be defined as having multiple negation which we would nevertheless wish to exclude, such as a German sentence like *Er hat kein Geld, kein Haus, keine Freunde*. A generative grammarian would consider this as three underlying clauses, with deletion under identity. We might loosely say here that three sentential units corresponding to the same 'slot' in the sentence are negated, and thus that the sentence does not contain mutiple negation.

A preliminary survey was made of a number of older Yiddish texts. All of these texts

looked at had the feature of double negation, though there were clear differences in the
type of doubly negated constructions occurring and in the percentage of potential double
negations realized as double negations. The following is a list of the texts examined with
examples of the structures found:

Cambridge Codex (1382)
das er ni keyn vort fargas (2: 175)
der ni keynen bukhshtabn geshrip nokh gelas (3: 77)

Shmuelbukh (Augsburg 1544, published by Falk and Fuks 1961)
far donder un far blits kaan mensh kaan shtikn gesakh (verse 192)
nun hon ikh al maan lebtog ni kaan zind geton (verse 1232)

Kubukh (Verona 1595, discovered and republished, Rosenfeld 1984)
fun kaanem vor er nit zat (p. 4)
ikh mag itsunder nit redn mit kaan menshn (p. 43)

Maysebukh (Basle 1602)
derhalbn zol kaan mensh nit hofartik zaan ven er shoun a gedule hot (p. 48)
den es ver nit faan az a meylekh zelt kaan vaab nit hobn (p. 190)

Megiles vints (Amsterdam 1648, republished Shmeruk 1962/3)
nimant niks hot darum ton visn
aakh kaanem yehudi kaan gelt tsu gebn kaan shultman kaanem kaans
zol ton brengen (verse 10)
der zakhn kontn mir nit visn kaan grunt (verse 48)

Simkhes hanefesh (Fürth 1727, republished Shatzky 1926)
kaan lust un kaan freyd in em tu nit shparn (p. 2)
yom shabes kaan herts iz nit batribt (p. 3)

Takones hakehile dekohol koudesh ashkenazim asher beamsterdam (1737)
das kaan abgeynder parnes nit virt al tsetl habekhire (p. 11)

London Jewish Letters (early 18th century, published Maitlis 1955)
maan braankhe hot aakh kaan hayer (=English 'hire') nit (no. 2)

To these we can add the numerous examples of double negation observed by Lockwood
(1975: 9–11) in the *Jüdische Privatbriefe aus dem Jahre 1619* (Landau and Wachstein 1911).
Lockwood concludes that 'there are no obvious structural criteria for the use of double
against single negatives' (1975: 11). Herzog (1965: 57) in a study of *Seyfer refues* (1790)
notes the form *keyn refue nit,* although this is described as 'modern use'. Copeland and
Süsskind (1976) in their study of Herz's *Ester, oder di balonte tugent* (1828) comment on
the double negative *kaan man gilt niks in houz* (2.20, 1976: 131).

It is clear therefore that double negation was a general feature of written Western Yiddish
(as it is of course of Eastern Yiddish) and even given the methodological problems associated
with these texts, we would be justified in concluding that it was a feature of early spoken

Yiddish as well. This is not of itself surprising, but it should be put in the context of the various statements made in the literature about the origins of double negation, where double negation is implicitly discussed as solely an Eastern Yiddish feature. Sapir (1915: 234) writes: 'In syntax the double negative may be mentioned as an archaic feature though something should perhaps be ascribed to Slavic influence', and the same balance is struck by Willer who finds the parallel both in older and dialectal German and in Polish: 'In MHG and in contemporary popular dialects two negatives (as in Polish) give a negative thought' (Willer 1915: 418–9, my translation). Kagarov (1926: 425) attacks the idea that the morphology of Yiddish is Germanic and its syntax Slavic, criticizing a tendency to compare Yiddish with modern standard German (he may have had Veynger in mind, given the following remark: 'In yidish kenen zayn etlekhe farneynungen in zats un der zats hit op dem negativn kharakter (in daytsh iz farkert)' Veynger 1913: 35). Kagarov concludes that double negation is a 'kharakteristisher shtrikh fun di slavishe shprakhn, ober vayt nit fremd af dorem daytshe dialektn' (1926: 425). The main contention of Kagarov's article is that neither Slavic nor Hebrew have had more than a weak influence on Yiddish syntax and that 'zayn bazis zaynen di zelbe mitlhoykhdaytshe, mitldaytshe un di andere dialektn, vos hobn geleygt dem grunt far der morfologye un der leksik fun yidish' (1926: 428). M. Weinreich seems to lean more to Slavic influence to explain the predominance of double negation in modern Yiddish: 'in mitlhoykhdaytsh iz di toplte farneynung bloyz eyne fun di meglekhkaytn un af vifl zi bagegnt zikh in hayntike mizrekhdike daytshe dialektn, derklert men zi mit slavisher hashpoe' M. Weinreich 1973, volume 2: 191). U. Weinreich shares the same general caution about too specific an attribution of influence: 'the non-contradictory use of repeated negative words has been noted in both Yiddish and colonial German. The double negative is common in older and modern non-standard German, but the multiplication of negatives in excess of two may be a feature of Slavic origin' (1958: 15). Weinreich's tentative claim about negation in excess of two must be at least qualified, given the possibility in German dialects of multiple negation (see Merkle 1976: 156, and Hildebrand 1890: 222, cited in Wells 1985: footnote to 108, where the following sentence is quoted from a 14th century Alemmanic legal document: *und sol kain herr liegend gut noch kain hus von kainem* [*Mann*] *noch Kainer* [*Frau*] *ze Nuwkilch erben in kainem Weg),* and given the structure cited above from *Megiles vints* (verse 10): *aakh kaanem yehudi kaan gelt tsu gebn kaan shultman kaanem kaans zol ton brengen* ('in addition, to give no money to any Jew, no debtor should bring anything to anybody'). It might be argued that this sentence is especially emphatic, or that in general double negation in West Yiddish is merely used to stress negativity, whereas in East Yiddish negation in excess of two is not especially emphatic. It is however difficult to evaluate the 'emphaticness' of a given utterance (see discussion in Lockwood 1975, cited above); the whole of *Megiles vints* is emphatic, since it deals with a pogrom against the Jews of Frankfurt, and it would be circular to call certain utterances emphatic simply because they contain double or multiple negation. This illustrates one of the difficulties involved in interpreting statistical counts: if double or multiple negation is being used emphatically or as a sign of colloquial register, then comparison between texts on the basis of statistics alone becomes problematic. However it remains to be shown that in general double negation has an emphatic function, though Veynger (1913: 35) suggests that the difference between Eastern Yiddish *nisht a sakh* and *nisht keyn sakh* is in terms of emphasis. There is clearly a need both for further detailed textual analysis, of statistical research on the model of Pensel (1981), with close study not only of the incidence of double negation in general, but of specific kinds of double negation (compare for example *ikh hob nisht keyn tsayt,*

ikh hob keyn tsayt nisht, keyn tsayt hob ikh nisht, tsayt hob ikh nisht, as well as the various possible structures with *keyner* and *nimant,* sometimes alternating in the same text, different words for 'nothing' and so on).

We can see from this brief survey of the literature that no general consensus obtains as to the precise origin of double negation in Yiddish, but it can justifiably be claimed that the linguists cited above were thinking of East Yiddish when discussing the origins of the double negative in Yiddish, since MHG and Slavic are juxtaposed as potential sources.

We should next look briefly at the German background to the consideration of double negation. Grimm (1873: 461) calls double negation in German 'eine heimische Regel' and attacks 'die lateinisch geschulten Schulmeister' for driving out 'die angeborene deutsche Regel'. Von Polenz (1978: 98) represents the opposing position, that the influence of Latin was beneficial: "Was von lat. Einfluss als wertvolle Bereicherung der dt. Sprache unangefochten geblieben ist, sind vor allem die syntaktischen Mittel begrifflicher Klarheit und Präzision. So wird nach lat. Vorbild vom 16. bis 18. Jh. die deutsche Möglichkeit der doppelten Verneinung . . . in der dt. Schrift-und Hochsprache verdrängt." The existence of this ideological split among Germanists should lead to a certain circumspection in dealing with accounts of double negation. Grimm could be suspected of wishing to multiply the number of examples of double negation to support his championship of it. Indeed Pensel (1981: 320) claims that the drop in the number of multiply negated sentences from the period 1470–1530 to the period 1670–1730 (from 1.8% to 0.6% of all negated simple sentences) is not reflected in accounts of the double negative, given the number of examples adduced in the *Deutsches Wörterbuch,* Paul's *Grammatik* and Kehrein's *Grammatik,* 'wo noch viele Belege für diese Art der gehäuften Negationen angeführt werden'. Pensel's study could prove extremely valuable for comparison between the development of the German literary standard and of the Yiddish literary standard (Kerler 1985), since some measure of the extent of the divergence of the Yiddish literary language from the German can be given. The frequency of double negation in texts such as *Megiles vints* and the *Maysebukh* suggests the at least partial independence of written Yiddish from developing norms of modern standard German and thus when placed in a wider context can contribute to the evaluation of the linguistic and especially sociolinguistic status of Western Yiddish texts, serving as a measure of the influence, or lack of it, of written German on written Western Yiddish.

Pensel's study confirms Kagarov's association of double negation with South German. In the first period examined (texts from 1470–1530) the highest proportion of doubly negated sentences is found in West Upper German, then East Central German, with an average level in East Upper German and West Central German, and North German well below the average (Pensel 1981: 306–7). We cannot base too much on Pensel's figures, since they deal with a period later than the generally accepted dating of the origin of Yiddish, but they fit in with the current trend in the search for the origins of Yiddish that looks to South and East Central German dialects for parallels with Yiddish (see King 1979 and this volume).

We should now turn to the Eastern Yiddish structure *nisht keyn* (as opposed to *keyn . . . nisht*). A preliminary search through the Germanist literature on negation (e.g. Grimm 1873: 457–492, Hildebrand 1890, Paul 1920: 334–7, Kürschner 1983, Wells 1985) revealed only one reference to this specific structure, though it is probable that a more exhaustive search will find evidence of it, perhaps in discussions of colonial German. Merkle (1976: 155) rejects the analogous structure *need koan* as a possibility in Bavarian German, although

he shows that Bavarian German favours double negation and multiple negation even up to quadruple negation (1976: 156). It is not always clear from discussions whether the structure is not found, or whether it is not regarded as a separate structure from the very common *kein . . . nicht*. J. Strauss reports hearing the form *nicht kein* from a speaker from Essen, West Germany (personal communication). Lockwood (1975: 11) notes that the structure *nisht keyn* does not occur in the 17th century Prague letters, and that the construction 'seems, according to the examples given by Kehrein, not to have been current in German at that time either'. Lockwood goes on to argue that *nisht keyn* is a pattern of Slavic origin: 'in the EY pattern, *nit,* although it does not go so far as to take over the pre-verbal position of its Slavic equivalent, does enter into a partnership with the verb rather than the negated noun itself, such a relationship being characteristic of the Slavic particle, as it was of the earlier German *ne* [. . .] alongside this new Slavicized fashion, the old style persists into Eastern Yiddish today'. However Robinson (1986: 10) notes, among other doubly negated structures, the following in the *Kav hayosher* (Frankfurt 1709: 28): *zolst nit kaan tsoyberay broukhn.* This still leaves open the question of the existence of this form in West Yiddish (Koidenover was born in Vilne, see Erik 1979: 309) but we can assume that the form is not a very recent innovation in Eastern Yiddish. A great deal of further research needs to be done on this topic and the many parallel topics that are relevant to our understanding of the relationship between West and East Yiddish and of the extent to which West Yiddish texts reflect spoken usage (Kerler 1985). If the structure *nisht keyn* were to be shown to be purely an East Yiddish phenomenon, this would be *prima facie* evidence for the Slavic influence for which Lockwood argues.

However the parallel between the pre-verbal Slavic *nie* and East Yiddish *nisht* as in *nisht keyn* does not seem particularly strong. The Slavic particle always appears before the verb, whereas the Yiddish *nisht* not only follows the verb but can easily be separated from it: Polish *nie mam czasu* 'I have no time', *on nigdy nikomu nic nie mòwi* 'he never says anything to anybody' as compared with Yiddish *ikh hob nisht keyn tsayt, ikh hob dokh nisht keyn tsayt, keyn tsayt hob ikh nisht* and *'in london iz nishto nisht keyn baytog, nisht keyn inderfri, in london iz shtendik farnakht'* (Sholem Aleichem). We should not dismiss the possibility of Slavic influence out of hand, but it seems premature to look to Slavic to account for the origin of a specific feature merely because it cannot be found in German. It might be argued that the (allegedly) freer word order of Slavic made it possible for the pattern *ikh hob keyn tsayt nisht* to alternate with a newer form *ikh hob nisht keyn tsayt.* Again though, we should stress that the Slavic model in this case is an uncertain one, especially given the fixed position of the negative particle *nie.* The well established status of *nisht keyn* seems to argue against it being a recent innovation as a result of Slavic influence (this is not to imply that all Slavic influence is necessarily recent). In question 001 141 of *The Language and Culture Atlas of Ashkenazic Jewry.* Columbia University (LCAAJ) informants were asked to translate into Yiddish the sentence 'they don't speak German'. Two basic variants were given: *zey redn nisht/niks/nit daytsh* and *zey redn nisht/nit keyn daytsh.* The form *nisht keyn* dominated in the Eastern area (i.e. Eastern East Yiddish), the form with *nisht* (or variant) was found in the West and especially the South West of the speech territory. It seems therefore that the *nisht keyn* structure is found in areas least under the impact of West Yiddish and/or German. We should however carefully distinguish absence of German and West Yiddish influence from presence of Slavic influence. West Yiddish would have been in a situation somewhat analogous to that of a creole that remains in contact with the 'higher prestige' cognate source language. Thus it is probable that a

form of post-creole speech continuum existed between West Yiddish and German (for discussion of this term see Decamp 1971, Day 1974), whereas Eastern East Yiddish would have developed 'independently'.

It seems therefore most plausible to argue that *nisht keyn* is an independent Yiddish development. Danielsen (1968) in a detailed study of the indefinite pronominal negative in OHG and MHG, gives a framework within which a hypothesis about the origin of the East Yiddish *nisht keyn* may be formulated. Simply put, it seems plausible to argue that *nisht keyn* is a reflex of MHG *nechein* (with variants such as *nehein, enhein, inhein, enchein, nekein, ichkein*), under analogy with the form *ni keyn* 'never any', often 'not any, no' and the form *keyn . . . nisht.* (An outline of the history of these forms and their development from OHG *nohein, nihein, nohhein, nihhein* is presented in Danielsen 1968: 99). The first factor that should be considered in the prevalence of the form *ni keyn* 'never any' and cognates in both MHG and Early written Yiddish (see examples cited above from the *Cambridge Codex* and *Shmuelbukh*). On these forms Grimm writes the following (1873: 460): 'Das im 14. 15. 16. jh. so häufige *nie kein* (. . . *niechein* neben *nichein* schon in den md. Sachsenspiegel) mag urspr. ein verkleidetes *nekein* sein; findet sich doch *nie* gleich *ne* nor dem Verb . . . *nie* ist da nur starkes *nicht*, wie schon mhd. diesz *nie kein* ist der Sache nach wie eine Auffrischung des ahd. *nih-ein*. Ebenso findet sich *dekein*, alter *dochein*, in alter frische hergestellt in *doch kein* . . . und *nekein*, urspr. *nochein*, in *noch kein* . . . hierher gehört auch das *ichkein* . . ., und dem *nie kein* entsprechend *ie kein* irgend ein . . .'. Confirmation of this process is given by Danielsen: 'Vom 12. Jh. begegnen wir hauptsächlich im Mitteldeutschen und seltener im Alemannischen der Neigung zur Erhöhung des *e* > *i* in der negativen Vorsilbe. Auch dem Bairischen ist das Phänomen nicht fremd. Das Ostfränkische hat nur *ni–*. Eine gewisse Beeinflussung durch die Negation *nie* liesse sich hier geltend machen (vgl. die nicht sehr verbreiteten Formen *niehein, niechein)*'. In a footnote is added the form *niekein* found in a 14th century manuscript (Danielsen 1968: 95). Semantic overlap between *never* and *not* can for example also be observed in colloquial English, where *never* is frequently used as an emphatic *not*. The fact that Eastern Yiddish replaced German *nie* with the form *keynmol . . . nisht* would have allowed the overlap to be generalized without the danger of confusion that might arise in German between *nikein* 'not any' and *ni(e) kein* 'never any'. Thus we have a tendency to reanalyse *nechein* and its cognates as *niechein,* or even *nienchein* (Danielsen 1968: 98), in conjunction with the Eastern Yiddish loss of *nie* which might have served as a barrier to an analogy of *nechein* and variants with *kein . . . nisht/nit.* Danielsen advances what he calls a 'Kollisionstheorie' (i.e. the colliding of different variants of *nechein*) to account for various changes in the form of the indefinite negative in German, as well as for the eventual supremacy of *kein* (1968: 101). We might postulate that the Jews of this period, with different migration patterns and a different geographical taxonomy of German speaking territory (see M. Weinreich 1973, volume 1, chapter 1 and Katz, this volume), would have developed different 'collision forms' from the coterritorial non-Jews. For example, Jews in Austro-Bavarian territory (see Gilbert 1984: 31 for a map of Jewish migration northwards into South German territory) up to the 14th century would have been in contact with the form *nechein,* or *nehein,* whereas in Middle German *kein* had become dominant by the 13th century (Danielsen 1968: 102). If we assume northward and eastward migration and fusion between East Central German and Austro-Bavarian features (King 1979: 8–9), then we would have a 'collision' in the period pre-14th century of speakers in contact with *nechein/nehein* and those in contact with *kein*. We can hypothesize that a fusion form **niçkejn* emerged (with

raising of *e>i* as discussed above), which under application of the general change from German *ç*>West Yiddish *š* (cf West Yiddish *iš* 'I', *ništ* 'nothing, not') would give a form such as *nish(t) keyn*. Alternatively, and perhaps more plausibly, we can postulate that *nechein/nichein* became **nišejn* under the change discussed above, which would be reanalysed as **niš+ejn,* which on contact with German (and early Yiddish) *kein* and *ni kein,* and given the presence of the structure *keyn . . . nisht* in early forms of Yiddish would yield **niškejn,* Yiddish *nish(t) keyn*. The form *nekein* is also attested in MHG (Danielsen 1968: 101). The argument outlined above is clearly speculative in detail, but can serve as an illustration of the possibility of combining detailed information about early German dialects with factors in the history of Yiddish (e.g. German *ç*> West Yiddish *š,* loss of *nie* 'never' in Eastern Yiddish).

We should now briefly look at the history of the forms for 'nothing' and 'not' in East and West Yiddish. In West Yiddish literature, the 'standard' seems to have become *niks* for 'nothing' and *nit* for 'not', though this is only an impressionistic finding that would need to be examined in detail. It seems clear though that the older form in Yiddish for 'not' was *nisht*. This is suggested by the predominance of *nisht* forms in fixed forms and expressions such as *nishtik* 'trivial', *tsenishtn* 'destroy', *tsu nisht makhn* 'frustrate', *nishtl* 'trifle', *gornisht iz nisht* and by the implicational scaling found in responses to LCAAJ question 103110. Informants were asked to translate the sentence 'he didn't eat anything' into Yiddish. The following variants (omitting certain phonetic details) were obtained:

ikh hob gornish(t) gegesn

ikh hob gornit gegesn

ikh hob ni(t) gegesn gornit

ikh hob ni(t) gegesn gornish(t)

ikh hob nish(t) gegesn gornish(t)

ikh hob gornit nit gegesn

ikh hob gornish(t) nit gegesn

ikh hob gornish(t) nish(t) gegesn

ikh hob nit gegesn gornish(t) nit

Thus *nit* can accompany either *gornisht* or *gornit,* but *nisht* accompanies just *gornisht* (there was one exception). We have in Beranek's Atlas (1965: map 99) information on the distribution of terms for 'nothing' in West Yiddish. The form *nisht* is found in the North and Central East, and *niks* in the South and West. Itzik Feitel Stern (1833) in the introduction to his *Lexicon der jüdischen Geschäfts und Umgangssprache* divided German Jews into those in the North who say *nisht* and those in the South who say *niks*. Unfortunately, neither Beranek nor Itzik Feitel Stern give any information about the distribution of forms for 'not'. However it seems probable that at least for a time over

much of West Yiddish speech territory the terms for 'nothing' and for 'not' were homophonous: In the North *nisht,* in the South *niks.* U. Weinreich in his study of Transcarpathian Yiddish (1964: 253) gives the West Transcarpathian form for 'not' as *niks,* and this is confirmed by the three informants from this area for LCAAJ question 103 110. These same informants have the form *gorniks* 'nothing', instead of what we might expect historically, namely *niks.* It seems likely therefore that the replacement of *nisht* 'not' by *nit* 'not' in West Yiddish, and the de-emphasizing of *gornisht/gorniks/gornit* (compare German *nichts* as against *garnichts*) in Eastern and West Transcarpathian Yiddish is a reaction to the widespread homophony of the forms for 'nothing' and those for 'not'. In German dialects, the form *nischt* also exists in both meanings, but the areas do not overlap (compare Wrede 1951: map 73 'nothing' with Eichhoff 1977, volume 2: map 116 'not'). The possibilities for instability in this part of the negative system can be illustrated from sentences such as *ikh her nisht* 'I can't hear, I hear nothing' where the negative particle could be glossed as the negative 'adverb' 'not' or the negative substantive 'nothing'.

Mention should also be made of a construction observed by U. Weinreich (1964: 254), the negative imperative *niks vaants* 'don't cry' in West Transcarpathian Yiddish which is analogous to the Lithuanian Yiddish form *nit veynt* (U. Weinreich 1958: 383). Weinreich suggests Hungarian influence in the one case and Slavic in the second. Weinreich's suggestion of independent developments leading to analogous forms in the two areas is perfectly plausible, though we should also consider the possibility that these forms represent remnants on the periphery of the East Yiddish speech territory of a feature with originally a much wider distribution. A study currently in preparation by Ulrike Kiefer of Columbia University involving the comparative dialectology of East Yiddish and German will allow individual distributional facts to be placed in an overall context and thus contribute to their evaluation.

The purpose of this paper has been to show that the study of Yiddish morphology and syntax (see King, this volume) can make a significant contribution to our understanding of the history of Yiddish. A general history of the morphology and syntax of older Yiddish texts would add greatly to our knowledge of the development of Yiddish as a whole. Furthermore, the study of East Yiddish, given that large areas of East Yiddish speech territory were removed from continuous co-territorial German influence, can also throw light on the origins and early history of Yiddish. By the cautious comparative study of Eastern Yiddish and MHG (the importance of the Slavic framework notwithstanding) we can frame hypotheses about early Yiddish and put a comparative history of the West Yiddish and German literary languages in some sociological and sociolinguistic perspective.

REFERENCES

BERANEK, F. J. 1965 *Westjiddischer Sprachatlas.* Marburg/Lahn.

BESCH, W. *et al.* (eds) 1983 *Dialektologie: ein Handbuch zur deutschen und allgemeinen Dialektforschung.* Walter de Gruyter, Berlin.

COPELAND, R. and SÜSSKIND, N. 1976 *The Language of Herz's Esther. A study in Judeo-German Dialectology.* University of Alabama Press.

DANIELSEN, N. 1968 Die negativen unbestimmten Pronominaladjektiva im Alt- und Mittelhochdeutschen. *Zeitschrift für deutsche Sprache* **14,** 92–117.

DAY, R. 1974 Decreolization: co-existent systems and the post-creole continuum. In Decamp, D. and Hancock, I., 1974, 38–45.

DECAMP, D. 1971 Towards a generative analysis of a Post-creole Continuum. In Hymes, D., 1971, 349–370.

DECAMP, D. and HANCOCK, I. (eds) 1974 *Pidgins and Creoles: Current Trends and Prospects.* Georgetown University Press.

EICHHOFF, J. 1977 *Wortatlas der deutschen Umgangssprache,* 2 Vols. Francke, Berlin.

ERIK, M. 1979 *Di geshikhte fun der yidisher literatur.* Congress for Jewish Culture, New York.

FALK, F. and FUKS, L. (eds) 1961 *Das Schemuelbuch des Mosche Esrim Wearba,* 2 Vols. Van Gorcum, Assen.

FUKS, L. 1957 *The Oldest Known Literary Documents of Yiddish Literature,* 2 Vols. Brill, Leiden.

GOLDWASSER, M. 1982 *Azhoras Noshim:* a linguistic study of a 16th century Yiddish work. *Working Papers in Yiddish and Eastern European Jewish Studies* No. 33. Yivo, New York.

GRIMM, J. and GRIMM, W. 1854–1960. *Deutsches Wörterbuch,* 16 Vols. Leipzig.

HAKKARAINEN, H. 1967 *Studien zum Cambridger Codex* 1. Turun Yliopisto, Turku.

HERZOG, M. I. 1965 Grammatical features of Markuze's *Seyfer Refues.* In Weinreich, U. 1965, 49–62.

HILDEBRAND, R. 1890 Gehäufte Verneinung. In *Gesammelte Aufsätze und vorträge zur deutschen Philologie und zum deutschen Unterricht.* Teubner, Leipzig.

HYMES, D. 1955 'Positional analysis of categories: a frame for reconstruction' *Word* 11, 10–23.

HYMES, D. (ed.) 1971 *Pidginization and Creolization of Languages.* Cambridge University Press.

KAGAROV, Y. 1926 Di grunt stikhye fun yidishn sintaksis. In Weinreich, M., Prilutski, N. and Reyzen, Z., 1926, pp. 425–428.

KATZ, D. 1980 The wavering Yiddish segolate: a problem of socio-linguistic reconstruction. *International Journal of the Sociology of Language* 24, 5–27.

KATZ, D. 1983 Zur Dialektologie des Jiddischen. In Besch, W. *et al.,* 1983, pp. 1018–1041.

KATZ, E. 1963 Six Germano-Judaic Poems from the Cairo Genizah. PhD Dissertation, University of California, Los Angeles.

KERLER, D. B. 1985 From declining Western Yiddish to the nascent Eastern Yiddish standard: concepts, sources and strategies. Paper delivered to Autumn General Meeting of The Linguistics Association of Great Britain, September 1985.

KETTMANN, G. and SCHILDT, J. (eds) 1981 *Zur Ausbildung der Norm der deutschen Literatursprache auf der syntaktischen Ebene (1470–1730) der Einfachsatz.* Akademie Verlag, Berlin.

KING, R. D. 1979 New Perspectives on the History of Yiddish: the evidence of the German component. Paper delivered to the International Conference on Research in Yiddish Language and Literature Oxford, 6–9, August, 1979.

KÜRSCHNER, W. 1983 *Studien zur Negation im Deutschen.* Gunter Narr, Berlin.

LANDAU, A. 1901 Die Sprache der Memoiren Glückels von Hameln. *Mitteilungen der Gesellschaft für jüdische Volkskunde* 1 Heft, 7, 20–68.

LANDAU, A. and WACHSTEIN, B. (eds) 1911 *Jüdische Privatbriefe aus dem Jahre 1619.* Vienna.

LOCKWOOD, V. 1975 Negation in a sample of 17th century Western Yiddish. *Working Papers in Yiddish and East European Jewish Studies* No. 14.

LÖTZSCH, R. 1974 Slawische Elemente in der grammatischen Struktur des Jiddischen. *Zeitschrift für Slawistik* 19, 446–457.

MAITLIS, J. 1955 London Yiddish letters of the early 18th century. *Journal of Jewish Studies* 6, 153–165, 237–252.

MARCHAND, J. 1959 Review of Fuks, 1957. *Word* 15, 383–394.

MERKLE, L. 1976 *Bairische Grammatik.* DTV, Munich.

PAUL, H. 1920 *Deutsche Grammatik,* Vol. 4. Niemeyer, Halle.

PENSEL, F. 1981 Die Satznegation. In Kettmann, G. and Schildt, J., 1981, 287–326.

ROBINSON, E. 1986 A study of the language of the *Kav Hayosher.* Unpublished paper, Columbia University.

ROSENFELD, M. (ed.) 1984 *The Book of Cows: a Facsimile Edition of the famed Kubukh.* London.

SAPIR, E. 1915 Notes on Judeo-German phonology. *Jewish Quarterly Review* 6, 231–266.

SHATZKY, J. (ed.) 1926 *Simkhes hanefesh.* Maisel, New York.

SHMERUK, Kh. (ed.) 1962/3 *Megiles vints.* Hebrew University, Jerusalem.

ITZIK FEITEL STERN 1833 *Lexicon der jüdischen Geschäfts und Umgangssprache.* München.

TAVYOV, Y.-Kh. 1914 [The Slavic Elements in Yiddish]. *Hašiloah* 30, 139–150.

VEYNGER, M. 1913 *Yidisher sintaksis.* Warsaw.

VON POLENZ, P. 1978 *Geschichte der deutschen Sprache.* De Gruyter, Berlin.

WATKINS, C. 1964 Preliminaries to the reconstruction of Indo-European sentence structure. *Proceedings of the 9th International Conference (1962) of Linguists* **1964,** 1035–1042.

WEINREICH, M. 1960 Old Yiddish Poetry in Linguistic-Literary Research. *Word* **16,** 100–118.

WEINREICH, M. 1973 *Geshikhte fun der yidisher shprakh* 4 Vols. Yivo, New York.

WEINREICH, M., PRILUTSKI, N. and REYZEN, Z. (eds) 1926 *Filologishe shriftn 1* Kletskin: Vilne.

WEINREICH, U. 1958 Yiddish and colonial German in Eastern Europe: the differential impact of Slavic. In *American Contributions to the 4th International Congress of Slavicists,* Moscow, September 1958, pp. 1–53.

WEINREICH, U. 1964 Western traits in Transcarpathian Yiddish. In *For Max Weinreich on his 70th Birthday,* pp. 245–262.

WEINREICH, U. (ed.) 1965 *The Field of Yiddish 2: Studies in Language, Folklore and Literature.* Mouton, The Hague.

WELLS, C. J. 1985 *German. A Linguistic History to 1945.* Clarendon, Oxford.

WILLER, J. 1915 Żargon żydowski na ziemiach polskich. *Encyklopedia Polska* **2,** division 3.1, 397–424.

Language & Communication, Vol. 7, Supplement, pp. 39–46, 1987.
Printed in Great Britain.

0271-5309/87 $3.00 + .00
Pergamon Journals Ltd.

THE ORIGIN OF THE *O* VOWEL IN SOUTHEASTERN YIDDISH

JEAN JOFEN

Baruch College in the City University of New York

Southeastern Yiddish is the Yiddish spoken in Rumania and Bessarabia. Very little is known about the Jews who originally settled these countries and even less about the places of their origin. However, theories have been advanced on that subject. The most prevalent theory is that Southeastern Yiddish is a synthesis of Polish and Lithuanian Yiddish.

It is the object of my study to point out, on the basis of linguistic as well as historical evidence, that this is not so; that this territory was also settled by Jews who had Bavarian dialects as the basis of their language and who followed the course of the Danube to settle this territory.

Because of the dislocation and extermination of the greatest part of the Jewish community of all of Eastern Europe it has become impossible to study Yiddish dialects in their place of origin. I was, however, successful in showing that research could be conducted exclusively with immigrants and that meaningful and distinctive isoglottic lines could be obtained and the dialects classified and distinguished on the basis of this information. This is one of the contributions I have made to linguistic geography (Jofen 1964) and it has subsequently led to a more detailed work in this field.

'The Southeastern Dialect' is characterized by the large number of *o* and *ey* phonemes, and by the small number of *a* phonemes in stressed syllables. Another characteristic is the tendency towards monophthongization: *ey > i, beyzem > bizem* 'broom' and *ou > u, frou > fru* 'woman'. We also find in this dialect the tendency towards fricativization, viz., *ou > ov, trouerik > troverik* 'sad' (Jofen 1964: VI).

I will now discuss each of these characteristics. The most outstanding characteristic of Southeastern Yiddish is the appearance of *o* for historical *ă*.

1. The *o* phoneme: In this dialect there is hardly a short *a*. Instead, we find *o* in words of Germanic, Slavic and Hebrew origin—cf. *tots* 'tray', *khosene* 'wedding', etc.

The only German dialect which shows this phenomenon is the Bavarian.

> Eine reiche Quelle des unechten "o" ist die Neigung des bairischen "a" sich zu verdumpfen. Wir können sie durch die Jahrhunderte verfolgen (Weinhold 1867: 37).

Ayrer rhymes *man: son* (Ayrer 1865: 813). We also find in old chronicles: *ohtzehen* in 1300 (*Altenburg Urkundenbuch* 1865: n 85). *Ohzik* in 1285 (*Wittelsbach Urkundenbuch* 1857: 158).

A sixteenth century document explicitly states that:

> 'a' der erste Buchstabe hat bei den Teutschen eine grosse Gemeinschaft mit dem 'o', weicht einer dem andern, steht einer für den andern, und sprechen die Bauern gemeiniklich 'o' wo dei Stetten 'a' brauchen. Es sprechen auch gemeiniklich diesen ersten Buchstaben die Baiern aus, dass er mehr dem 'o' gleich ist denn dem rechten 'a' so die Schwaben und Walhen reden (Aventini 1566: V).

This is very important for Yiddish dialect study because some Yiddish linguistics have long claimed that Swabian is much more representative of Old Yiddish than is Bavarian. Thus

Max Weinreich: "The Old Yiddish period (1250–1500) is still very much connected with the Swabian dialect" (M. Weinreich 1940: 47).

My contention is that *o* in *mome* 'mother', *tote* 'father', is the old Bavarian *o* which the Jews brought with them when they left Bavaria.

What was the history of the Jews in Germany and especially in Bavaria? We find that Jews had come with the Roman army to the Rhein and Main. We find in the Urkundenbuch of the city Speyer: 'Cum ex Spirensi villa urbem facerem, putavi milies amplificare honorem loci nostri, si et Judaeos colligerem' (*Urkundenbuch der Stadt Speyer*, I, No. 11). ("When I wanted to make a city of the village Speyer I felt that I would increase the glory of our city a thousandfold if I also settled a great number of Jews").

We also learn that "Die wichtigste Niederlassung der Juden in Bayern war in Regensburg. Der Donauhandel hat hier zahlreiche Juden ansässig gemacht. Schon um die Jahrtausendwende erscheint hier ein Ghetto ein 'habitaculum iudaeorum'" (Bauerreiss 1953).

The first persecution of Jews in Bavaria is reported from Passau in 1200 (Schmid 1929), and in 1298 from Rottingen and Iphofen (Browe 1926: 46). The persecutions found their central focus in Deggendorf. There we find an inscription on a church from the middle of the 14th century: "Anno domini 1337 des nachste Tag nach sankt Michelstag wurden die juden erslagen di stat si anzunden do wart gotes leichnam funden. Daz sahet frauen und do huab man das Gotshaus ze baun an." Bauerreiss, *Pie Jesu* (36).

The second wave of persecution of Bavarian Jewry was triggered by accusations that Jews poisoned the wells and brought about the 'black death'. A third wave broke out in Munich in 1442 "und 40–80 Prozent der damaligen jüdischen Bevölkerung wurden ausgewiesen. Ihr Gotteshaus wurde von dem Münchner Arzt Dr. Hans Hartlieb in eine Kirche verwandelt" (Kraft: 679).

The Jews were driven out of Augsburg in 1440 (Stetten 1865); of Munich in 1442, and Landshut and Würzburg in 1450. "Am längsten hat sich die jüdische Gemeinde in Nürnberg erhalten, aber das Jahr 1500 sah keine Juden mehr in Nürnberg" (*Deutsche Chroniken* Vol. I). Thus for nearly two hundred years Jews were excluded from Bavaria, but succeeded in establishing themselves again during the war of the Spanish succession. Thus the 14th and 15th centuries saw the German Jews in their flight to the East.

I believe, from historic evidence, that the Jews of Bavaria moved along the Danube southeastwards, through Hungary ("Historisch bewiesen ist es dass die Juden sich in der Walachei gegen 1367 kurz nach der Gründung dieses Fürstentums unter Ladislaus Bessarab niedergelassen haben nachdem sie von Ludwig dem Grossen aus Ungarn vertrieben wurden" (Bernstein 1918: 15). We also find records of many Jewish settlers in the Walachei—"Sie betreiben den Pferdehandel in der Moldau von Anfang des 16. Jahrhunderts" (Bernstein 1918: 16).

If I postulate that the Jews of Bavaria colonized Southeastern Europe by the route of Hungary I will of course have to demonstrate many more similarities between Southeastern Yiddish and Bavarian as well as traces of Bavarian dialects in Hungarian Yiddish.

I began by showing the *o,* in place of the short *a*. This is a distinguishing mark of Bavarian. It is interesting that another group of Bavarians, not Jews, who settled in Austria in the 14th century also maintain this distinguishing characteristic of Bavarian. "Südlich von Laibach dehnt sich das Gottscheeland aus, das bayrische Siedler seit dem 14. Jhdt

bebauen'' (Martin 1939: 158). In investigating the dialect of Gottschee we find: "In unserer Ma ist die Entwicklung des *a* weitergediehen als sonst. Bei Länge führt sie durchwegs, bei Kürze nur in einem Teile des Gebietes unterstützt von Konsonanten welche die Rundung fordern zu *u* sonst zu *o*. Ausserdem stellt zich zwischen *o* und gewissen darauf folgenden Konsonanten (*r, l, n*, und Dental) ein Gleitlaut ein: *juər, miər*" (Tschinkel 167). Even more evident is the development of *a* to *o* in the spelling of family names. *Saller: Soller; Kramer: Kromer; Falkner: Folkner* (Obergfoell 1887).

In my Atlas I divided Yiddish dialects into Northern and Southeastern on the basis of the development of MHG *u* as per isogloss 81 *froy: frou: fru* 'woman' and isogloss 82 *oyskern: ouskern: uskern* 'sweep' and to a more limited extent isogloss 83 *yoykh: youkh: yukh* 'broth' and isogloss 84 *groypn: groupn: grupn* 'barley' (Jofen 1964: 45).

This monophthongization is also found in Bavarian: "Neben dem alten Diphthong *au* hat der bayrische Dialect einen jüngeren aus *u* entwickelt. Er tritt einzeln im 12. Jahrhundert auf" (Weinhold 1867: 76). Otacker (1745: 669) rhymes: *pflum: goum* and Weinhold remarks: "Der Schluss auf die starke Entwicklung des *u > ou* im 13. Jahrhundert im bairischen Dialect ist hiernach gerechtfertigt" (Weinhold 1867: 102).

Another distinguishing feature of the Southeastern dialect unearthed in my Atlas is the fricativization of *ou* to *ov*—*trourik > troverik* 'sad'; *zour > zover* 'sour'. This too we find in the Bavarian Dialect: "*u* vor *r* wird gewöhnlich *awe* geschrieben, indem *r* einen Vorschlag erzeugte: *Mauer > Mawer* (c. 1155, M.B. XXVIII, Weinhold 76). Also from Mundartgedichte: Matheis (1954: 36)

An ganz' n Tag geht's so dahin
Vor lauter Trawigkeit (Matheis 1954: 36).

We find parallels also in the consonant systems. Bavarian and Yiddish have voiceless stops *p* and *k* where modern German has voiced *b* and *g*. Compare *nepl* (*Nebel*) (Herberstein 1557: 302) *topan* (*toben*) *kegn* (*gegen*) (Notizblatt 6; 367). We find unreal *t* in Bavarian and Yiddish in *destwegen, anderscht, nachert* (Weinhold 148). Loss of *n* is manifest in Yiddish in the numbers *fuftsn* (*funfzehn*) and *fuftsik* (*fünfzig*). In Bavarian there is no loss of *n*, but the grammar of Gottschee's dialect has *vufsain, vuftsikh* (Tschinkell 136).

We find *m* instead of *w* in both languages in the personal pronoun *mer, mar, mir* instead of *wir*.

The loss of *h* in part of the Yiddish territory, especially the Southeastern part, (also the ahistoric prefixation of "inorganic" *h* in words beginning with a vowel) is one of the riddles in bilingual dialectology. Some Yiddish linguists try to explain it as due to influence of neighbouring Slavic dialects:

The specific geographic distribution of /h/ loss [. . .] is even more mysterious than the mere fact of such a loss [. . .]. Another puzzle is the loss of /h/ precisely in the territory of Ukrainian where *h* (< *g*) plays so important a role, and the preservation of /h/ in the territory of Polish, where *h* is the most marginal of phonemes, occurring only in loanwords from German, Czech and Ukrainian, if not popularly replaced by /x/. If contact lies at the root of the Yiddish innovation, we should have found precisely the reverse distribution" (U. Weinreich 1963: 347, 348).

Thus the attempt to explain loss of /h/ by Slavic influence did not lead Weinreich to any positive result and we therefore return to German dialects to come up with a solution.

Weinhold (1867: 192) remarks: "Ferner zeigt sich *h* in älteren Quellen nicht selten vocalischen Anlaut vorgetreten." He cites the following examples: *halmahtigun (Allmächtigen), Massman* (1839), *hatam (Atem)* in *Salzburger Glossen III* (295–314); *Heperhart (Eberhard)* (Muspilli 1832: 42, 8.); *hevigon (ewigen)* (Muspilli 9, 2.) *hostern*

(Ostern) (Altenburger Urkundenbuch 1865: 99). From Tirol he also reports: *Henkel (Enkel).* He finds that "In dem sog cimbrischen Catechismus von 1602 kommt dieses *h* öfter vor, so wie umgekehrt anlautendes *h* abfällt." U. Weinreich (1958: 225) reports *ba hakh* 'by you' in Podolie.

Since we know that aphaeresis and anaptyxis go hand in hand we must also consider the loss of an *h* phoneme in this territory. On this point we find, unfortunately, only few words in Bavarian: *alben (Halben)* (Diemer 1849: 342, 9) but we do find many examples in Alemannic: "Der alemannisch nicht seltene Abfall von anlautendem *h* kommt bairisch so gut wie nicht vor" (Weinhold 1867: 193). Weinhold tries to explain the loss of *h* as a continuing process. We know that in the 9th century *h* disappeared in combinations like: *hw, hl, hr, hn*. The epenthesis of *h* before vowels can be seen as an extension of hiatus where it was originally inserted to separate two vowels: *niehe, gereuhen*.

It is interesting that this *h* before vowels is also reported from Gottschee: "Vor die Vokale tritt zuweilen h als starker gehauchter Einsatz: *Hanapark (Annaberg)*" (Hauffen 1895: 24).

As for the confusion of sibilants, which we find in Northeastern Yiddish but not in Southeastern Yiddish, I would ascribe it to Slavic influence, probably, as Weinreich (1963: 353–354) claims, under the influence of Polish *mazurzenie*.

The Yiddish shares some interesting features with Bavarian. Both have plural ending *-len* in the word *mantlen (Oberbairisches Archiv)*, vs. *Mäntel* in modern German.

The nouns: *almer, spital, spitz, parschon (Person)* are all masculine in Bavarian and Yiddish vs. feminine in modern German, while *die Schoz* is feminine in Bavarian and Yiddish but masculine elsewhere.

The diminutive forms in *l* are common to both Yiddish and Bavarian, in names like: *Lipperl, Pepperl* (Weinhold 1867: 244).

Weinhold reports an interesting list of names from Bavaria, not mentioning whether they are Jewish. "Die verkleinernde Kraft der *z* aüssert sich nur an den Eigennamen, die sich in ältester Zeit sehr oft finden: *Geza, Genza, Raza, Riza, Chuonzi*" (Weinhold 1867: 246). All these names are very prevalent in Southeastern Yiddish today and my atlas informant for Berdichev is called *Minze*. The Bavarian forms of names which are much more prevalent in the Ukraine further strengthen my theory.

The old dual which has been given up in almost all German dialects was lost in prehistoric times, but was retained in the personal pronoun in Gothic and Norse—"Go. duals of the 2nd pers. are still preserved in the modern Bav. dialects [. . .]: *os* 'you' (nom.), *enk* 'you' (acc.), *enker* 'your' are duals from a historical standpoint, but plurals in their present meaning" (Prokosch 1939: 230). Weinhold adds: "Ein Hauptvorzug und Merkmal des bairischen Dialects sind die dualen Formen. Leider haben wir bis zum Endes des 13. Jh. keine Belege dafür obschon sie natürlich in lebendiger Volksrede bestanden haben müssen. Schon bei den ältesten Schriftstellern, die sie haben (Otacker, C. 451. 1314) ist die duale Bedeutung dieser dualen Formen schwankend oder ganz in die plurale übergegangen (Grimm, *Grammatik der deutschen Sprache*. 973) für die folgende Zeit ist dies noch mehr der Fall." The dual forms: *ez* (nom.), *enker* (gen.), *enk* (dat.), *enk* (acc.) which are found in the Bavarian are also found in Southeastern and Hungarian Yiddish.

Weinhold (1867: 291) notes further that "mit Ausnahme des Kärntischen Lesachthals (Lexer, 59) haben alle Gegenden unsers Gebiets jetzt diese-ts. Im 17. Jahrh. war es sogar in die schlesische Mundart eingedrungen: In Wenzel Scherffers Gedichten s. 641 lesen wir:

"Venue rieff: Frau was wolltets haben? Wolltets füllen einen Graben? O gehts heim und spinnt dafür." My own Atlas (Jofen 1964) documents from community 43 (Hungary) "ɛts ət zejn dɔrt a vildə xaje" (you will see there a wild animal).

Yiddish still retains the verb *"turn"* 'be allowed' which we find in Bavarian only up to the 17th century—"Das Zeitwort scheint im 17. Jahrhundert vom dem Dialect aufgegeben zu sein. Die einzige Spur in den heutigen Mundarten des Gebietes ist das von Höfer # 90 neben dürfen aufgeführte deuren" (Weinhold 1867: 330). We find, however, from before: *(ix) turr, (Fastnachtspiele aus dem fünfzehnten Jahrhundert, 1851: 37, 24), (er) thur* (Herberstein 1557: 99).

The lexicon too shows that Southeastern Yiddish has words known only in Bavarian: Map LII in my Atlas investigates the expressions for 'stammer'. From community 53 the informant reported: *ea kaketst* 'he stammers'. Weinhold (1867: 192) reports: *"w fällt ganz aus: so steht kirre zu got. quairrus und quirren; kerren zu querren, kackezen zu quackezen, Nestkack zu Nestquack.*

From Gottschee, too, Tschinkel reports *kikkatsn* 'stottern'; he leads it back to OHG *gicchazzen,* MHG *gigzen.* Lessiak (1903: 151) tries to find an etymological link with *krakketən* 'schreien', *krächzen.*

> Solche Mädchen gibts nicht vil,
> Wie ich gerne haben will
> die nich häggeln, wenn sie gehen
> oder schakeln wo sie stehen (Schmeller 1872: II, 366).

Otherwise the word would be *shoykeln.* cf. *kaufen—koyfn, laufen*—loyfn.

The Bavarian form *penzen* 'bitten, drängen, erstreben'(Pangkofer 1854) might throw some light on Yiddish *bentshn* 'bless, say grace after meals' which has never been adequately explained.

Max Weinreich explains Southeastern Yiddish as a synthesis of Lithuanian (Northeastern) and Polish (Mideastern) Yiddish. He contends that the Ukraine was settled by both Polish and Lithuanian Jews but concedes that the theory cannot explain the Yiddish of Eastern Galicia, Bukovina and Moldavia, which he finds to be on the whole identical with the dialect of the Ukraine: "Es iz ober ba mir geblibn a kashe, vi azoy zikh an eytse tsu gebn mitn dyalekt fun mizrekh galitsye, bukovine, moldeve, vos es iz identish bederekh klal mitn dyalekt fun ukrayne" (M. Weinreich 1940: 59).

On the basis of my linguistic findings both phonetic and lexical and on the basis of historic evidence there can be no doubt that Southeastern Yiddish can not be explained as a fusion of the Polish and Lithuanian alone but must also be viewed as an offspring of Bavarian. A similar indication is given by Birnbaum who notes that the path of the dialect is mainly from the south, probably over the Carpathian mountains from the west: "Der veg fun dem dyalekt tsit zikh der iker fun dorem, aponim iber di karpatn, fun mayrev" (see M. Weinreich 1940: 59).

My contention is that the Jews, after they were expelled from Bavaria, moved right along the Danube through Austria-Hungary towards Rumania. To strengthen this theory, I will now demonstrate that elements of Bavarian phonology and lexicon are to be found also in the Yiddish of Hungary.

The possessive pronoun in Bavarian is *enker.* "Ir kommt allmählich seit Ende des 12. Jahrhunderts auf: noch im 13. Jahrhundert überwiegt sehr bedeutend die Verwendung des Gen. von Personalpronomen. Ausser dem *ihr* besitzt der Dialect ein junges aus dem Dat.

Pl. *iin* gebildetes *ihnen* 'iner' das übrigens auf eine Mehrzahl und den Höflichkeitsplural sich bezeiht: *Ihner Hut, Ihnes Kleid"* (Weinhold 1867: 374). These polite forms of the Bavarian are still maintained in the Yiddish of Hungary.

My atlas turns up the forms *amper* 'pail' from communities 40 (Kassa), 41 (Miškolc), 42 (Szeged), 43 (Szatmar), 44 (Munkacs) and 45 (Huszt). The form is reported by Schmeller for Bavaria.

Map XLIX shows *smayte* 'sour cream' for communities 41, 43, 44 and 45. Schmeller reports it as *der Schmete* 'dicke Milch'.

Map XXXIV shows *snoutsn* 'moustache' for communities 40–45. Schmeller reports "der Schnauzbart auch wohl bloss der Schnauz." Community 43 reports *"beyusn"* for 'moustache' which Schmeller has as *"bouzn"* 'Haarknoten'.

Max Matheis (1954: 43) reports *brätl* 'stew'—

> Und os habn gar a Brätl gricht
> Dass eah grad d'Fetten glanzt im G'sicht
> Drum essts di Täg enk, Kugelrund
> solangs enk schmeckt, solang seids gsund.

Bratl is still used in Hungarian Yiddish for 'stew'.

Matheis (1945: 12) also reports from Bavaria *štaad*—

> Bauern nemt' enk no a Schnüpfi
> und klopft's d'Pfeife aus schö staad.

In Hungarian Yiddish one encounters even today:

> Az mə gayt shtāt
> kimt mən vāt ('if you go slow, you reach far').

The form *shiplink* for 'seven' we find in the expression *shipe zibele* 'seven month old baby'.

There is another area in which I can point out a link between Bavarian, German and Hungarian and Southeastern Yiddish. This area is folklore. I will begin with an object that has up to now been considered specifically Jewish. The object is *khale* 'loaf of white bread used on the Sabbath and holidays'. Uriel Weinreich (1962: 31) reports that "the hallah was especially embellished by twists of dough representing hands, keys and other objects. Ladders and birds, for example have been used in season in order to symbolically facilitate the ascent of prayers to heaven. . . . If ornamental bread forms are a Jewish innovation due to Slavic baking patterns their endowment with religious symbolism and especially their association with particular holidays unknown to the Christian neighbours testify to the sublety and creativeness of the adaptation process."

As I pointed out at the beginning of this article it is possible to learn something about Bavarian speech and culture from the people of Gottschee.

Hauffer (1895: 47) reports from Gottschee:

> An den heiligen drei (Weihnachtsabend, Silvester, und Vorabend des Dreikönigsfestes) wird in Gottschee der Tisch mit einem weissen Tuche bedeckt. Darauf werden 3 oder mehrere feine Weissbrote gelegt. Die kleineren heisen Wächter (bochtr) und Nachbarn (nochparn) das grösste Shiplink (wohl von Sippe, Schroer vermutet von mhd. sip also ein siebgrosses Brot). Der Shiplink ist mit allerlei aus Teig gebacken Figuren, dem Christkind in der Wiege, Tauben, Hühnern, Bindern, Schweinen und einem geflochtenen Rand versehen. Am Dreikönigstage wird er erst angeschnitten und an die Hausgenossen vertheilt, auch die Thiere erhalten Stückchen davon ins Futter gemengt, damit sie vor Behexung gereit bleiben.

Thus we see that it is not a custom that originated with the Jews but was taken over by them.

Up to this day Hungarians bake small *khales* which they call *bokhter*.

Many Bavarian superstitions are retained in Jewish lore. They are not confined to

Southeastern Yiddish but travel fast over the the entire speech territory. Cf. *Wenn man über ein Kind hinschreitet, so wächst es nicht mehr* 'if you step over a child it will not grow'; *Wer einem andern unter den Füssen durchschlüpft, der wächst nimmer* 'if you slip through the feet of another person, you will not grow'; *Wer zum Fenster hinaussteigt und nicht wieder hinein, der wächst nicht mehr* 'if you climb out of a window and not back, you will not grow' (after Panzer 1954).

Many superstitions deal directly or indirectly with death. *Wenn eine schwangere Frau über ein Grab geht, so stirbt ihr Kind* 'if a pregnant woman goes over a grave her unborn child will die'. For this reason pious Jews even today do not permit a pregnant woman to go to a cemetery, even though there is no basis for the prohibition in Biblical or Talmudic Law.

Superstitions connected with some mishap are: *Wem etwas ins Aug fällt, der halte den Atem, bis er dreimal über entgegengesetzten Arm gespuckt hat* 'if something falls into your eye, hold your breath till you spit three times over your other arm'.

> Ein Kind wirft den Milchzahn auf den Boden und sagt:
> Maus, Maus Maus
> Da hast du einen beinernen Zahn
> Gib mir einen eisernen dran

'if you lose a tooth you should say: Mouse, mouse, mouse here you have a tooth of bone, give me an iron one instead'. The Yiddish variant is

> Mayzl, mayzl, mayzl
> gib mir an ayzernem
> na dir a beynernem.

Wenn jemand etwas erzält und niesst dazu, dann ist es wahr 'when someone sneezes while he is telling a story it is usually the truth'. Yiddish has *Genosn bam emes*. Yiddish folklore explains it in this fashion: A lie can be planned but the truth comes straight out and can not be planned just as one can not plan to sneeze.

Many superstitions are connected with marriage. *Welches Mädchen in den Bronnen schaut, entdeckt ihren Bräutigam* 'if a girl looks into a well she will see her bridegroom'.

In this article I attempt to chart a new course and show how much can be explained and learned in the history of Yiddish if we leave aside one of the theories held in high esteem till now, namely that Southeastern Yiddish has to be explained as a fusion of the Polish and Lithuanian.

REFERENCES

Altenburger Urkundenbuch. 1865 Vienna.

AVENTINI, J. 1566 *Chronica.* Frankfurt am Main.

AYRER, 1865 *Ayrers Dramen.* Stuttgart.

BAUERREIS, R. 1853 *Kirchengeschichte Bayerns.* Erzabtei St. Otilien.

BAUERREIS, R. *Pie Jesu.*

BERNSTEIN, S. 1918 *Die Judenpolitik der rumänischen Regierung.* Copenhagen.

BROWE, P. 1926 Die Hostienschändigung der Juden im Mittelalter. *Rom. Quartalschrift* **34.**

Deutsche Chroniken, Vol. I. Nurnberg.

CHAFE, W. L. (ed.) 1952 *Symposium on Language and Culture.* Proceedings of the Annual Spring Meeting of the American Ethnological Society. Seattle.

DIEMER, J. 1849 *Deutsche Gedichte des 11 und 12. Jahrh.* Vienna.

Fastnachtspiele aus dem fünfzehnten Jahrhundert, 1851. Stuttgart.

HAUFFEN, A. 1895 *Die deutsche Sprachinsel Gottschee.* Graz.

HERBERSTEIN, (Freiherr V.) S. 1557 *Selbstbiographie.* Vienna.

JOFEN, J. 1964 *A Linguistic Atlas of Eastern European Yiddish.* Michigan.

JOFFE, J. A. 1954 Dating the Origin of Yiddish dialects. In Weinreich, U. 1954, pp. 102–121.

KRAFT, B. *Andechser Studien.*

LESSIAK, P. 1903 "Die Mundart von Pernegg in Kärnten". In *Beiträge zur Geschichte der deutschen Sprache und Literatur* p. 28.

MARK, Y. (ed.) 1958 *Yuda A. Yofe bukh.* Yivo, New York.

MARTIN, B. 1939 *Die deutschen Mundarten.* Leipzig.

MASSMANN, 1839 *Kleine Sprachdenkmale des 8–12 Jahr.* Quedlinb.

MATHEIS, M. 1954 Bayrisches Bauernbrot. In *Mundartgedichte.* Straubing.

MUSPILLI, 1832. Munich.

Oberbairisches Archiv. Munich.

OBERGFOELL, 1887 *Gottscheer Familiennamen.* Göttschee.

Otackers Reimchronik, 1745. Ratisb.

PANGKOFER, J. 1854 *Gedichte in Altbayrischer Mundart.* Nurnberg.

PANZER, F. 1954 *Bayrische Sagen und Braüche.* Göttingen.

PROKOSCH, A. 1939 *A Comparative Germanic Grammar.* Philadelphia.

Salzburger Glossen III.

SCHMID, W. A. 1929 Zur Geschichte der Juden Passau's. In *Zeitschrift für die Geschichte der Juden in Deutschland I.*

SCHMELLER, A. 1872 *Bayriches Wörterbuch.* Stuttgart.

STETTEN, V. 1865 Geschichte der reichsfreien Stadt Augsburg. *Chroniken der deutschen Städte,* p. 4.

Urkundenbuch der Stadt Speyer.

TSCHINKEL, H. *Grammatik der Gottscheer Mundart.*

WEINHOLD, K. 1867 *Bairishe Grammatik,* Berlin.

WEINREICH, M. 1940 Yidish. In *Algemeyne entsiklopedye, Yidn B.* Dubhov-fond, Paris.

WEINREICH, U. (ed.) 1954 *The Field of Yiddish. Studies in Yiddish Language, Folklore, and Literature.* Linguistic Circle of New York, New York.

WEINREICH, U. 1958 Di klangike struktur fun a podolyer reydenish. In Mark, 1958, pp. 221–231.

Wittelsbach Urkundenbuch, 1857. Munich.

WEINREICH, U. 1962 Culture Geography at a distance. Some Problems in the Study of East European Jewry. In Chafe, 1952, pp. 27–39.

WEINREICH, U. 1963 Four Riddles in Bilingual Dialectology. In *American Contributions to the Fifth International Congress of Slavists,* The Hague, pp. 335–359.

Language & Communication, Vol. 7, Supplement, pp. 47–60, 1987.
Printed in Great Britain.

0271-5309/87 $3.00 + .00
Pergamon Journals Ltd.

THE PROTO DIALECTOLOGY OF ASHKENAZ

DOVID KATZ

Oxford Centre for Postgraduate Hebrew Studies and St Antony's College, Oxford

I. Primacy of historical reconstruction

First impressions frequently deceive, and so it is that the seeming *a priori* priority of written evidence in the recovery of lost states of language is illusory. It was Saussure (1916: 297–300) who eloquently proclaimed the superiority of retrospective (reconstructive) recovery of language history over prospective (paper trailing) work. The logic is all too simple. Documents are subject to a thousand and one doubts: paleographic (who, when and where?), linguistic (what unconscious normative model, whose language if anybody's, how accurately transcribed?), and interpretive (how receptive to accurate analysis by a researcher living in a time when not a single native contemporary of the writer survives?). Comparative reconstruction in the right hands, undertaken with the necessary safeguards (including overwhelming consistency of correspondences and accurate retrieval of data) is a vastly more powerful and accurate tool because the evidence (the corpus of forms discovered) is empirically visible and confirmable to the observer. This argument over 'primacy' is not an abstraction of preferred forms of evidence by historians vs linguists (thought that surely plays a role too), but a methodological dilemma every historical linguist must face. The conscientious worker will of course never ignore any piece of evidence, whatever its provenance. The question is, which evidence will he confront with which, and that is a question he confronts every day of his working life.

In the historiography of oldest Yiddish, the contrast between documentary extrapolation and reconstruction is rather more stark than on average. That is true for two reasons. Firstly, there is virtually nothing surviving in the vernacular from the earliest generations of Ashkenazic history in medieval central Europe. And secondly, those documents from later generations that do survive exhibit a far greater than usual gap between spoken and written language. That gap results from the relatively late emergence of YIDDISH CONSCIOUSNESS among Ashkenazic Jewry (see Marchand, Miller, Rosenfeld, in this volume; Katz 1986a on a similar situation in the history of Yiddish Studies). That alone is somewhat analogous to the position of other European vernaculars in medieval times. But there is a critical difference. Those vernaculars generally stood in sociolinguistic complementation to a nonsimilar classical language (usually Latin), while Yiddish on its native German language territory, in addition to standing in sociolinguistic complementation to Hebrew and Aramaic in the thousand year state of INTERNAL ASHKENAZIC TRILINGUALISM (Katz 1985: 98), also stood in complementation to coterritorial variants of German transparently cognate, even to the most naive observer, with the Germanic Component within Yiddish. More often than not it was some form or other of German literary language that provided the normative model for Yiddish writing. Nearly all of Old Yiddish literature reflects varying degrees of TARGET CONFORMIZATION and ACTUAL CONFORMIZATION with a German based normative model. Both may be subsumed by retrospective application over the whole history of Yiddish literature of the Yiddish term DAYTSHMERISH ('Germanish', esp. 'Germanized Yiddish of the late nineteenth and early twentieth century Yiddish press and radical literature'). Genuine

Yiddish specificities in older Yiddish literature frequently represent the "failings" of the writer insofar as features of his actual language surface, notwithstanding his greater-than-average repressive efforts on that score. Older Yiddish literature is frankly unfaithful to the real language of its writers, far in excess of the usual speaking-writing gap. This has long been recognized by Yiddish philology (see Avé-Lallemant 1858–1862, III: 205; Shulman 1898: 44; Borokhov 1913: 354; Reyzen 1920: 26–27; Shtif 1922: 184, 189, 191; Erik 1928: 85, 336–337, 370–371; Tsinberg 1928: 82; M. Weinreich 1928: 22, 28).

II. Empirical validity of Proto Yiddish

By definition, no protolanguage can have EMPIRICAL REALITY insofar as no modern observer can experience it as a spoken vernacular the way a contemporary variety can be experienced, and that is no more than to say that water is wet. Moreover, protolanguages, like historical linguistics generally, are out of fashion, and their alleged overdoing in the nineteenth century is often demonstrated by references to such exaggerated (but methodologically important) exercises as Schleicher's (1868) reconstructed Indo-European fable. The continued implicit contention of some modern masters that one goal of historical linguistics is recovery of the "ancestor language" (Hoenigswald 1960: 119) contrasts with the view that the "end result of reconstruction is vastly less interesting [. . .] than the assumptions and procedures that advance us toward that reconstruction" (King 1969: 155).

By shifting the debate from empirical reality to EMPIRICAL VALIDITY, a much broader consensus is to be hoped for. The empirical validity of protolanguage *X,* as of anything else, depends on the strength of the evidence invoked. The three crucial factors here are the QUANTITY, QUALITY and CERTAINTY of the consistent correspondences discovered and methodically arranged by the historical linguist from spoken (i.e. empirically real) varieties of language. It is hence as measurable a linguistic entity as any on a continual scale ranging from the wildly conjectural to the logically irrefutable. And in my own view, Yiddish is a splendid example of this latter end of that scale. Marchand (1960: 41) correctly sees in Yiddish "a unique opportunity to be of service to the scholarly world", among other reasons, by providing for the testing of "the theory of unified protolanguages" (Marchand 1960: 41). Although my conclusion is opposite to Professor Marchand's (1965: 249 and this volume), it is he who has invaluably framed the question for us all.

Three factors are paramount. First is the early, and ultimately, vast, multidirectional geolinguistic expansion of Yiddish throughout central and eastern Europe. The resulting contiguity and coterritoriality with a *multitude* of German and non-German dialects facilitates confrontation of the Germanic Component with evidence from German, free from fear of longterm ongoing impact by any one variety of German that would cloud protolanguage conclusions. Second is the contiguity and coterritoriality of Yiddish with *no* Semitic dialect that could have fed its Semitic Component. This state of affairs facilitates confrontation with appropriate forms of Northwest Semitic free from fear of continuing impact from that quarter. Finally, investigation of the mechanisms and chronology of FUSION between both components within Yiddish over time and space—bearing in mind the first two factors—take conclusions on PROTONESS well beyond the danger threshold of COINCIDENCE (a concept referred to variously in the literature, e.g. "parallel development"). These happy historical circumstances render Yiddish a protolanguage laboratory of rare potential.

There is, in fact, astounding consistency of correspondence between any Yiddish dialect and any other Yiddish dialect over time and space vis à vis the two pan-Yiddish cognate

donor language groups (Germanic and Semitic; the Slavonic Component is by and large limited to Eastern Yiddish and to recent centuries). This is evident via four paramaters of correspondence, for which examples are offered to illustrate the methodology. The case can of course only be proven relative to quantity, quality and certainty of a vastly greater corpus, and a monograph on the subject is in preparation. No claim is made, of course, that all Yiddish can be traced to a unitary ancestor variety. The claim is that a significant portion of Yiddish in time and space exhibits clear signs of derivation from a protolanguage.

(1) SYSTEMATIC CORRESPONDENCE of the systems of stessed vocalism of all Yiddish dialects, Western and Eastern (Birnbaum 1923; Fischer 1934 [see now Bin-Nun 1973: 183–238], U. Weinreich 1958a: 223; M. Weinreich 1973: II, 321–382; Katz 1983a: 1021–1031). Thus, Southwestern Yiddish (SWY, "Swiss-Alsatian") and Midwestern Yiddish (MWY, "Central German") *ŭ* is systematically cognate with (= ‖) Northwestern Yiddish (NWY, "Netherlandic") *ŏ* ‖ Southeastern Yiddish (SEY, "Ukrainian") *ɪ* ‖ Mideastern Yiddish (MEY, "Polish") *ĭ* ‖ Northeastern Yiddish (NEY "Lithuanian") *u*, hence e.g. SWY, MWY *gŭzmə*, 'exaggeration' *hŭnt* 'dog' ‖ NWY *gŏzmə, hŏnt* ‖ SEY *gɪzmə, hɪnt* ‖ MEY *gĭzmə, hĭnt* ‖ NEY *gúzmə, húnt*. The correspondence obtains in *all* old items in the language.

(2) ANALOGOUS FUSION between Germanic and Semitic in all varieties of Yiddish (Katz 1979; 1982: 284–285; 1985: 95–96). The point of departure is provided by the normalized stock language cognates in Tiberian (the standard phonological system of Hebrew and Aramaic, codified on the western shores of the Sea of Galilee in the late first millennium), and Middle High German (MHG). In the above cited example, it is evident that fusion between the *u* vowels in Tiberian *gŭzmṓ* and MHG *hunt* set in *before* the Yiddish shifts that processed the vowel regionally, resulting in *ĭ* in MEY, in *ŏ* in NWY, or in anything else anywhere else; otherwise these two would not be fused throughout Yiddish. The same is true in the arena of the more volatile long vowels and diphthongs. Take for example vowel 22 — SWY *ɛj* ‖ MWY *ē* ‖ NWY *ɛj* ‖ SEY *ej* ‖ MEY *aj* ‖ NEY *ej*, hence e.g. SWY *mɛ́jlə* "it doesn't matter; anyway", *éjbik* 'forever' ‖ MWY *mḗlə, ḗbik* ‖ SEY *méjlə, éjbik* ‖ MEY *májlə, ájbik* (‖ Tiberian *mḗlṓ*, MHG *êwic*). It would take quite a coincidence for all the locally differentiated Ashkenazic Hebrew and Aramaic liturgical reflexes of Tiberian ṣere (= *ē*) and all the locally differentiated dialectal reflexes of MHG <ê> to "happen to fuse" everywhere. Still, coincidence is possible. Where the chance of coincidence is significantly reduced is in the application of analogous fusion throughout the vowel system. Indeed, analogous pansystemic fusion is the historical phenomenon that has enabled Yiddish dialectology to adopt numbers representing diaphonemic correspondences (U. Weinreich 1958a: 225–226; M. Weinreich 1960; Herzog 1965: 228; Katz 1983a: 1021–1024), such that the Yiddish dialectologist can speak of, say, *vowel 11*, rather than "a vowel cognate with Tiberian A fused with MHG X in Southwestern Yiddish but not applicable in Mideastern Yiddish where Tiberian A is fused with MHG Y and Tiberian B is the fusion partner of MHG X". Had separate "Yiddishes" arisen at separate points of time and space, this hypothetical state of LOCAL FUSION would surely have resulted. A Semitic Component vowel would have fused with one local realization here, with another there. A protolanguage is indicated by the aplication of analogous fusion geographically over the vast expanse of Ashkenazic speech territory, and structurally throughout the stressed vowel systems of Yiddish dialects.

(3) CONGRUENT ANOMALIES vis à vis the stock languages. The traditional historical linguist's exceptions to sound laws (measured against the correspondences holding in the overwhelming majority of cases) are anomalies compared with the bulk. Congruent

anomalies are exceptional in the same way in all known varieties of the target language (Katz 1982: 287–293; 1985: 95–96). Thus for example, vowel 41 (short ɔ in all Yiddish dialects) is expected in Yiddish reflexes of MHG *hocker,* based on the usual correspondence (e.g. MHG *ort, woche, wolf* and Pan Yiddish ɔrt 'place', vɔx 'week', vɔlf 'wolf'). That an expected cognate MHG 'dictionary form' doesn't match the usual correspondences between MHG and the Germanic Component of Yiddish in itself proves nothing; there were after all, many variants of any item in German dialects, as everywhere else. What is striking is congruence, the consistent appearance of the same unexpected reflex (in terms of the diaphonemic system) throughout Yiddish. In this case, it happens to be vowel 42 (SWY ɔu ‖ MWY ō ‖ NWY ɔu ‖ SEY ɔj ‖ MEY ɔj ‖ NEY ej), hence SWY hṓukər 'hunchback' ‖ MWY hṓkər ‖ NWY hṓukər ‖ SEY hɔ́jkər ‖ MEY hɔ́jkər ‖ NEY héjkər. Similarly, vowel 52 (SWY ū̃ ‖ MWY ū ‖ NWY ū ‖ SEY i ‖ MEY ī ‖ NEY u) is expected in the Yiddish cognate of Tiberian məzūzɔ̄́ (e.g. Tiberian bəθūlɔ̄́, ḥavrūθɔ̄́, malbūším and SWY besū̃lə 'virgin', xavrū̃sə 'bunch; crowd; (traditional) study pair', malbū̃šəm 'clothing' ‖ MWY besū́lə, xavrū́sə, malbū́šəm ‖ NWY besū́lə, xavrū́sə, malbū́šəm ‖ SEY bsílə, xavrísə, malbí'šəm ‖ MEY bsílə, xavrísə, malbíšəm ‖ NEY bsúlə, xavrúsə, malbúšim). What turns up everywhere, however, is vowel 51 (SWY ŭ ‖ MWY ŭ ‖ NWY ŏ ‖ SEY ɪ ‖ MEY ĭ ‖ NEY u), hence SWY məzŭ́zə 'traditional door post marker; mezuzah' ‖ MWY məzŭ́zə ‖ NWY məzŏ́zə ‖ SEY məzízə ‖ MEY məzĭ́zə ‖ NEY məzúzə (Katz 1978a; 1978b: 27–30).

(4) CONCRETE DISPARITY of realization is needed to clinch a proof for systematic correspondence, analogous fusion or congruent anomaly. If the systems of stressed vocalism in Yiddish dialects were concretely (= phonetically, physically) identical or highly similar from Strassbourg to Poltava, that state of affairs would severely weaken any case for protoness, in consequence of the possibilities of coincidence and more recent transdialectal borrowings coming into play. It is precisely the documentation of systematic correspondence, analogous fusion and congruent anomaly in items exhibiting radically differing concrete realizations that serves to recover a state predating the phonological evolution of any of the varieties examined.

III. Semitic component proto vocalism

The phonetic realization of any stressed vowel phoneme in a Yiddish dialect is invariably identical for both the Germanic and the Semitic Component in that dialect. The dynamic phonology of the Semitic Component, however, differs radically in a number of ways, the two most salient of which are penultimate stress assignment (and the resulting shift of stress upon suffixation) and, to the point here, the salient morphophonemic alternations conditioned by the syllable boundary features open vs. closed, hence SWY šéjdəm 'ghosts' ~ sg. šéd, sóufər 'scribe' ~ pl. sófrəm, and švṓxəm 'praises' ~ sg. švắx ‖ MWY šḗdəm ~ šéd, sóufər ~ sófrəm, švṓxəm ~ švắx ‖ NWY šéjdəm ~ šéd, sóufər ~ sófrəm, švṓxəm ~ švắx ‖ SEY šéjdəm ~ šéd, sójfər ~ sófrəm, švúxəm ~ šváx ‖ MEY šájdəm ~ šéd, sójfər ~ sófrəm, švúxəm ~ švắx ‖ NEY šéjdəm ~ šéd, séjfər ~ sófrəm, švóxəm ~ šváx. Amongst the high vowels, alternation has become vestigial, but enough traces survive to warrant their inclusion (e.g. MEY dínəm 'laws', with MEY i_{32} ~ sg. dĭn, with MEY $ĭ_{31}$; NWY xŭšəm 'senses', with NWY u_{52} ~ sg. xŏš, with NWY $ŏ_{51}$).

Thus, Pan Yiddish exhibits alternations in the Semitic Component (only) that are not cognate with any known alternations in the stock languages—Hebrew and Aramaic. To put it in terms of the numbering system of diaphonemic Yiddish vocalism, these open vs closed syllable alternations are 22 /___šʲ ~ 21 /___Cšʲ, 42 /___šʲ ~ 41 /___Cšʲ, 12 /___šʲ ~ 11 /___Cšʲ, 32 /___šʲ ~ 31 /___Cšʲ, 52 /___šʲ. ~ 51 /___Cšʲ. The

mystery of these alternations has intrigued many. The currently accepted standard theory was founded, albeit in rather primitive form, by the Hebrew poet Avrom Dov-Ber Lebensohn, better known as Odom Hakoyheyn (= Adam Hakohen in Israeli pronunciation), an acronym for Avrom Dov-Ber Mikhalishker, after his native Lithuanian village Mikhalishek. Lebensohn (1874: 19–25) postulated that the vocalism of the Semitic Component derived from a five vowel system that underwent lengthening in open syllabic position, leading to the rise of long vowel reflexes. In the century to follow, massive supplementary evidence came in to support his theory. Tshemerinski (1913: 61–63) and Veynger (1913: 79–81) adduced parallels with the conditioning environments for the familiar lengthening of MHG short vowels in open syllables. Moreover, researchers of early Hebrew and Aramaic manuscripts emanating from Ashkenazic territory found graphemic evidence of a prevailing five vowel system (§5 below). In short, a consensus emerged from both Germanic and Semitic researches that a five vowel Semitic Component system had undergone Open Syllable Lengthening (e.g. M. Weinreich 1973: II, 20–21, 334, 352–354; Birnbaum 1979: 60, 63–65). For a more detailed history of scholarly views on the subject, see Katz (1982: 149–181).

I have proposed in detail elsewhere (Katz 1977; 1979: 54–76; 1982: 182–314) that internal, comparative and transcomponent reconstruction (this last method entailing a modified invocation of the comparative method upon the interaction of the components within a fusion language) demonstrate unequivocally that the standard theory is untenable. Suffice it here to say rather informally that there are simply far too many vowels in the identical phonological environment to be derived from a primeval five. Thus, for example, vowel 25, cognate with Tiberian stressed open syllabic segol (SWY $\bar{e}$ ‖ MWY $\bar{e}/\bar{\imath}$ ‖ NWY $\bar{e}$ ‖ SEY $\imath/\bar{\imath}/ej$ ‖ MEY ej ‖ NEY ε) represents the lengthened /e/ phoneme (originally short 21) lengthened under Germanic impact—e.g. SWY $b\acute{\bar{e}}g\partial d$ 'garment' ‖ MWY $b\acute{\bar{e}}g\partial d/b\acute{\imath}g\partial d$ ‖ NWY $b\acute{\bar{e}}g\partial d$ ‖ SEY $b\acute{\bar{e}}jg\partial d/b\acute{\imath}g\partial d$ $b\acute{\imath}g\partial d$ ‖ MEY $b\acute{e}jg\partial d$ ‖ NEY $b\acute{e}g\partial d$. Vowel 22 cannot be generated by any rule or shift because its environment overlaps with 25; 22 is originally long. The same proof, albeit rather more involved, obtains regarding vowel 13 which is the genuine lengthened /a/ phoneme (originally short 11) in both components, rendering it impossible that 12 represents a vowel lengthened from the same /a/ from which 13 derives. That proof is clinched by the two lone dialects of Yiddish where 12 and 13 never merged in the Germanic Component—SWY and MWY where vowel 13 (cognate with MHG a) while lengthened under the impact of Germanically engendered Open Syllable Lengthening, remained unrounded $\bar{a}$ (hence e.g. $z\acute{\bar{a}}g$ 'say' ‖ MHG sag) while originally long 12 (cognate with MHG $\hat{a}$) appears as $\bar{o}$ (hence e.g. $n\acute{\bar{o}}dl$ 'needle' ‖ MHG $n\hat{a}del$). Semitic Component open syllabic qames always appears as unambiguous 12, i.e. $\bar{o}$, hence e.g. SWY, MWY $x\acute{\bar{o}}sn$ 'bridegroom', (<Tiberian $h\underset{\cdot}{o}\theta\acute{o}n$ via Stress Shift, Posttonic Reduction and assorted consonantal shifts), never *$x\acute{a}sn$. The status of open syllabic qames as an originally long vowel is thereby demonstrated.

The reconstructed proto vocalism of the Semitic Component yields a ten vowel system along the lines of

*$\bar{\imath}_{32}$	*$\bar{u}_{52}$
*$\breve{\imath}_{31}$	*$\breve{u}_{51}$
*$\bar{e}_{22}$	*$\bar{o}_{42}$
*$\varepsilon_{21/25}$	*$\bar{\mathfrak{z}}_{12}$
	*$\mathfrak{z}_{41}$

*$a_{11/13}$

IV. The candidate Northwest Semitic cognates

Having postulated this ten vowel Semitic Component protosystem, the next step is to confront it with the known systems of Northwest Semitic (Hebrew and Aramaic) vowels to see if a match is in sight. In sharp contrast to standard theory, a derivation from a five vowel Palestinian system is impossible, based on the evidence of Yiddish dialectology. The system is even more remote from the Babylonian system in which pathaḥ and segol are merged. The Northwest Semitic type with which the reconstructed vocalism of the Semitic Component is closest is the ten vowel quantity distinguishing Kimchian interpretation of Tiberian vocalism originated by Joseph Kimchi (Qimḥi) and elaborated upon by his sons Moshe and David in twelfth and thirteenth century Spain (see M. Kimchi [1509–1518: 11], D. Kimchi 1532: [86], 1545: 48a). From the perspective of the history of linguistics, it is noteworthy that the Kimchis saw fit to frame highly specific phonological environments to correspond with unitary diacritics they regarded as multivalent. The charge that the Kimchian system was contrived has been effectively refuted in recent decades. Chomsky, who originally ascribed the Kimchian system to "the influence of the Latin languages employed in the Provence" (1952: 31), retracted this view (1977: 177, xxvii) in the face of Bendavid's (1958) impressive metrical and philological evidence. Alternatively, an imperfect but respectable matchup of Proto Yiddish vocalism can be made with the seven vowel Ben Asher version of Tiberian vocalism (cf. Ibn Ezra 1546: 134; Baer and Strack 1879: 11–12; Schramm 1964: 29).

But there is still an insoluble noncompatibility between even the Kimchian interpretation of Tiberian vocalism and the stressed vowel system of the Semitic Component in Yiddish. The Pan Yiddish Semitic Component alternations of long vowels in open syllables with short vowels in closed syllables render a system like the Kimchis' tenable as a prospective donor system in open syllables only. In closed syllables, the oppositions 11: 12, 21: 22, 31: 32, 41: 42 and 51: 52 would be systematically neutralized in favour of the short member of each pair as is the case in every modern dialect of Yiddish. Along with the segmental phonology of the proto Semitic Component, we must reconstruct its dynamic phonology, and the salient rule here is quite simply V $\rightarrow$ [-long]/____C$\breve{S}$. Hence I posited a hitherto unknown Northwest Semitic vowel system that most resembles the Kimchian interpretation of Tiberian vocalism (distinguishing five long/tense vs. five short/lax) in open syllabic position but is closest to a five vowel Palestinian type system in closed syllablic position (Katz 1979: 77–78).

V. Manuscript evidence: methodology

It is easy enough to say, as we have done, that the vowel system from which the Semitic Component derives happens to coincide with nothing else known, and that conclusion is certainly in concord with the proposed primacy of evidence via reconstruction from all the known varieties of the language (cf. above §I). It is a ten vowel system (*$\bar{\imath}$, *$\breve{\imath}$, *$\bar{e}$, *ε, *$\bar{\jmath}$, *a, *$\bar{o}$, *$\breve{\jmath}$, *$\bar{u}$, *$\breve{u}$) in which *$\bar{\imath}$ $\rightarrow$ *$\breve{\imath}$, *$\bar{e}$ $\rightarrow$ *ε, *$\bar{\jmath}$ $\rightarrow$ *a, *$\bar{o}$ $\rightarrow$ *$\breve{\jmath}$ and *$\bar{u}$ $\rightarrow$ *$\breve{u}$ in closed syllabic position, the neutralization resulting in a reduced five vowel inventory. We are left with the dilemma of reconciling these results with a number of incompatible systems—the five vowel Palestinian system, the seven or ten vowel Tiberian system, and the five vowel system evident in early Ashkenazic Hebrew and Aramaic manuscripts (demonstrated inter alia by rampant confusion of qameṣ/pathaḥ and ṣere/segol). There need be no qualms about demonstrating a hitherto unknown Northwest Semitic system midway between two known systems, Tiberian and Palestinian, as a service of Yiddish

linguistics to Semitics. In fact, it is not at all difficult to imagine a ten vowel system neutralized contextually to five in a time and place for which ten-in-all-environments and five-in-all-environments are well documented. Such "compromise dialects" are neither typologically suspect nor rare in occurrence.

It is far more difficult to accept the lack of conciliation between the Semitic Component in Yiddish with the overwhelming evidence of twelfth and thirteenth century Hebrew and Aramaic liturgical manuscripts on Ashenazic territory, written by and for the primeval Ashkenazic population. Yalon, researching medieval Ashkenazic manuscripts, uncovered massive scrambling of the Tiberian graphemes qameṣ (‖ Yiddish vowel 12) with pathaḥ (‖ Yiddish 11) and ṣere (‖ Yiddish 22) with segol (‖ Yiddish 21) in these manuscripts (the diacritic system is such that confusion among the remaining vowels is only rarely evident graphemically). His conclusions have repeatedly been reconfirmed by further investigation (Yalon 1930: 204–205; 1937–1938: 62–66; 1938–1939: 11; 1942: 27; 1964: 19; Klar 1951: 75; Bet Arye 1965: 34–37, 102; Eldar 1976; 1978: 16–32). Yalon and many of his followers conclude, not unreasonably, that the Semitic Component in Yiddish once had a five vowel system that underwent expansion triggered by Germanic open syllable lengthening. Those manuscripts making use of the Tiberian sublinear vowel graphemes, but exhibiting confusion in their distribution revealing an underlying five vowel Palestinian type pronunciation are known in the field as "Palestinian-Tiberian" manuscripts (Allony 1964). It is rather difficult to accept M. Weinreich's "Babylonian Renaissance", a scenario whereby Babylonian teachers brought Tiberian (i.e. northern Palestinian) vowels to medieval German Jews leading to their abandoning their erstwhile five vowel (i.e. southern Palestinian) system and shifting to the later known Ashkenazic system as a conscious normative effort (1954: 93–99; 1973, II: 31–32).

It is liturgical manuscripts that display the most interesting deviations from Tiberian standards. Biblical texts tend to be well normalized divulging little of the phonology of the *pointer,* the specialist scribe who inserted the vowel diacritics and who may or may not be the scribe of the letters per se in a given case. The meticulous modern scholars who have studied these documents have done so from the viewpoints of codicology and the history of Hebrew pointing rather than phonology per se. Moreover, such phonological interests as they have had have been from the perspective of the history of Hebrew vocalization systems, over a millennium after the demise of ancient Hebrew as a vernacular. The following methodological guidelines for the study of medieval Ashkenazic Hebrew and Aramaic manuscripts are proposed for the elucidation of historical *Yiddish* phonology, and it is hoped they may in some degree be useful for Hebrew phonology as well; far more can be learned about Hebrew and Aramaic liturgical pronunciation in the context of the phonological system of the readers' everyday phonologies in their roles as speakers of their everyday vernacular than in the context of scribal pointing variants per se.

(1) GRAPHEMIC VS PHONOLOGICAL SIGNIFICANCE. It is vital that instances of nonstandard vowel pointing resulting from variant pointing tradition or just plain ignorance of the prestigious Tiberian norm not be bunched together with instances truly signifying phonological features. With no claim being made for complete accuracy, it is proposed that all features can be affixed to a scale ranging from clearly insignificant (e.g. the graphic variants of qameṣ—whether its vertical portion is a bar or a dot) to probably insignificant (e.g. confusion between 'ultrashort' ă, ĕ and ɔ̆ and their 'just plain short' counterparts— a, ε and ɔ), to clearly significant (e.g. confusion between a and ɔ̄, and between ε and ē, which points to a five vowel Palestinian type system). Classification of a manuscript on

phonological grounds should generally be limited to those criteria demonstrably phonological.

(2) STRUCTURAL COMPATIBILITY WITH THE SEMITIC COMPONENT. It was U. Weinreich (1958a) who unmasked "Chancery Yiddish" (the heavily Hebraicized Yiddish of certain communal documents) on the grounds that the Hebrew elements therein do not jibe with the known and universal fusion formulas whereby Germanic and Semitic are joined in Yiddish, and that numerous constraints (e.g. against the conjunction 'and' being other than Germanic) are violated. All the more must the student of medieval central European Hebrew and Aramaic manuscripts be aware of this constraint. A deviation in pointing in an obscure inflection may represent nothing more than grammatical ignorance on the part of the pointer. If however, we find, say, that a simple noun adhering to a common nominal paradigm attested throughout Yiddish is pointed in a deviant manner, we will have discovered something of the pointer's phonology.

(3) LEXICAL COMPATIBILITY WITH THE SEMITIC COMPONENT. Carrying caution a stage further, one would limit the investigation of the manuscript to lexical items known beyond doubt to be extant in Yiddish. By thus restricting investigation of a liturgical nonspoken language on the basis of the evidence provided by cognates in an everyday spoken language, results are further desirably confined to the phonological systems of speakers rather than the normative aspirations of pointers.

(4) ISOLATION OF THE CONDITIONING ENVIRONMENT. Whenever a form deviating from the Tiberian (or any other) norm is discovered, its phonetic environment must be isolated just as in fieldwork with speakers.

(5) CORRELATION WITH NON-PHONOLOGICAL EVIDENCE. Following upon all the above, classifications of manuscripts would be correlated with non-phonological data. The two most important areas are codicology—to determine if the ordering and variants of prayer texts reveal their period and provenance, and paleography—to determine the degree to which the writing can elucidate these.

VI. Western vs eastern Proto Ashkenaz

The Jewish civilization of central (and later, eastern) Europe that has come to be known as Ashkenaz was in its earliest phases, beginning around a thousand years ago, divided into two distinct cultural centres. The best known is the Rhineland, centred upon the three communities of Speyer, Worms and Mainz, known by the acronym *Shum,* after the first letters of their Jewish names. That is the Rhineland territory then known as either *Rinus* (i.e. Rhine, Rhineland) or *Loter* (after Lotharingia) where Rabeynu Gershom, whose best known edict forbade polygamy, lived and worked (see Finkelstein 1924: 111–138). Gershom's role in breaking European Jewry away from the Orient, and in the founding of Ashkenaz has been splendidly analyzed by M. Weinreich in a framework of cultural history (1951; 1964).

Now, it is no diminution of the status of Loter in the formation of Ashkenazic Jewish culture to claim, as we do, that the language we know as YIDDISH, in all its geographic and temporal variation, simply does not derive from Loter. The Germanic based language spoken by Rhineland Jewry that *could have* become Yiddish, but didn't, was, quite simply, lost, though not without a trace—proper names and a few relic forms survive as borrowings into the Germanic based language of Jews of a more easterly territory that spread throughout the lands that came to be subsumed by Ashkenaz, including, of course the Rhineland itself,

and that language known to us via its many later incarnations, is Yiddish. The evidence is overwhelming. As King (1979: 7–8) puts it, "Yiddish bears hardly any trace of having been derived from or influenced by a dialect from the western part of Germany, i.e. by the Rhineland" and "No linguist, using the evidence of Yiddish and German dialects [. . .] would arrive at the conclusion that the Rhineland is the cradle of Yiddish". Indeed, the debate within the Germanist camp is between those who find East Central German features of paramount importance (Gerzon 1902: 131) and those who find more congruence with Bavarian (Mieses 1924; 270; King 1979). Bin-Nun (1973: 77–85) and Birnbaum (1979: 71–76) tend to support synthesis of both. But to the point here is that nobody has found points of congruence with Rhineland dialects of German, and the Rhineland family trees of Yiddish seem to derive at least in part from the noble but historically invalid method of adopting a wished-for pedigree.

It is the second area of early Jewish settlement upon the territory that was to become Ashkenaz that lies on territory coterritorial or contiguous with German dialects that are the serious candidates for being donors to the Germanic Component in Yiddish—the Jewish cultural area known as *Peyhem* (/péjhəm/'Bohemia') or *Estraykh* ('Austria'), names that like so many in Jewish history became divorced from the narrower geographic sense of their etymons and acquired significance as cultural configurations. A word on the self definition of each Jewish area in the Middle Ages is necessary. Among the most salient conscious differences between Jewish cultural areas are those expressed in the applicable local *mínheg* 'custom, tradition' or *núsekh* 'version' of the exact texts used and the internal ordering of those texts within the daily and festival prayerbooks. Bearing in mind the frequency (thrice daily) of the prayers and the ultimate sanctity they assume within the cultural framework of the analyzed society—and that is at the end of the day the framework that matters—it is hardly surprising that the most minute difference could help identify an individual's communal, ergo geographical homeland and, crucially, that *mínheg* and *núsekh* would be pivotal factors in the cultural self identification of a community and its perceptions of other communities outside. The modern historian of Yiddish must fit the known language divisions into the puzzle. And in the international cultural differentiation within earliest Ashkenaz (that term being applied in part retrospectively), the great Jewish centres situated in the general vicinity of the Danube—Regensburg, Nürnburg and Rothenburg—were all part of the *Eastern* rite—Peyhem or Estraykh—although they were in later centuries realigned and linked to the Western rite, when both stood in contradistinction to the *new* Eastern rite of eastern Europe—*Poyln* ('Poland'). But it is the primeval state that is relevant to the matters at hand, and in that state, Regensburg, Nürnberg and Rothenburg are unambiguously part of the early Eastern rite, as opposed to the Rinus/Loter based Western rite of the Rhineland (cf. Goldshmid 1970: 14). Regensburg housed the oldest Jewish quarter on German speaking soil (cf. Aronius 1902: 139–142; Brann *et al.* 1963: 285–305; Wasserman 1972), and settlement in Nürnberg and Rothenburg was scarcely younger. Now it is true that this earliest Eastern rite did not at the very outset boast the same calibre of Talmudic (ergo cultural) luminaries as Rinus/Loter but it was not long before the Danube centre—the Eastern Ashkenaz of those days—caught up. In the thirteenth century the Maharam of Rothenburg (Meyer ben Borukh) was acknowledged by all Ashkenazim as the outstanding rabbinic authority of the generation.

VII. The proto dialectology of Ashkenaz

Two hanging threads remain. First—Yiddish, a language bearing no intimate affinity

with German dialects of the medieval Jewish Rhineland centre. Second—a large corpus of medieval Hebrew and Aramaic liturgical manuscripts that betray a five vowel system similar to that of the Palestinian system of vocalization, the medieval French Jewish cultural area and the Sephardic tradition, but nothing suggestive of Yiddish. The obvious answer is that those pointers of these manuscripts who were Ashkenazim at all were Loterians, Rhineland westerners who spoke a Germanic based language in the western dialect regions of earliest Ashkenaz, whose Hebrew and Aramaic reading tradition and vernacular Semitic Component were in fact characterized by a five vowel system.

There are three corroborative proofs, one circumstantial, one correlative and one definitive. Circumstantially, the open syllabic congruence of the vowel system of the Proto Semitic Component with the norm—the classical Tiberian system—renders all those manuscripts exhibiting a Tiberian type system elusive. They can equally represent the work of a pointer trained in Tiberian and that of a Danube region resident and they therefore sadly fail to pinpoint ''Danube'' in the way the five vowel pointers leave their ''Rhine'' trademark on everything they touch. Every traditional Yiddish speaker knows when to apply long vowels in closed syllables in Ashkenazic Hebrew and Aramaic based inter alia on his knowledge of their nonneutralized allomorphs in open syllables in the Semitic Component of his everyday Yiddish; hence, for example, any nonsecularized MEY speaker who has *šéd* 'ghost', *sɔ́d* 'secret' and *klál* 'rule' in his everyday Yiddish will know, with the barest minimum of traditional education, that their Ashkenazic Hebrew forms are, in his dialect, *šájd, sɔ́jd,* and *klɔ́l* (the history of the anomaly of this last case, shortening of 12 to 41 in the Ashkenazic of the dialect rather than to 11 as in its Yiddish, is outside the scope of the present paper). And that knowledge derives largely from his native Yiddish where the open syllabic allomorphs, *šájdəm* 'ghosts', *sɔ́jdəs* 'secrets' and *klúləm* 'rules' serve to apprise him of the underlying forms which turn up on the whole as the surface forms in the liturgical language. The moral of the story is that the Danube region pointer had vastly less difficulty in mastering Tiberian pointing than his five vowel Rhineland counterpart, because Tiberian phonology matched his own to a great extent, and it is therefore no wonder that most Danube manuscripts betray little that is interesting in the way of deviations from Tiberian norms.

A very different tale is told by the manuscripts exhibiting promiscuous confounding of vowels, nearly all of which, even when reexamined as per the principles proposed above in §V, show the Yalon school to be correct in its assessment. Thus, for example, British Library Add 27205 has *paním* (p 41b) for *pɔ́ním* 'face' (pathaḥ for qameṣ). Munich MS Heb 617/Staatsbibliothek 21 has *ḥéseð* (p 126a) for *ḥéseð* 'righteousness' (ṣere for segol); my sincere thanks to Mr Hermann Süss for kindly arranging for a swift microfilming of the MS. The famed *Vormzer makhzor,* the 1272 Worms makhzor (festival prayerbook) containing the oldest known purportedly Yiddish sentence (cf. M. Weinreich 1963), is no different, exhibiting forms such as *bəraxa* (p 97b, after Bet-Arye 1965: 35) for *bərɔ́xɔ́* 'blessing' (pathaḥ for qameṣ twice). I for one am convinced that no Yiddish speaker, proto or otherwise, could have penned any of these diacritics because the relevant oppositions in open syllabic position — pathaḥ ‖ Pan Yiddish vowel 11 vs qameṣ ‖ 12, and segol ‖ 25 vs ṣere ‖ 22 — are valid in all Yiddish dialects, and these three lexical items happen to have 12, 25 and 12 respectively, hence SWY *pɔ́nəm, xésəd, brɔ́xə* ‖ MWY *pɔ́nəm/ púnəm, xésəd/xísəd, brɔ́xə/brúxə* ‖ NWY *pɔ́nəm, xésəd, brɔ́xə* ‖ SEY, MEY *púnəm, xéjsəd, brúxə* ‖ NEY *pɔ́nəm, xésəd, brɔ́xə.*

Correlatively, the researcher is fortunate to have substantial evidence from contemporary comments on *bney khes* and *bney hes*. The *bney khes* were the Danube region Jews who realized Tiberian ḥet = [ḥ] consonantally, possibly as voiceless velar spirant [x] while the *bney hes,* the Rhinelanders, couldn't, and merged it with [h] or lost it altogether. It is not often that rabbinic talent was turned toward phonology and the motives relate to pronunciation norms of sacred texts. M. Weinreich (1958) brilliantly collated the available evidence and produced a schematic map showing which western cities are documented *hes* territory, and which eastern ones are in *khes* country. Now the incontrovertible fact is that [x] appears in all its historical positions in all the components of Yiddish and in all the dialects of Yiddish. As happens not infrequently in Yiddish historical linguistics, it becomes fashionable to cite exceptional cases to no end (e.g. *mékṇ* 'erase' cf. the Hebrew root *mḥq*) and ignore the overwhelmingly applicable generalization. It is a cornerstone of linguistic methodology that a feature found in every known period and every known variety of a language was probably there all along, unless proof exists to the contrary. In this case as in many others, Weinreich (1958: 108) invoked his "Babylonian Renaissance" to account for the later "reintroduction" of *x*. It is fascinating for the history of Yiddish linguistics that a giant of Weinreich's stature ignored his own substantial findings both in German dialectology and the medieval rabbinic *khes–hes* evidence in adhering tenaciously to the Loter theory, at the expense of explaining away yet another problem via Babylonia. At the same time, it is a tribute both to Weinreich's thoroughness in assembling data and his genius at structuring data into coherent conceptual systems that his findings can often be used as forcefully to argue against his own theses as for them.

Definitive proof can only derive from a manuscript matching the system arrived at via reconstruction. One has thus far been examined that corroborates the proto vocalism proposed for the Semitic Component in Yiddish (Katz 1977; 1979: 54–76; 1982: 294–311; cf. above §III). It is Oxford Mich 617/627, a festival prayerbook completed in 1258 by one Yehude ben Shmuel Zlatman (Zeltman?). This MS, analyzed according to the principles proposed in §V above, yields the predicted Proto Yiddish phonological configuration. Confusion of ṣere with segol and of qameṣ with pathaḥ is limited to closed syllabic position, hence *ješ* (p 10b) for *jēš* 'there is' (segol for ṣere), *kəlal* (p. 54a) for *kə/ɔ/l* 'generality, rule' (pathaḥ for qameṣ), etc. In open syllables, pointing follows Tiberian norms, hence *bəhēmɔ̄* (p 19b) 'animal', *ḥɔ̄xɔ̄m* (p 25a) 'wise man'. Most significantly, the Oxford MS exhibits systematic morphophonemic alternation conditioned by the syllable boundary. In a number of cases alternation is cognate with Pan Yiddish alternation, e.g. *šəvɔ̄ḥɔ̄* 'praise (Aramaic determinate form)' (p 115a) ~ *šəvaḥ* (absolute), cf. SWY *švɔ̄xəm* 'praises' ~ sg. *švɑ̆x* ‖ MWY *švɔ̄xəm/švŭxəm* ~ *švɑ̆x* ‖ NWY *švɔ̄xəm* ~ *švɑ̆x* ‖ SEY *švúxəm* ~ *šváx* ‖ MEY *švúxəm* ~ *švɑ̆x* ‖ NEY *švɔ́xim* ~ *šváx*. In other instances, would be Yiddish alternation has been obliterated by Stress Shift (from ultimate to penultimate) and ensuing Posttonic Reduction, both under Germanic impact. All the more illuminating to learn from the MS that final Semitic Component syllables (later processed by Stress Shift and Reduction) once underwent alternation in earliest Ashkenaz, just as nonreduced vowels meeting the structural description of Closed Syllable Shortening do today. Hence, *gannɔ̄vim* 'thieves' (p 109a) ~ sg. *gannav* (p 105a), an alternation lost in the modern language where the final syllable is processed by Posttonic Reduction, giving Pan Yiddish *gánəv*. The pointer of Yehude ben Shmuel Zlatman's prayerbook hails from the Danube regions, congruent with the eastern dialect region of earliest Ashkenaz, whence Yiddish derives. Although there isn't a single explicitly "Yiddish" word in the entire work, it may have more to say about earliest Yiddish than the renowned 1272 sentence in the Worms makhzor.

It has become customary, in the tradition of Max Weinreich, to seek out a "symbolic founder" of a Jewish cultural area. In the rise of the easterly regions of Old Ashkenaz, centred in Regensburg and its environs in the Danube Basin, it was Yehude Khosid (Yehuda Heḥasid), also known as Rabbi Yehude of Regensburg (*c.* 1150–1217), who was the central figure in the far reaching ethical and mystical *Khasidey Ashkenaz* movement and the principal author of its key work, the *Seyfer khasidim* (see Dan 1968). Like the Maharam of Rothenburg after him, Yehude Khosid, too, was a native of the Rhineland who moved eastward and became a beloved leader in the Danube centre. The edicts attributed to Yehude Khosid frankly had less impact on Jewish history than Gershom's in Loter. The most famous forbid an author to sign his name to a book, and a man from marrying a woman who has the same name as his mother.

REFERENCES

ALLONY, N. 1964 Ezehu hanikud shelanu bemakhzor vitri? *Bet mikra* **17**, 135–144.

ARONIUS, J. 1902 *Regesten zur Geschichte der Juden im fränkischen und deutschen Reiche bis zum Jahre 1273. Bearbeitet unter Mitwirkung von Albert Dresdner und Ludwig Lewinski.* Leonhard Simion, Berlin.

AVE-LALLEMANT, F. C. B. 1858–1862 *Das deutsche Gaunerthum in seiner social-politischen, literarischen und linguistischen Ausbildung zu seinem heutigen Bestande,* IV vols. F. A. Brockhaus, Leipzig.

BAER, S. and STRACK, H. L. 1879 *Die Dikduke HaTeamim des Ahron ben Mosche ben Ascher und andere alte grammatish-massorethische Lehrstücke zur Feststellung eines richtigen Textes der hebräischen Bibel.* L. Fernau, Leipzig.

BENDAVID (FAYERSHTEYN), A. 1958 Minayin hakhaluka litenuot gedolot uketanot? *Leshonenu* **22**, 7–35, 110–136.

BEN ZEEYV, Y. 1874 *Seyfer talmud leshoyn ivri.* Romm, Vilna.

BESCH, W., KNOOP, U., PUTSCHKE, W. and WIEGAND, H. E. (eds.) 1983 *Dialektologie. Ein Handbuch zur deutschen und allgemeinen Dialektforschung.* Walter de Gruyter, Berlin, New York.

BET-ARYE, M. 1965 Nikudo shel makhzor kehilat kodesh vermayza *Leshonenu,* **29**, 27–46, 80–102.

BIKL, S. and LEHRER, L. (eds.) 1958 *Shmuel Niger bukh.* Yivo, New York.

BIN-NUN, J. 1973 *Jiddisch und die deutschen Mundarten unter besonderer Berücksichtigung des ostgalizischen Jiddisch.* Max Niemeyer, Tübingen.

BIRNBAUM, S. A. 1923 Übersicht über den jiddischen Vokalismus. *Zeitschrift für deutsche Mundarten* **18**, 3–4, 122–130.

BIRNBAUM, S. A. 1979 *Yiddish. A Survey and a Grammar.* Manchester University Press, Manchester & University of Toronto Press, Toronto.

BOROKHOV, B. 1913 A gerus fun far dray hundert yor [= review of Landau and Wachstein 1911]. In Niger, 1913, pp. 351–356.

BRANN, M. 1963 *Germania Judaica. Band I. Von den ältesten Zeiten bis 1238. Nach dem Tode von M. Brann herausgegeben von. I. Elbogen, A. Freimann und H. Tykocinski.* J. C. B. Mohr (Paul Siebeck), Tübingen.

CARMON, E. (ed.) 1976 *Kheker veiyun.* University of Haifa, Haifa.

CATALÁN, D. (ed.) 1958 *Estructuralismo e Historia* [= *Miscelánea Homenaje a André Martinet,* II]. Universidad de La Laguna.

CHOMSKY, W. 1952 *David Ḳimḥi's Hebrew Grammar (Mikhlol). Systematically Presented and Critically Annotated.* Dropsie College for Hebrew and Cognate Learning, Philaldelphia & Bloch Publishing, New York.

CHOMSKY, W. 1977 *Halashon haivrit bedarkhey hitpatkhuta.* Rubin Mass, Jerusalem.

DAN, Y. 1968 *Torat hasod shel khasidut ashkenaz.* Mosad Bialik, Jerusalem.

ELDAR (ADLER), I. 1976 Leverur mahuto vegilgulav shel hanikud haerets-yisraeli-teveryani. In Carmon, 1976, pp. 39–48.

ELDAR (ADLER). I. 1978 *Masoret hakeria hakedam-ashkenazit. Mahuta vehayesodot hameshutafim la ulemasoret sefarad. Vol. 1: Inyaney hagaya venikud* [= *Eda velashon. Pirsume mifal mesorot halashon shel edot yisrael* Morag, S. (ed.) 4]. Magnes, Jerusalem.

ERIK, M. 1928 *Di geshikhte fun der yidisher literatur fun di eltste tsaytn biz der haskole tkufe. Fertsnter—akhtsnter yorhundert. Mit 35 bilder un melodyes.* Kultur lige, Warsaw.

FINKELSTEIN, L. 1924 *Jewish Self-Government in the Middle Ages.* Jewish Theological Seminary of America, New York.

FISCHER, J. 1934 Das Jiddische und sein Verhältnis zu den deutschen Mundarten unter besonderer Berücksichtigung der ostgalizischen Mundart. Unpublished doctoral dissertation: Ruprecht-Karls Universität, Heidelberg [partially published as Fischer, 1936; published in full as Bin-Nun, 1973].

FISCHER, J. 1936 *Das Jiddische und sein Verhältnis zu den deutschen Mundarten unter besonderer Berücksichtigung der ostgalizischen Mundart. Erster Teil—Lautlehre (einschliesslich Phonetik der ostgalizische Mundart). Erste Hälfte: Allgemeiner Teil.* Oswald Schmidt, Leipzig.

FISHMAN, J. A. (ed.) 1985 *Readings in the Sociology of Jewish Languages,* Vol. I. E. J. Brill, Leiden.

GELBER, M. H. (ed.) 1986 *Identity and Ethos. A. Festschrift for Sol Liptzin on the Occasion of his 85th Birthday.* Peter Lang, New York, Berne, Frankfurt am Main.

GERZON, J. 1902 *Die jüdisch-deutsche Sprache. Eine grammatisch-lexikalische Untersuchung ihres deutsches Grundbestandes.* J. Kauffmann, Frankfurt am Main [published same year as *Die jüdisch-deutsche Sprache. Eine grammatisch-lexikalische Untersuchung ihres deutsches Grundbestandes. Inaugural-Dissertation zur Erlangung der Doctorwürde der Hohen Philosophischen Facultät zu Heidelberg vorgelegt von Jacob Gerzon aus Köln a. Rh.* S. Salm, Köln].

GOLDSHMID, D. 1970 *Makhzor leyamim noraim lefi minhage bene ashkenaz lekhol anfehem.* Koren, Jerusalem.

GÜDEMANN, M. 1888 *Geschichte des Erziehungswesens und der Cultur der Juden in Deutschland während des XIV und XV Jahrhunderts* [= *Geschichte des Erziehungswesens und der Cultur der abendländischen Juden während des Mittelalters und der neueren Zeit, III*]. Alfred Hölder, Vienna.

HERZOG, M. I. 1965 *The Yiddish Language in Northern Poland. Its Geography and History.* Indiana University, Bloomington & Mouton, The Hague.

HOENIGSWALD, H. M. 1960 *Language Change and Linguistic Reconstruction.* University of Chicago Press, Chicago.

IBN EZRA, A. 1546 *Sefer tsakhot badikduk.* Daniel Bomberg, Venice.

KAHLE, P. 1930 *Massoreten des Westens II.* W. Kohlhammer, Stuttgart.

KATZ, D. 1977 First Steps in the Reconstruction of the Proto Vocalism of the Semitic Component in Yiddish. Unpublished paper presented to the Department of Linguistics, Columbia University.

KATZ, D. 1978a Semantic Classes Resistant to a Yiddish Sound Shift. Unpublished paper presented to the Department of Linguistics, Columbia University.

KATZ, D. 1978b Genetic Notes on Netherlandic Yiddish Vocalism. Unpublished paper presented to the Department of Linguistics, Columbia University.

KATZ, D. 1979 Der semitisher kheylek in yidish: a yerushe fun kadmoynim. Paper placed before the First International Conference on Research in Yiddish Language and Literature at the Oxford Centre for Postgraduate Hebrew Studies, 6–9 August [Hebrew translation = Katz 1986b].

KATZ, D. 1982 *Explorations in the History of the Semitic Component in Yiddish.* Unpublished doctoral dissertation: University of London.

KATZ, D. 1983a "Dialektologie des Jiddischen" in Besch, Knoop, Putschke & Wiegand 1983, pp. 1018–1041.

KATZ, D. 1983b Yidish in tsvelftn un draytsetn yorhundert: evidents fun hebreishe un aramishe ksav-yadn. Paper placed before the Second International Conference on Research in Yiddish Language and Literature at the Oxford Centre for Postgraduate Hebrew Studies, 10–15 July.

KATZ, D. 1985 Hebrew, Aramaic and the rise of Yiddish. In Fishman, 1985, pp. 85–103.

KATZ, D. 1986a On Yiddish, in Yiddish and for Yiddish. Five hundred years of Yiddish scholarship. In Gelber, 1986, pp. 23–36.

KATZ, D. 1986b Hayesod hashemi beyidish: yerusha mimey kedem. In *Hasifrut,* **10,** 3–4, **(35–36),** pp. 228–251.

KIMCHI, D. 1532 *Sefer mikhlol.* Constantinople.

KIMCHI, D. 1545 *Sefer Mikhlol.* Daniel Bomberg, Venice.

KIMCHI, M. [1509–1518] *Mahalakh shevile hadaat.* Pesara.

KING, R. D. 1969 *Historical Linguistics and Generative Grammar.* Prentice-Hall, Englewood Cliffs, NJ.

KING. R. D. 1979 Evidence of the German Component. Paper placed before the First International Conference on Research in Yiddish Language and Literature at the Oxford Centre for Postgraduate Hebrew Studies, 6–9 August.

KLAR, B. 1951 Letoledot hamivta beyemey habenayim. *Leshonenu* **17,** 72–75.

LANDAU, A. and WACHSTEIN, B. *Jüdische Privatbriefe aus dem Jahre 1619. Nach den Originalen des K. U. K. Haus-, Hof- und Staatsarchivs im Auftrage der historischen Kommission der Israelitischen Kultusgemeinde in Wien.* Wilhelm Braumüller, Vienna, Leipzig.

LEBENSOHN, A. [=*A*vrom *D*ov-Ber *M*ikhalishker] Hakoyheyn ben Khayim "Yisroyn leodom". Subtextual commentary in Been-Zeev, 1874.

MARCHAND, J. W. 1960 Three basic problems in the investigation of early Yiddish. *Orbis* **9.1**, 34–41.

MARCHAND, J. W. 1965 The origin of Yiddish. In *Communications et rapports du Premier Congrès International de Dialectologie générale* (Louvain du 21 au 25 août 1960) pp. 248–252.

MIESES, M. 1924 *Die jiddische Sprache. Eine historische Grammatik des Idioms der integralen Juden Ost- und Mitteleuropas.* Benjamin Harz, Berlin, Vienna.

NIGER, S. (ed.) 1913 *Der pinkes. Yorbukh far der geshikhte fun der yidisher literatur un shprakh, far folklor, kritik un biblyografye. Ershter yorgang.* B. A. Kletskin, Vilna.

REYZEN, S. 1920 *Gramatik fun der yidisher shprakh. Ershter teyl.* Sh. Shreberk, Vilna.

SCHLEICHER, A. 1868 Eine Fabel in indogermanischer Ursprache. *Beiträge zur vergleichenden Sprachforschung auf dem Gebiete der arischen celtischen und slawischen Sprachen* **5**, 206–208.

SHTIF, N. 1922 *M. Gideman, Yidishe kultur geshikhte in mitlalter* [=annotated translation of Güdemann 1888]. Klal-farlag, Berlin.

SAUSSURE, F. d. 1916 *Cours de linguistique générale. Publié par Charles Bally et Albert Sechehaye.* Librairie Payot, Lausanne, Paris.

SCHRAMM, G. M. 1964 *The Graphemes of Tiberian Hebrew.* University of California, Berkeley, Los Angeles.

SHULMAN, E. 1898 Imkey Sofo. *Hashiloyakh* **4**, 37–46, 106–112, 221–229.

TSHEMERINSKI, K. 1913 Di yidishe fonetik. In Niger, 1913, pp. 47–71.

TSINBERG, Y. 1928 Der kamf far yidish in der altyidisher literatur. *Filologishe shriftn* **2**, 69–106.

VEYNGER, M. 1913 Hebreishe klangen in der yidisher shprakh. In Niger, 1913, 79–84.

W[ASSERMAN], H. 1972 Regensburg. In *Encyclopaedia Judaica* **14**, 35–37.

WEINREICH, M. 1928 *Bilder fun der yidisher literatur geshikhte. Fun di onheybn biz Mendele Moykher Sforim.* Farlag Tomor fun Yoysef Kamermakher, Vilna.

WEINREICH, M. 1951 Ashkenaz: di yidish-tkufe in der yidisher geshikhte. *Yivo bleter* **35**, 7–17.

WEINREICH, M. 1954 Prehistory and early history of Yiddish. Facts and conceptual framework. In Weinreich, U. 1954, pp. 73–101.

WEINREICH, M. 1958 Bney-hes un bney-khes in ashkenaz: di problem—un vos zi lozt undz hern. In Bikl and Lehrer, 1958, pp. 101–123.

WEINREICH, M. 1960 Di sistem yidishe kadmen-vokaln. *Yidishe shprakh* **20**, 65–71.

WEINREICH, M. 1963 A yidisher zats fun far zibn hundert yor (analiz fun gor a vikhtikn shprakhikn gefins). *Yidishe shprakh* **23**, 87–94.

WEINREICH, M. 1964 Ashkenaz in algemeyn yidishn gerem. *Goldene keyt* **50**, 172–182.

WEINREICH, M. 1973 *Geshikhte fun der yidisher shprakh. Bagrifn, faktn, metodn,* IV vols. Yivo, New York.

WEINREICH, U. (ed.) 1954 *The Field of Yiddish. Studies in Yiddish Language, Folklore and Literature* [=Publications of the Linguistic Circle of New York, 3]. New York.

WEINREICH, U. 1958a A Retrograde sound shift in the guise of a survival. An aspect of Yiddish vowel development. In Catálan, 1958, pp. 221–267.

WEINREICH, U. 1958b Nusakh hasoferim haivri-yidi. *Leshonenu* **22**, 54–66.

YALON, H. 1930 (Review of Kahle, 1930). *Leshonenu* **3**, 202–207.

YALON, H. 1937–1938 Sheviley mivtaim. *Kuntresim leinyaney halashon haivrit* **1**, 62–78.

YALON, H. 1938–1939 Diukim beferush Rashi al tere asar. *Kuntresim leinyaney halashon haivrit* **2**, 9–11.

YALON, H. 1942 Hagiya sefaradit betsarefat hatesfonit bedoro shel Rashi uvedorot sheleakharav. *Inyaney lashon* **1**, 16–31.

YALON, H. 1964 *Mavo lenikud hamishna.* Mosad Bialik, Jerusalem.

Language & Communication, Vol. 7, Supplement, pp. 61–71, 1987.
Printed in Great Britain.

0271-5309/87 $3.00 + .00
Pergamon Journals Ltd.

PREWAR SOVIET THEORIES ON THE ORIGINS OF YIDDISH*

DOV-BER KERLER

Oxford Centre for Postgraduate Hebrew Studies and Lincoln College, Oxford

The theme of the first Winter Symposium is the origin of Yiddish. The theme of this paper is the origin of Yiddish as seen through the eyes of prewar Soviet Yiddish linguistics. This imposing branch of Yiddish philology was brutally brought to an abrupt end by Soviet authorities.

Those who research the history of Yiddish tend to rely on far reaching if not always conclusive reconstructions. Some measure of reconstruction will also be necessary for the historian of Soviet Yiddish linguistics: not everything that was researched reached print, and more material was prepared for publication than was published. It is well known that not all topics were considered equally acceptable for research, and in certain periods there was perhaps a fear even to reflect on those things that were in the normal run of events not permitted public expression. When we seek to ask what Soviet Yiddish linguists had to say about the origin of Yiddish we find that several of them had more to say than they actually expressed aloud or published in their articles.

It may be that the very existence of organized research into Yiddish linguistics in the Soviet Union was from the outset permissible only to meet purely practical—and temporary—ends. The greatest priority was of course given to practical research: language standardization, the methodology of language teaching, the theory and practice of translation from Russian (and sometimes Ukrainian) into Yiddish, orthographic reforms, and the preparation of terminological dictionaries and word lists. These are the central and most prominent themes and concerns of research into Yiddish in the Soviet Union. The preponderance of these themes in Soviet Yiddish linguistics has naturally caught the interest of recent researchers (e.g. Schaechter 1977, Kahn 1972/3, Peltz 1981, 1985, Peltz and Kiel 1985, Hutton 1983).

It should be stressed that, from the ideological point of view, topics such as the origin of Yiddish were not 'popular' in the Soviet Union. Anyone showing too much interest in the older periods of the history of Yiddish was liable to be awarded with a whole string of epithets such as 'Bourgeois-recidivist Yiddishist' or 'Yiddishist (= nationalist = chauvinist) petty-bourgeois eclectic' (cf. Greenbaum 1978: 45, 85ff.).

Nonetheless not everything in Soviet Yiddish linguistics was directed towards pure normativism (= standardization) and language planning (= Sovietization, the construction

*I am grateful to Dovid Katz for constant encouragement and guidance and to Chris Hutton for translating the paper from the Yiddish manuscript, and to both for comments on earlier drafts. Needless to say, responsibility for errors and shortcomings rests with me. The research on which this paper is based was supported, in part, by the Memorial Foundation for Jewish Culture (New York). Special thanks are due to Didi Rosen for love and support in this as in all things.

of a 'Soviet Yiddish' cf. Volobrinski 1934; Shklyar 1934; Spivak 1935; Zaretski 1935; Fridland 1940). In any case, practical linguistic research requires prior historical and dialectological research as a basis for normativization. This serves to some extent as the justification for Mordkhe Veynger's (1890–1929) interest in Yiddish dialectology (1928b: 676). Likewise, Elye Spivak (1890–1952), in his consideration of new word formations in Yiddish, looks back as far as the glosses of the 13th century (1939: 170) and to the linguistic monuments of the 15th century (1939: 179).

Furthermore, there were among the Soviet Yiddish linguists those such as Mordkhe Veynger and Nokhem Shtif (1879–1934) who had long (i.e. from their pre-Soviet days) had an explicit interest in the history of Yiddish.

What then can one learn about the views of Soviet Yiddish linguists on the origins of Yiddish? Firstly one might mention the course outlines and the general surveys of the history of Yiddish that appeared in the Soviet Union: Kalmanovitsh (1921), Kagarov (1923), Shpilreyn (1926), Gitlits (1940), Falkovitsh (1940). It might appear that Kalmanovitsh's *Konspekt* has little relevance to organized Yiddish research in the Soviet Union. The *Konspekt* was published relatively early, just as Soviet research was getting organized, and the author left the Soviet Union a short time later and became one of the leading scholars of the Vilna Yivo. Nonetheless one can discern in it several of the concepts and conclusions that could be characterized as standard for interwar Soviet Yiddish linguistics.

Kalmanovitsh divides the history of the language into two periods. The first is called *yidish-daytsh* (1922: 4) which begins somewhere in the MHG period when Yiddish 'developed independently out of a MHG dialect or a mixture of several MHG dialects' (1922: 3) on the linguistic territory 'between the Middle Rhine and the Danube (*loc. cit.*). It is not known precisely when Yiddish came to be perceived as a distinct linguistic entity, but probably 'in different places at different times' (1921: 4). His second period begins at the end of the 15th, and beginning of the 16th century, when Yiddish is 'already complete as an independent linguistic construct' (*loc. cit.*). Kalmonovitsh also mentions the fusion character of the language and the considerable impact on its structure of Hebrew and Aramaic, which 'not only provided lexical material, but also influenced to a considerable extent its syntactic development and played a part in the formation of its phraseology' (1922: 3).

Kagarov (1923) treats the matter of the contribution of German dialects to the formation of Yiddish at greater length. He notes also 'the existence of *ivre-taytsh* ['di gemishte hebreish-daytshishe shprakh'] as an independent language distinct from the German vernacular going back to the expulsions from Austria in 1420 and from Saxony (Germany) in 1432' (1923: 7).

It is not clear from Kagarov's article whether he considers that Yiddish (as distinct from MHG on the one hand and *ivre-taysh* on the other) arose first on German speaking territory or not until the refugees from the expulsions left German speaking territories and 'settled partly in Holland, partly in Poland and Lithunia' (1923: 7). At the outset Kagarov writes that 'the skeleton, the Germanic structure of the language, stems from the German dialects of the 14th to the 16th centuries' (1923: 5). He later moves his dating for the origin of Yiddish forward, explaining that 'until the middle of the 15th century the Jews of Germany spoke the local dialects of that country, just as they at first spoke French in Western Germany' (1923: 7).

It is to a much earlier period that Shpilreyn points in his *Konspekt* (1926) where he speaks of 'the first informations about Yiddish in chronicles of the 12th and 13th century' (1926:

5). What we designate today as older Western Yiddish (*yidish-daytsh* for Kalmanovitsh, *yidish-taytsh* for Gitlits (1940: 49) and Falkovitsh (1940: 8) and *ivre taytsh* for Kagarov) is characterized as ultimately German interlayered with Hebrew'' (1926: 6).

All these studies stress the obvious fusion character of Yiddish, citing the non-Germanic components, especially the Semitic, as decisive factors in the origins of Yiddish (most notably Falkovitsh 1940: 8). However it is clear that these works lack a refined grasp of the history of Yiddish, one that would have characterized precisely the fundamental distinctions between Western and Eastern, older and modern, spoken and written varieties of Yiddish. This retrospectively speaking, major defect in these studies derives from their methodological and popularizing purposes, the only exception being Gitlits (1940). In general their authors did not report the results of independent in depth research into the history and origins of the Yiddish language.

In addition to these general surveys there are a number of articles that have either an incidental or a direct relevance to the topic at hand. Several of them present explicit theories as to the origin of Yiddish (Veynger 1913, 1926, 1928a, 1929, Grande* 1930) and others define a set of underlying relations and concepts of a philological and historiographical nature that are, in part, relevant to this subject (Shtif 1913, 1922, 1928, 1929a, 1929b, 1932).

Mordkhe Veynger first began to develop a theory of the origin of Yiddish in his early work 'Dialektologishe bamerkungen', published in Noyakh Prilutski's *Zamlbikher* in 1912. In this article Veynger takes a position on the historical development of Yiddish and Yiddish dialects and proposes the following retrospective scenario:

> From time immemorial Jews have lived in Germany. As was the case in other countries, they spoke the language of the surrounding population in Germany. And this population spoke differently in every town and in every village. This diversity in early Germany is the driving factor behind the creation of the Yiddish dialects (Veynger 1912: 130–131).

Veynger arrives at an estimate for the age of Yiddish by considering the source of the modern (i.e. Eastern Yiddish) dialects. For him, their origin is to be sought not in Eastern Europe, but in Germany itself (1912: 131–132). In his treatment of the dialectal realization of the *oy* diphthong as *uv* (*groy ~ gruv; bloy ~ bluv*) and as *ov* (*zoyer ~ zover; boyen ~ boven*) he concludes that 'the *v* [. . .] is not a recent phenomenon—it is in actual fact not only a *MHG* but an *OHG* feature (from the 8th to the 12th century)' (1912: 132).

Among Veynger's later, Soviet writings, his first lengthy article 'Vegn yidishe dialektn' (1926) is of special significance. Although certain aspects of the study are treated in a theoretically and methodologically superior manner in later works in *Tsaytshrift* 2 and 3 (1928a, 1928b; cf. Shtif 1929a, 1: 32–35), we do not find there an account of what Nokhem Shtif later characterized as 'Veynger's theory'.

The 1926 article opens with a declaration in which the history of Yiddish is presented as a topic in its own right:

> What purpose do we have in mind in publishing these materials on Yiddish dialects? Firstly, they serve as a source for a Yiddish atlas. Secondly, no history of the Yiddish language, no historical grammar can be constructed without these dialectal materials (Veynger 1926: 181).

In his final chapter Veynger discusses a series of phonetic phenomena in Yiddish 'in connection with analogous facts in German' (1926: 202). Here he explains, among other things, the inorganic *h,* and *h* dropping in Southeastern Yiddish. Rejecting Gerzon's (1902) theory of Slavic influence, he points to the existence of this phenomenon in both MHG and OHG:

> I believe that this phenomenon in Yiddish is a *purely Germanic one*. We should work on the assumption that *the h in Yiddish dialects is a survival from the distant past* and it is quite possible that this phenomenon

leads us back to sources considerably older than MHG, which is generally considered the earliest possible source for Yiddish. It is quite possible *that the origins in Yiddish of the feature under discussion are to be found actually in OHG* (Veynger 1926: 203).

This is the key point of Veynger's theory: present day Yiddish dialects stem from Germany and their source—and therefore the source of Yiddish in general—must be sought not in the MHG period but as far back as the OHG period. Veynger brings further evidence for his theory in citing the collapse of *s* and *š* in Lithuanian Yiddish: 'It transpires that in OHG there was a possible process as a result of which *sk* became *sch,* and a second process which resulted in *s*' (1926: 204). Veynger cites the following examples: OHG *skap,* Y. *sof* ~ *šof;* OHG *skuld,* Y. *suld* ~ *šuld;* OHG *fisk,* Y. *fis* ~ *fiš*; OHG *waskan,* Y. *vasn* ~ *vašn*; OHG *himlisc* Y. *himlis* ~ *himliš*. He concludes:

> I consider that this *sh* ~ *s* alternation [that is preserved in several German and Yiddish dialects—DBK] is a survival of OHG *sk* > *s,* and in this phenomenon I find further evidence that the origin of Yiddish belongs not to the MHG but to the OHG period. (Veynger 1926: 205).

Interestingly, Uriel Weinreich in his classic article on *sabesdiker losn* (1952) did not reject out of hand Veynger's theory, leaving it as a hypothesis to be tested by further research into the history and structure of the Yiddish sound system (U. Weinreich 1952: 367, 369).

Veynger's explanation of the inorganic *h* in SEY and the *s* ~ *sh* alternations in NEY concludes with the following remark:

> Weinreich (*Shtaplen*, p. 36), on the basis of Yiddish linguistic research hitherto, maintains that 'it is absolutely certain that the Yiddish language did not emerge before the MHG period'. A series of facts—the inorganic *h,* the *š* as against Lithuanian *s,* and others—bear witness to the fact that we can make this further step in solving the problem of the dating of the origins of Yiddish. (Veynger 1926: 265).

The main contentions of Veynger's theory are described briefly and with greater circumspection in his posthumously published *Yidishe dyalektologye* (1929: 27–28).

After Veynger's death Shtif published a detailed critique of Veynger's dialectological studies. His most important objections were (1) that even if we accept Veynger's reconstructions (and Shtif is at pains to show why they cannot be correct), why does he insist that the source for certain phonetic alternations in Yiddish must be OHG, given the fact that they are also found in the MHG period (1929a, 2: 7–9)? (2) that 'Veynger did not approach the study of Yiddish merely as a Germanist: he approached it with the hypothesis (more precisely, a certainty) that all phonetic properties of Yiddish dialects should be traced to German of the earliest periods (OHG). He neither raises nor refutes the possibility of influence from elsewhere (the Slavic languages)' (1929a, 2: 21).

The second point of Shtif's criticism can be explained in part by Veynger's outlook on Yiddish from the point of view of a Germanist who saw Yiddish as primarily and perhaps even exclusively a Germanic language:

> Yiddish by virtue of its fundamental linguistic character belongs to the Germanic languages. Adequate research into Yiddish is only possible in the context and on the basis of Germanic linguistics in general and German linguistics in particular (Veynger 1926: 27).

It seems unlikely that even Yiddish philologists researching the 'Germanic foundations' of Yiddish would be ready to accept such a categorical declaration as axiomatic for research into Yiddish.

Veynger's fundamental commitment to the Germanist approach also explains his silence on the question of the role of the Semitic and Slavic components in the historical evolution of Yiddish. But how can we explain the first point of Shtif's criticism? What was it that drove Veynger to push back the origins of Yiddish as far as OHG? As Shtif puts it, when discussing Veynger's reconstruction of *s* < *sk*:

> The question is how and why [does Veynger need—DBK] to trace the *ancestry* [*Yikhes* in original; my emphasis—DBK] of *s* in White Russian and Lithuanian dialects all the way back to OHG? At the most it is a survival from the *MHG* period (Shtif 1929a: 2: 7).

It would seem that no complete answer can be given to this question, but one plausible hypothesis is that Veynger, his Germanist approach notwithstanding, was something of an ideological Yiddishist.

In the pre-Soviet phase of his career Veynger wrote for publications that were Yiddishist in both the philological and ideological senses, including Noyakh Prilutski's (1912) *Zamlbikher 1* and Niger's (1913) *Pinkes* where he writes that:

> the sounds that are produced by a Jew while praying are in no way Hebrew sounds. There is one and only one name appropriate for them: *Yiddish sounds,* those that we hear when we speak Yiddish. This follows from the fact that *the laws of development that gave rise to Hebrew in its present form are the same laws that operate in Yiddish.* I (Veynger 1913: 79).

We also know that his approach to the standardization of Yiddish orthography vis-à-vis the traditional spelling systems was ambivalent (cf, Zaretski 1929: 4, 6–7) and that for a while he was an active Bundist (see the biographical information in *Di yidishe shprakh* 1929, 1: 2). Finally it is well known that the issue of a 'respectable' age for Yiddish was an important feature of Yiddishist apologetics in the first decade of the 20th century. Shtif, in his pre-Soviet classic work of ideological Yiddishism *'Yidn un yidish'* writes that *'One does not ask questions about the ancestry of a language,* any more than one would ask them about a mother. No people chooses the language it would like, just as no one chooses his own mother' (1919: 39). Thus it is most interesting to find on the same page, a few lines further: "But this old-German language, this Yiddish, that we have been speaking, writing, thinking and feeling in, has been a Jewish language for *one thousand years.* It was a thousand years ago that it became *our* language." In the Soviet Union, even in the more 'liberal' times of the 1920s, no one dared show even the slightest, covert sign of ideological Yiddishism. My conjecture is that Veynger insisted on locating the origin of Yiddish not in the MHG but in the OHG period as a reflex of his Yiddishist leaning and leading the resultant tendency to seek the maximal antiquity for the language.

Another Soviet Yiddish linguist who paid special attention to the history of Yiddish was Nokhem Shtif. In addition to his numerous studies of normative syntax and stylistics, Shtif also published important studies on older written texts and on specific stages in the history of Yiddish. And although he did not actually formulate a 'credo', we can all the same attempt to reconstruct his individual approach to the history of Yiddish on the basis of the works published in *Di yidishe shprakh.* (See Fig. 1).

Like Veynger, Shtif too had a pre-Soviet Scholarly period. It was then that he underwent the transformation from Bal-Dimyen (his first pseudonym) to Shtif. Not only did he collaborate on the Vilner *Pinkes,* he was the primary founder of the Yiddish Scientific Institute in 1925. In Shtif's pre-Soviet writings the kernel of his later intellectual development can be discerned. In a review of Pines' *Geshikhte fun der yidisher literatur* (Shtif 1913) he sets out his own position on research into Yiddish, from which it can be seen that he is a Yiddishist in the philological sense, i.e. Yiddish represents for him an object of research in its own right (1913: 317–321). In his footnotes to Güdemann's *Geschichte des Erziehungswesen und der Cultur der Juden in Deutschland* which he translated in part into Yiddish, Shtif comments on the rules of Old Yiddish spelling, which Güdemann discusses on the basis of *Seyfer hamides* of 1542 (Shtif 1922: 148–9, 180–3, 184–6). The term *yidish-daytsh* is used only in the translation of Güdemann's text. In Shtif's own notes one encounters only 'development of Yiddish' (1922: 16), 'rules of Old Yiddish spelling' (1922:

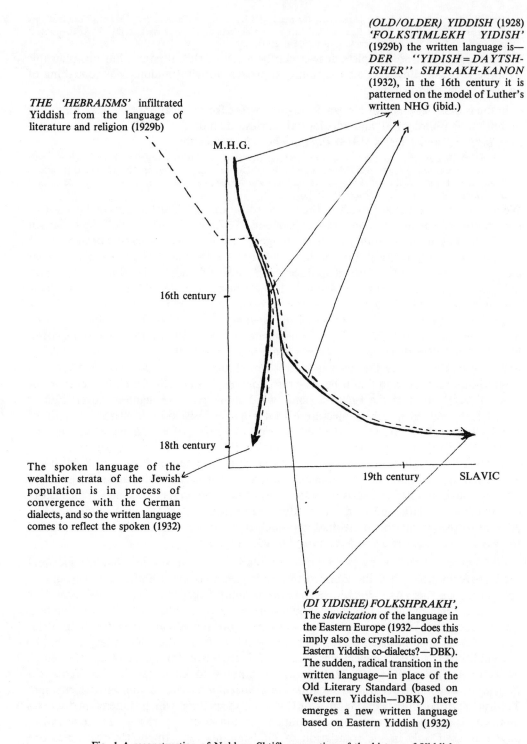

(OLD/OLDER) YIDDISH (1928)
'FOLKSTIMLEKH YIDISH'
(1929b) the written language is—
*DER "YIDISH = DAYTSH-
ISHER" SHPRAKH-KANON*
(1932), in the 16th century it is
patterned on the model of Luther's
written NHG (ibid.)

THE 'HEBRAISMS' infiltrated
Yiddish from the language of
literature and religion (1929b)

M.H.G.

16th century

18th century

The spoken language of the
wealthier strata of the Jewish
population is in process of
convergence with the German
dialects, and so the written language
comes to reflect the spoken (1932)

19th century   SLAVIC

(DI YIDISHE) FOLKSHPRAKH',
The *slavicization* of the language in
the Eastern Europe (1932—does this
imply also the crystalization of the
Eastern Yiddish co-dialects?—DBK).
The sudden, radical transition in the
written language—in place of the
Old Literary Standard (based on
Western Yiddish—DBK) there
emerges a new written language
based on Eastern Yiddish (1932)

Fig. 1 A reconstruction of Nokhem Shtif's perception of the history of Yiddish.

148, 180; cf. especially 81), and he uses the term *yidish-daytsh* only in inverted commas (1922: 180, 189, 191). My thanks to Professor Khone Shmeruk for referring me to Shtif's footnotes to Güdemann's book.

Shtif's ideas would probably have changed in the course of time, but on becoming a Soviet scholar he was forced into an abrupt shift of direction (for an instructive Soviet interpretation of the shift cf. Slutski 1935: 85). It was clear that he could no longer continue to operate openly as an ideological Yiddishist (his contribution to ideological Yiddishism is still in need of adequate evaluation) and he was less and less in a position to allow himself the luxury of research into such 'eclectic' or 'bourgeois' topics as Old and older Yiddish, not to mention the origins of Yiddish. It is also very difficult to assess whether the dramatic turnabout in Shtif's position with regard to the history of the Semitic component (cf. Peltz 1981: 46, 50–52, Katz 1985: 88) was forced upon him or was truly philological.

Shtif's writings comprise a series of conceptualizations that bears witness to his maturity as a historian of Yiddish. More than other Soviet Yiddish linguists he stressed the fundamental importance of the distinction between spoken and written language (1932, 1: 5ff.). In addition he gave an account of the external influences on written Yiddish (1932, 1: 4–5, 7) and emphasized the split between Eastern and Western Yiddish under the impact of the Slavicization of the former and the 'New High Germanization' of the latter (1932, 1: 5). Shtif characterizes both older spoken Yiddish (1929b: 13, 14, 21) and Eastern Yiddish (1932, 1, 2) as *folkshprakh,* sometimes also as *folkstimlekh yidish.* Older written Yiddish he terms *der yidish-daytshisher shprakh kanon* (1932 1, 2—the term *yidish-daytsh* is used consistently in inverted commas). It is clear from Shtif's writings that he was above all a Yiddishist in the philological sense. Approaching Yiddish as an object of research in its own right, he looked back on the entire history of the language as the history of *Yiddish* in contrast to others who described its earlier stages as *yidish-daytsh,* or *taytsh,* or *ivre-taytsh.* Shtif's consciousness of the names for Yiddish can be seen from his pioneering article on the subject in *Yidishe filologye* (Shtif 1924).

Paradoxically, much can be learned from Shtif's polemical article 'Di sotsyale diferentsiatsye in yidish—di hebreishe elementn in der shprakh' (Shtif 1929b, cf. Spivak's 1935a: 21 critique on this article). Explaining that Hebraisms had not begun to "infiltrate" Yiddish under the impact of religious practice and literature until the 15th and 16th centuries, he writes that up to the 14th, 15th and 16th centuries Jews in Germany knew and used *Yiddish* words (i.e. of Germanic origin) for concepts and objects, for which later only or principally the Hebrew word was acceptable' (1929b: 13, cf. Hutton 1984: 24-25).

Unfortunately Shtif did not concern himself specifically with the issue of when, where and how Yiddish arose. From his criticism of Veynger's theory we learn that he located the origin of Yiddish in the MHG period, somewhere on German-speaking territory. It is also certain that he conceived the history of the language as the history of Yiddish and if he had discussed its origins he would have spoken of the origins of *Yiddish.*

Rejecting any decisive role for Hebraisms in the original development of Yiddish, Shtif also characterizes the 'pre-Hebraized'—that is, according to him—the older elements of the language, as Yiddish. It is clear that in structural terms the Germanic component is for Shtif the principal component of the Yiddish language. Taking into account his evocation of the "Hebrew lexical invasion" (= "di hebreyshe okupatsye") the emergence of Yiddish was for Shtif a process of an independent ethno-linguistic development. His perception of the history of Yiddish thus differs from the generally accepted characterization of it as a FUSION LANGUAGE (on which cf. M. Weinreich 1973 I: 32–35).

It is perhaps symptomatic to the nature of Yiddish linguistics in the Soviet Union that the second researcher who devoted himself explicitly to the topic of the origin of Yiddish was not a Yiddish specialist but a distinguished Soviet Semitist at the beginning of his career: Bentsien Grande (1891–1974). In April 1930 he delivered a paper in the 'Subsection for Materialist Linguistics in the Communist Academy' of Moscow. The paper was entitled 'An attempt to apply the Japhetidological approach to the history of Yiddish'. We know that Grande was supposed to publish the paper in the Kiev journal *Di yidishe shprakh* (see Shtif's footnote in Zaretski 1930: 71). Unfortunately I was unable to find any such article either in that journal or in other Soviet or Soviet Yiddish linguistic publications. All that we know about Grande's paper is set down in Zaretski's short but detailed report (1930).

Here is not the place to go into a detailed account of Marrist-Japhetidological linguistics (for a discussion see Mark 1935, Raskin 1978: 259–262; for a contemporary authentic Soviet Yiddish account of that time cf. Gitlits 1935), but it is clear that Grande's theory of the origin of Yiddish is not only conceived under the inspiration of Japhetidology but wholly based upon it. Interestingly, Grande even consulted the Academician Marr himself (Zaretski 1930: 74). Today Grande's lecture may seem little more than an academic curiosity rather than a consistent theory of the origins of Yiddish. But this attempt is itself of interest. Grande approaches the origins of Yiddish (just as Veynger had previously) by way of a synchronic analysis of contemporary Yiddish. The reconstruction of the history of a language on the basis of synchronic analysis (internal reconstruction) is a perfectly legitimate and productive method in modern linguistics. Grande restricted himself to Northeastern Yiddish, and his analysis was based exclusively on the far from structural preconceptions of Japhetidological methodology.

Given that Zaretski's article is itself a treatment of Grande's lecture, I will limit myself here to citing excerpts from it:

The attempt has been made [. . .] to derive Yiddish (that is the phonetic side of the language) from modern German dialects. Later it was assumed that Yiddish derives from Middle High German; Veynger even considers that we should look for the roots of Yiddish in Old High German. But no answer can be given to this question, because the question itself is badly phrased. We cannot say that what was earlier a uniform German gradually split into German and Yiddish—this is an Indo-Europeanist approach and not a Japhetidological formulation of the question. The correct formulation is the following: which layer of the prehistoric human language can still be residually detected in Yiddish. Yiddish (Grande is concerned only with the Lithuanian-White Russian dialect) is an 'o-language' (i.e. Yiddish *o* corresponds to German *a: vos/was*). The following relation has been observed in Japhetic languages: the 'o-languages' have 'sharp' sibilants and the 'a-languages' have 'blunt' sibilants. In 'sharp' languages there is generally a collapse of the phonemes *s* and *š*. Could not the same be said of Yiddish? It turns out that it can. Yiddish (Lithuanian Yiddish) is an 'o-language'—and has 'sharp' sibilants. The phonemes *s* and *š* are confused. Both phenomena (the *o* and the confusion of *s* and *š*) are old—the historical manuscripts testify to that, both in their orthography (*s* as *š*, *o* against German *a*) and in poetry, by their rhyme scheme. In this way we can see confirmed in Yiddish the same relationship found in the Japhetic languages. Against Shtif's contention that the sibilant features of Lithuanian Yiddish are due to White Russian impact we can cite the fact that 'sin' is used to designate *s* even in manuscripts written in Germany, i.e. before there was any White Russian impact. At that stage there existed already a single intermediate sound in place of the *s/š* distinction. [. . .]

At one time both Jews (in Germany) and Germans spoke a large number of local dialects. These dialects began to merge and coalesce. In this process, the local German dialects, that is those of the rural population, merged in one way, and those of the Jews in another. This is how German and Yiddish crystallized into separate languages. Why did Yiddish become crystallized specifically as an 'o-language'? This both is and is not a matter of chance. It was a chance from a purely linguistic point of view. But it would be possible to find out the reason, if one were to understand fully ther material culture of past generations of Jews in Germany. We can also assume, as was suggested to Grande by Marr in a private conversation, that the adoption by Jews in Germany of an 'o-language' could have been influenced by the linguistic habits they had brought with them to Germany. At this point Grande turns his attention to Hebrew. Hebrew, in the context of the

Semitic languages, is an 'o-language' (in contrast to Arabic, which is an 'a-language'). Hebrew must have persisted until a lot later than is generally thought. Grande is convinced of this given certain correspondences between Hebrew and Georgian. Hebrew could have persisted as a living language in certain remote areas up to the 3rd century C.E., that is to say, at a time when Jews could already have been in Germany. From this we can set up a theory: Jews in Germany originally spoke different local dialects. Given their earlier (Semitic) linguistic habits and the specific socioeconomic conditions under which they lived, they adopted precisely those dialects that had retained the ancient linguistic layer—the 'o-layer' (o as against a), 'sharp' sibilants as against 'blunt' sibilants. These same dialects in coalescing together formed the Yiddish language (Lithuanian Yiddish). In the course of a common socioeconomic way of life they came into contact with other dialects. These later coalesced to form the German dialects (Zaretski 1930: 72–74).

Raskin (1978: 260) sums up Japhetidology in the following way: 'There was little in the whole domain of language that was not subjected to Marr's interpretation and there are even a few ideas of his which do not sound too absurd, mostly when applied metaphorically rather than literally. It seems plausible to argue that several points made by Grande can be considered as useful metaphors, which, once removed from their context of Japhetidological methodology, might be applied productively. Firstly, Grande sets out the hypothesis that Hebrew in Yiddish is an inherited substratum (from the living spoken language!) which determined the original formation of Yiddish. Secondly, he saw the origins of Yiddish not in the splitting of early German into German and Yiddish, but in a process of independent formation by means of the convergence of different (Germanic?) dialects.

Zaretski (1891–1956), who was by no means a specialist on the history of Yiddish and is best known as a leading Soviet Yiddish syntactician and grammarian, also expressed an opinion on Grande's theory:

> Yiddish did not 'separate' from German. It arose through the convergence of different dialects—so much is clear even a priori, on the basis of the general presuppositions of the new approach to language. But this does not immediately solve the problem of when Yiddish originated, that is to say, of when this convergence took place, during the Middle High German or during the Old High German period? The lecturer [i.e. Grande—DBK] approaches the notion of phonetic law like an Indo-Europeanist. He accepts it a priori and seeks to justify it with data from Yiddish. This is all well and good: in Lithuanian Yiddish we have o (as against German a) and sibilant confusion. But Ukrainian Yiddish is also an 'o-language' (u and o belong in Japhetidological phonetics to the same group, in contrast with a) and there is no sibilant confusion to be found there. It seems much more plausible to contend as Shtif does that there was Slavic influence in Lithuanian Yiddish. True this does not explain the sibilant confusion (the fact that s and sh are written with the same letter) in older linguistic monuments that originate from Germany. [. . .] The theory of direct influence of Hebrew linguistic habits on Yiddish can be found in the work of the nationalist Mieses. But besides the fact that it remains to be proven that Hebrew was still a living language up to the 4th century, we know absolutely nothing about the German Jews of the 4th to the 11th centuries (Zaretski: 1930: 75–79).

It is thus evident that notwithstanding all kinds of extralinguistic and other limitations, several of the Soviet Yiddish linguists showed explicit interest in the origin of Yiddish. We have even managed to extrapolate two distinct theories—Veynger's and Grande's—about the genesis of Yiddish. Most of these articles were critically discussed, and in the case of Grande mentioned from a rather different perspective in Shklyar's 1932 retrospective review of Soviet Yiddish dialectological research.

If Veynger, a Germanist by training and in his approach to Yiddish dialectology sought the origins of Yiddish in the OHG period, was this not because he remained to some extent an ideological Yiddishist?

Shtif devoted himself openly to the study of the history of Yiddish. We can deduce from his Soviet writings that for him the earliest vernacular of Ashkenazic Jews should be considered as Yiddish. Thus we can say that Shtif was a Yiddishist in the philological sense. He would probably have agreed with the assertion that Yiddish is a Germanic language, but would have characterized it, from its very beginning, as *Yiddish,* not as *taytsh, yidish-taytsh* or *yidish-daytsh.*

Grande, notwithstanding that his attempt was not a particularly successful one, and given that this methodological presuppositions have a somewhat ludicrous air to the contemporary observer, nonetheless expressed in his theory a few important thoughts on the possible role of Hebrew in the original formation of the language (cf. Katz 1979 for an analysis of the Semitic component in Yiddish and the hypothesis, based on linguistic reconstruction, that the component is derived from a continous spoken tradition).

The historian of Yiddish philology who seeks to give an account of the various theories of the origin of Yiddish must take into consideration the modest but nonetheless noteworthy contributions of Soviet Yiddish linguists to this problem.

REFERENCES

FALKOVITSH, E. 1940 *Yidish—fonetik, grafik, leksik un gramatik.* Der emes, Moscow.

FISHMAN, J. A. (ed.) 1985 *Readings in the Sociology of Jewish Languages.* E. J. Brill, Leiden.

FRIDLAND, S. 1940 Vegn dem sovetishn yidish. *Ufboy—khoydish zhurnal far politik, visnshaft, literatur un kunst,* **2**, 38–48.

GERZON, J. 1902 *Die judisch-deutsche Sprache. Eine grammatisch-lexikalische Untersuchung ihres deutschen Grundbestandes.* Verlag von J. Kauffmann, Frankfurt am Main.

GITLITS, M. M. 1935 "Der forsherisher veg fun n. ya. mar." In *Afn shprakhfront,* second collection, pp. 99–113.

GITLITS, M. M. 1940 K voprosu o specifike i putyax razvitiya evrejskogo yazyka (yidish). *Yazyk i Myshlenie,* **12**, 47–56.

GRANDE, B. 1930 Opyt yafetidologicheskogo podxoda k istorii [yazyka] yidish (= "A pruv fun yafetidologishn tsugang tsu der geshikhte fun yidish"—fortrag gehaltn in der subsektsye far materialistisher lingvistik ba der komakademye in moskve—fartseykhnt loyt Zaretski 1930).

GREENBAUM, A. A. 1975 Hamekhkar hayehudi bivrit hamo'atsot (1917–1948). *Bekhinot,* **6**, 52–65.

GREENBAUM, A. A. 1978 *Jewish Scholarship and Scholarly Institutions in Soviet Russia 1918–1953.* Centre for Research and Documentation of East European Jewry, The Hebrew University, Jerusalem.

HUTTON, C. M. 1983 Normativism in Yiddish—Definitions and Categories. MA Essay, Department of Linguistics, Columbia University.

KAGAROV, E. 1923 Vegn dem bashtand un der ufshtamung fun yidish. *Yidish—ershte zamlung fun der yidisher filologisher komisye ba der tsentraler yidisher byuro fun folkombild.* Oysgabe fun dem ukrayinishn hoypt-komitet far profesyonel-tekhnisher un spetsyel-visnshaftlekher bildung un der tsentraler yidisher byuro bam folks-komisaryat far bildung, Kharkov, 5–8.

KAHN, L. 1972/3 Yidishe terminologishe komisyes—an iberblik. *Yidishe shprakh,* **31**, 35–42; 32, 1–8.

KALMANOVITSH, Z. 1921 *Yidishe gramatik. Konspekt fun leksyes geleyent far minsker lerer, mart 1921.* Melukhe-farlag fun vaysrusland, Minsk.

KATZ, D. 1979 Der semitisher kheylek in yidish: a yerushe fun kadmoynem. Metodn un meglekhkeytn. Unpublished paper placed before the First International Conference on Research in Yiddish Language and Literature at Oxford, 6–9 August.

KATZ, D. 1985 Hebrew, Aramaic and the Rise of Yiddish. In Fishman, 1985, pp. 85–103.

KREINDLER, I. T. (ed.) 1985 *Sociolinguistic Perspectives on Soviet National Languages. Their Past, Present and Future.* Mouton, Walter de Gruyter, Berlin, New York, Amsterdam.

MARK, Y. 1935 Di shprakh-teoryes fun akademiker N. Mar. *Yivo bleter,* **8**, 97–106.

NIGER, S. (ed.) 1913 *Der pinkes. Yorbukh far der geshikhte fun der yidisher literatur un shprakh, far folklor, kritik un bibliografye.* B.A. Kletskin, Vilna.

PELTZ, R. 1981 Dehebraization as an issue in the language planning efforts of the Soviet Yiddish linguistics. MA Essay, Linguistics Department, Columbia University.

PELTZ, R. 1985 The dehebraization controversy In Soviet Yiddish language planning: standard or symbol? In Fishman, 1985, pp. 125–150.

PELTZ, R. and KIEL, M. W. 1985 Di Yiddish-Imperye: the dashed hopes for a Yiddish cultural empire in the Soviet Union. In Kreindler, 1985, pp. 277–309.

PINES, M. 1912 *Di geshikhte fun der yidisher literatur.* B. Shimin, Warsaw.

PRILUTSKI, N. and LEHMAN, S. (eds.) 1912 *Noyakh prilutskis zamlbikher far yidishn folkor, filologye un kulturgeshikhte,* Vol. I. Nayer farlag, Warsaw.

RASKIN, V. 1978 Structuralism and after: notes on the current linguistic scene. In *Slacica Hierosolymitana* 2, 257–283.

SCHAECHTER, M. 1977 Four schools of thought in Yiddish language planning. *Michigan Germanic Studies,* 3.2, 34–66.

SHMERUK, K. (ed.) 1961 *Pirsumim yehudiyim bivrit hamo'atsot, 1917–1960.* [= *Jewish Publications in the Soviet Union 1917–1960.* Bibliographies compiled and arranged by Y. Y. Cohen with the assistance of M. Piekarz, introductions by Y. Slutski and Kh. Shmeruk.] "Galuyot" Series, The Historical Society of Israel, Jerusalem.

SHKLYAR, H. 1932 "Di yidishe dialektologishe forshung in sovetn-farband". In *Tsum XV yortog oktyaber-revoliutsye, literarish-lingvistisher zamlbukh,* pp. 141–163.

SHKLYAR, H. 1934 Di sovetishe naybildungen in yidish. *Lingvistishe zamlung,* 2, 46–90.

SHPILREYN, I. M. 1926 *Yidish. A konspekt fun a kurs in dem 2-tn moskver melukhishn univerzitet.* Shul un Bukh, Moscow.

SHTIF, N. 1913 Bal Dimyen [= Shtif] (review of Pines' *Di geshikhte fun der yidisher literature bizn yor 1890.* B. Shimin: Warsaw 1911). In Niger, S. 1913, pp. 313–348.

SHTIF, N. 1919 *Yidn un Yidish, oder ver zaynen "yidishistn" un vos viln zey? Poshete verter far yedn yidn.* Onheyb, Kiev.

SHTIF, N. 1922 *Yidishe kultur geshikhte in mitlalter (yidn in daytshland dos XIV un XV yorhudert).* [annotated translation of M. Güdemann's *Geschichte des Erziehungswesen und der Cultur der Juden in Deutschland waehrend des XIV und XV Jahrhunderts.* Alfred Hoelder: Vienna 1888.] Klal farlag, Berlin.

SHTIF, N. 1924 Loshn Ashkenaz, taytsh, leshoneynu, yidish undzer shprakh. *Yidishe filologye,* 1, 386–388.

SHTIF, N. 1928 Tsu der historisher antviklung fun yidishn oysleyg. *Di yidishe shprakh,* 8–9, 33–60.

SHTIF, N. 1929a M. Veyngers dialektologishe arbetn. *Di yidishe shprakh,* 14, 11–36; 15, 1–22.

SHTIF, N. 1929b Di sotsyale diferentsiatsye in yidish. Di hebreyishe elementn in der shprakh. *Di yidishe shprakh,* 17–18, 1–22.

SHTIF, N. 1932 Af der shvel funem 19-tn yorhundert. *Di yidishe shprakh,* part 1 "Di iberkerenish in der yidisher shrift-shprakh sof 18-tn onheyb 19-tn y[or]h[undert]" 29–30, 1–40; part 2 "Di slavizirung fun yidish" 32–33, 27–66.

SLUTSKI, B. 1935 "Der veg funem kh[aver] N. Shtif tsu bafrayen zikh fun zayn yidishistisher yerushe". In *Afn shprakhfront,* second collection, pp. 69–89.

SPIVAK, E. 1935 Problemes fun sovetishn yidish. *Afn shprakhfront, Kiev* 3–4, 28–76.

SPIVAK, E. 1935a "Vegn dehebreyizatisye un vegn dem hebreyishn 'element' in yidish". In *Afn shprakhfront,* second collection, pp. 3–22.

SPIVAK, E. 1939 *Naye vortshafung.* Melukhe farlag far di natsyonale minderhaytn in USSR, Kiev.

VEYNGER, M. 1912 Dialektologishe bamerkungen. In Prilutski, 1912, pp. 126–134.

VEYNGER, M. 1913 Hebreyishe klangen in der yidisher shprakh (notits). In Niger, 1913, pp. 79–84.

VEYNGER, M. 1926 Vegn yidishe dialektn. In *Tsaytshrift,* 1, 180–209.

VEYNGER, M. 1928a Vegn yidishe dialektn. In *Tsaytshrift,* 2–3, 614–651.

VEYNGER, M. 1928b Lingvistishe kartografye un der yidisher shprakhatlas. *Tsaytshrift,* 2–3, 653–676.

VEYNGER, M. 1929 *Yidishe dialektologye.* Melukhe farlag: Minsk.

VOLOBRINSKI, A. 1934 Der klasnkamf in der yidisher shprakh. *Lingvistishe zamlung,* 2, 91–123.

WEINREICH, M. 1973 *Geshikhte fun der yidisher shprakh—bagrifn, faktn, metodn.* YIVO, New York, vol. 1.

WEINREICH, U. 1952 Sabesdiker losn in Yiddish: a problem of linguistic affinity. *Word,* 8, 360–377.

ZARETSKI, A. 1929 Veynger der lingvist. *Di yidishe shprakh,* 14, 3–12.

ZARETSKI, A. 1930 Di yafetishe lingvistik un yidish. *Di yidishe shprakh* 21–22, 71–76.

ZARETSKI, A. 1935 Vegn sintaks fun sovetishn yidish. *Afn Shprakhfront,* 3–4, 170–191.

Language & Communication, Vol. 7, Supplement, pp. 73–81, 1987.
Printed in Great Britain.

0271-5309/87 $3.00 + .00
Pergamon Journals Ltd.

PROTO YIDDISH MORPHOLOGY

ROBERT D. KING

University of Texas at Austin

Yiddish comparative linguistics has been concerned much more with phonology than it has with morphology. This is neither novel or shocking. Historical reconstruction generally shows the same lack of proportion, the reasons for which are not hard to see: Phonological change is 'regular' in various senses, morphological change isn't; morphology is tied up with syntax in ways that make it hard to get a grip on, whereas phonology is relatively autonomous; and the linguistic realism of the reconstruction is probably more fraught with uncertainty for morphology that it is for phonology (see Hall 1950, 1960; Lloyd 1985; Pulgram 1961). In plain English, it is usually harder to reconstruct historical morphology that it is to reconstruct historical phonology.

The comparative method has been routinely applied to the reconstruction of various historical stages of Yiddish phonology. Thanks to the pioneering efforts of (among others) Fischer 1936 (= Bin-Nun 1973), Max Weinreich (1960a), and Uriel Weinreich (1958), we have a good understanding of the outlines of Proto Yiddish phonology even in the earliest forms of the language. Herzog (1965: 161–164) reconstructs vowel systems for Proto Southern Eastern Yiddish, Proto Northeastern Yiddish, and Proto Eastern Yiddish generally, and his reconstructions seem reasonable and sound to me. Reconstruction of the Proto Yiddish consonant system is even simpler since the various modern dialects disagree very little except in their vocalism.

There hasn't been very much in the way of a sustained effort to reconstruct early Yiddish morphology. Max Weinreich (1980), in the most comprehensive historical statement of the development of Yiddish to date (though his *Geshikhte* is at least as much a sociocultural history as it is a linguistic one), naturally touches on morphological developments again and again, as does Bin-Nun in the historical and sociological sections of his book (1973: 20–173), likewise Birnbaum (1979). Mieses (1924), in *Die jiddische Sprache*—his wonderful great pudding of a book consisting of long stretches of incomparable linguistic madness interlarded with unexpectedly brilliant *aperçus,* does what most others have done who write on the historical developement of Yiddish: pay sedulous attention to vowels and morphemes and lexical items, but not try anything bigger. This is at most very mild criticism: It isn't fair to criticize scholars for *not* doing something they didn't set out to do. It is simply an accurate statement of the research history to say that the systematic reconstruction of Proto Yiddish morphology has not yet been done.

The fact is that anyone who has ever written about the historical origins of Yiddish, and in particular about the German component, cannot avoid commenting on *some* oddity or other of historical morphology, e.g. the *ets/enk* pronouns of archaic Mideastern Yiddish, a feature anciently Bavarian (*pace* Marchand 1960: 40), or suffixes such as the diminutive *-l* and the intensive diminutive *-ele.* (See for example Birnbaum 1954 and Max Weinreich

1954.) Nonetheless, the reconstruction *per se* of Proto Yiddish morphology has not been undertaken.

Certain specific problems in morphological change in Yiddish have, on the other hand, attracted extensive and detailed treatments. I am thinking here of the collapse in Northeastern Yiddish of the three gender system of early Yiddish *der/dos/di* to two, *der/di* (or four or seven, depending on how one likes to count these things, cf. Herzog 1965: 101–124 and Wolf 1969). But this is obviously a late development specific to Lithuanian Yiddish and isn't 'Proto Yiddish' (which I date, I suppose, around 1200–1350). No German dialect has given up the three way gender distinction, though random shifts in individual words from one gender to another happen all the time in German dialects (see Schirmunski 1962: 443–445).

I think it might be a useful exercise to apply the comparative method to the reconstruction of Proto Yiddish morphology, to postulate from available dialect evidence what the earliest recoverable morphology was like. That this would require a lengthy monograph heavy with footnotes rather than a short paper hardly needs stating, but I think that it is possible in a paper even as brief as this one to discuss a few of the problems and to reach some preliminary conclusions which may tell us something about the origins of Yiddish. And that ultimately after all is what we are trying to do—to say true and interesting things about the origins of the Yiddish language.

The basic procedure involved in applying the comparative method involves comparing features found in the modern dialects and postulating the most plausible ancestral structure from which the later developments can be derived. We reconstruct a three gender system for Proto Yiddish because Mideastern Yiddish (MEY) has three genders and because the two genders of Northeastern Yiddish (NEY) are easily derived from a three gender system (and because of 'relic' morphological alternations like NEY *di bet* 'the bed', *af der bet > afn bet* 'on the bed'). It wouldn't make sense to derive the three gender system of Mideastern Yiddish from a putative *der/di* opposition in Proto Yiddish. Noun plurals formed by addition of the suffix *-im* (*poyer/poyerim* 'peasant') occur in all dialects of Yiddish, so one reconstructs a plural suffix *-im* for Proto Yiddish even though a suffix of that shape is not found in any of the variants of Middle High German (MHG)—and it is Middle High German of *some* kind from which Yiddish comes (an observation that must always be accompanied by all sorts of well-known qualifications, see Max Weinreich 1980: 422–433).

Certain sweeping generalizations can be made on the basis of a fairly superficial comparison of Northeastern and Mideastern Yiddish forms (I doubt incidentally that the addition of Southeastern Yiddish will alter significantly the reconstruction of morphology that results from NEY:MEY data, so I will deal here only with the latter two dialect areas). In the verb system we reconstruct for Proto Yiddish the following simple form classes and tenses: infinitive, imperative, past participle, present indicative, and present participle. All are found in cognate form in Mideastern Yiddish and Northeastern Yiddish. We do not reconstruct a preterite because no preterite is found solidly anywhere on Eastern Yiddish language territory. However, and this is the kind of thing I had in mind in saying that a monograph is ultimately needed to do the topic full justice, we *would* have to reconstruct a preterite if Western Yiddish were included in the date since earliest texts from Western Yiddish have preterites (cf. Birnbaum 1979: 146–149 and Bin-Nun 1973: 42–45). Preterite forms of the copula (*vor/vorn* 'was, were') are used by some writers of the second half of the nineteenth century such as Ayzik Meyer Dik (Max Weinreich 1980: 517),

though I tend to regard these as more likely affectations, *daytshmerizmen,* than inherited Eastern Yiddish forms. (But if they aren't, if in other words *vor/vorn* are in fact genuinely Eastern Yiddish, then all that does is further secure their position in the reconstruction of Proto Yiddish).

In adjectives we reconstruct a comparative ending *-er* and a superlative ending *-st.* That at least is straightforward. A more interesting question arises in regard to the number of adjective declensions in Proto Yiddish. Looking only at Northeastern and Mideastern Yiddish we would reconstruct one, but the inclusion of Western Yiddish would force us to reconstruct two, 'strong' and 'weak'. Middle High German used one set of adjectival endings after definite articles (*der blinde man* 'the blind man', *diu kleinen kinder* 'the little children'), a different set after indefinite articles and when no article is present (*ein blinder man* 'a blind man', *kleiniu kinder* 'little children'). There is no distinction in any variety of Eastern Yiddish: *der blinder man, di kleyne kinder, a blinder man, kleyne kinder.* At least some dialects of Western Yiddish maintain the strong:weak distinction, e.g. Alsatian Yiddish (Zuckerman 1969: 50–52), as does Standard German (for what that's worth).

Obviously it is vitally important to include Western Yiddish in the data for the reconstruction of Proto Yiddish; I chance a guess that Western Yiddish, whatever Western Yiddish actually *was,* will be possibly even more important for the reconstruction of Proto Yiddish morphology than it is for the reconstruction of Proto Yiddish phonology. (My formulation 'whatever Western Yiddish actually *was'* is a coy allusion to long standing and unresolved problems about the medieval German–Jewish nexus and the interpretation of documents, see Marchand 1959, 1960; Max Weinreich 1960b and Herzog 1978: 47–48). Methodologically it is probably best to reconstruct a Proto Eastern Yiddish on the basis of Eastern dialects alone and a Proto Western Yiddish on the basis of Western dialects alone, and then to reconstruct Proto Yiddish from the juxtaposition of the two. Among other things this procedure should make it clearer what is to be regarded as an innovation in Eastern Yiddish. In the instance of the adjective declensions we would attribute to Proto Western Yiddish strong and weak declensions and to Proto Eastern Yiddish a single undifferentiated declension; Proto Yiddish would then be reconstructed with two declensions, and the disappearance of the distinction is correctly seen to be an Eastern innovation.

Standard Yiddish has a single reflexive pronoun *zikh* in all persons and numbers: *ikh lern zikh, du lernst zikh, er lernt zikh, mir lernen zikh, ir lernt zikh, zey lernen zikh* 'to learn'. Birnbaum (1979: 250), speaking presumably in the first instance of Mideastern Yiddish, states that 'in the 1st and 2nd person most speakers do not use the real reflexive pronoun (*zex*) but the personal pronoun (*mex, dex, aax*)'. This usage is common in Mideastern Yiddish. One should consult the files of the Language and Culture Atlas of Ashkenazic Jewry to see how widespread the occurence of reflexive *mikh, dikh,* etc. is— and to try to detemine whether the distinctions that Birnbaum observed have anything to do with the influence of the 'hidden standard' (Schaechter 1969). The Middle High German situation is complex (cf. Paul and Mitzka 1960: §146, §217) but differentiated by person and number, as early Western Yiddish appears to be (Birnbaum 1979: 146–152). Presumably we would reconstruct Proto Yiddish with both strong and weak declensions.

It would be easy to continue in this way, stating big and fairly obvious generalizations about Proto Yiddish morphology and pointing out along the way aberrations that will eventually require scores of footnotes to explain. My purpose here, however, is more

programmatic. I want to demonstrate ways in which paying some attention to a systematic reconstruction of early Yiddish morphology may enlighten us about the origins of the German component of Yiddish. It will be adequate to my purposes to deal with one more category of Proto Yiddish morphology, the noun plural.

There are six major types of plural formation in both Northeastern and Mideastern Yiddish and, therefore, in Proto Yiddish:

A. Plural marked by *-n*.

B. Plural marked by *-s*.

C. Plural marked by umlaut alone.

D. Plural marked by *-er* (with obligatory umlaut if the noun has a back vowel).

E. Plural marked by 'zero' (no change, i.e. singular identical with plural).

F. Plural marked by *-im*.

(I subsume here under B two genetically distinct modes of pluralization: a) the 'Vov-Sof' ending *-(e)s* on words of Hebrew or Aramaic provenance, and b) an *s*-plural, the murky origins of which I will later discuss, on nouns not from Hebrew or Aramaic. Thus, for a): *melukhe/melukhes* 'state', *os/oysyes* 'letter of the alphabet', *kholem/khaloymes* 'dream'; for b): *feder/feders* 'pen', *hering/herings* 'herring', *bobe/bobes* 'grandmother'. *Synchronically*, in Proto Yiddish, I cannot see any reason to distinguish the two; I mean the two kinds of *s*'s must have *sounded* the same, which is why I treat them as a single way of forming plurals—synchronically).

Certain of these categories (A, D, E) derive more or less directly from the German component. A plural marked by *-n* was characteristic in Middle High German of feminine ô-stem nouns and *n*-stem nouns of all three genders, thus MHG *sache/sachen* 'thing', MHG *mensch(e)/menschen* 'person', compare Standard Yiddish (StY) *zakh/zakhn* and *mentsh/mentshn*. Almost no plurals in Middle High German were formed by umlaut alone (two exceptions: *bruoder/brüeder* 'brother', *vater/veter* 'father'), so that something similar to StY *tog/teg* 'day' would not have been possible. Umlaut plus *-e* is found in masculine *a*-stems (*gaste/geste* 'guest') and feminine *i*-stems (*kraft/krefte* 'strength'), and umlaut plus *-er* is found in strong neuter nouns such as *lamp/lember* 'lamb'. Zero plurals are found in assorted stem classes in Middle High German, e.g. *hirte/hirte* 'shepherd', *man/man* 'man', and *wort/wort* 'word'.

The number of nouns taking plurals in *-n* and *-er* (with automatic umlaut if a back vowel is present) has increased dramatically in Yiddish as compared with Middle High German. Thus, StY *veg/vegn* 'way', *tish/tishn* 'table', *yor/yorn* 'year', *tsimer/tsimern* 'room' versus MHG *wec/wege, tisch/tische, jâr/jâr, zimer/zimer(e)*; and StY *shteyn/shteyner* 'stone', *boym/beymer* 'tree', *noz/nezer* 'nose' versus MHG *stein/steine, boum/boume, nase/nasen*.

Most of the radical realignments we find in pluralization in the German component are the consequence of a single change in Yiddish: loss of final unstressed *-e* (apocope). If there is a single internal change that has done more than apocope to mould the countenance

of Yiddish I am not aware of it. It triggers more changes than anything else that happened in the history of Yiddish. Apocope often leads to homonymy between singular and plural, thus singular:plural *boum:boume* would become *boum:boum*. This is an ambiguity which Germanic languages generally, with the exception of North Germanic, do not gladly tolerate. The Germanic 'drift' is toward the requirement that a morphological opposition singular:plural must be manifested at the phonetic level by a phonetic accretion in the plural. Morphological 'transparency' is the order of the day. A Middle High German plural such as *nähte* 'nights' (Sing. *naht*) is doubly marked, once by umlaut, once by the suffix *-e;* and apocope still leaves a marked plural, a situation preserved in StY *nakht/nekht,* also StY *hant/hent* 'hand', *gast/gest* 'guest', and *zun/zin* 'son'. This establishes an analogical model for plural marking by the device of umlaut alone, paving the way for StY *tog/teg* 'day', *barg/berg* 'mountain', *shukh/shikh* 'shoe', and many others. Category C has grown enormously in size over time.

The number of zero plurals is small in Yiddish since a zero plural violates the 'transparency' principle discussed in the preceding paragraph. One would predict that the zero plurals called for in Standard Yiddish (e.g. *fish/fish* 'fish', *hor/hor* 'hair', *briv/briv* 'letter') will not always be the plurals found in folk speech. There is in general a good deal of fluctuation in plural formation in Yiddish though often for other reasons (see Uriel Weinreich 1960 and Herzog 1965: 150–156, 167–170).

The origin of the *s*-plural in Yiddish is a mystery. This form of plural is at home nowhere in *High* German territory, so it is not clear where this common, productive plural of Yiddish came from—whether from Romance (which Bin-Nun 1973: 28 argues for), whether from Low German (where it is frequent), whether from the Hebrew and Aramaic component. (There is an extensive discussion in Max Weinreich 1980: 408–412.) I think Low German can safely be ruled out since it has had no impact anywhere else on the structure of Yiddish. I find the arguments for a Romance origin (Loez) interesting and suggestive but not overwhelming: All that the Yiddish language itself tells us for certain about Romance influence is that a few lexical items were borrowed at a very early date. Anything beyond that is conjectural (though far be it from me to argue against making conjectures: I say only that the evidence for Romance influence comes almost exclusively from outside the language itself). To my mind the most reasonable assumption is that it all goes back to the common Hebrew plural 'Vov–Sof' present in numerous Yiddish words such as *milkhome/milkhomes* 'war', *matone/matones* 'present', and *mishpokhe/mishpokhes* 'family'. And again this is a natural consequence of apocope, which left Yiddish bereft of suffixes with which to signal phonetically the singular:plural distinction, so that whatever marking devices happened to be handy (like *-s* and umlaut) were generalized.

The *-im* plural is from the Hebrew and Aramaic component, no mystery there. It has extended itself into the German component in a handful of words (*poyer/poyerim* 'peasant', *dokter/doktoyrim* 'doctor'). One can only speculate about the cultural matrix of these few words that made them adopt this non-Germanic plural (**poyern* has always seemed perfectly reasonable to me).

There is obviously much more that can be said about this interesting and complex corner of historical Yiddish morphology, the noun plural. It is, from the perspective of a Germanist, a fascinating mixture of regular development from well known historical sources (Middle High German and Hebrew/Aramaic), fusion, sweeping analogical restructuring, and *hapax legomena*. The topic will no doubt someday attract the monograph it deserves.

Let me now turn to asking the kinds of questions for which this sketch of Proto Yiddish morphology was intended as a springboard. The major focus of my research interest in Yiddish has always been the question of origin, specifically the question of the dialect of medieval German from which Yiddish most directly derives, the question of the 'foundation dialect'. In other places I have argued for the Bavarian (more precisely, Bavarian–Austrian, or Austro–Bavarian) origin of Yiddish (King 1980: 422, and in Faber and King 1984: 396–399). There are important East Central German dialect traces in Yiddish to be sure, but they are swamped by the Bavarian ones. As we said: 'We do not think it can be seriously disputed that of all of the German dialects that have left an imprint on Yiddish, Bavarian has played the leading role by far, with East Central German in second place, and with *no other* German dialect having significant impact' (Faber and King 1984: 398).

The arguments we made for this conclusion almost all came from phonology: apocope, loss of final devoicing (and, this is absolutely crucial, the *causal* relationship between apocope and the loss of final devoicing, cf Kranzmayer 1956: 79), early unrounding of front rounded vowels, loss of vowel length, lack of umlaut in verb forms. The only morphological features cited in linking Bavarian and Yiddish were the *ets/enk* duals and the diminutive system.

Does the sketch of the reconstruction of the system of Proto Yiddish morphology I have attempted here help us in locating the German origins of Yiddish? The answer is both Yes and No. The loss of the strong:weak distinction in adjective declensions isn't found on German-speaking soil as far as I have been able to determine (by which I mean that I find no evidence of it in the most detailed and comprehensive treatment of German dialectology available to date, namely Schirmunski 1962: 470–471). The use of the third person reflexive pronoun (German *sich,* StY *zikh*) without diffferentiation as to person and number is found to some degree and in opulent variety throughout both High and Low German territory, but nowhere that I can find to the extent of Yiddish (Schirmunski 1962: 451–453). The absence of the preterite is almost uniform in Upper German, though often preserved in the verb 'to be' (as in Western Yiddish) and in the verb 'to have' (Schirmunski 1962: 489–491). The comparative *-er* and the superlative *-st* of Proto Yiddish are pretty much uniform over the German speaking territory.

None of these morphological features appears to be useful in locating the German dialect origin of Yiddish, though I have to stress the preliminary nature of this conclusion: It is not always easy to wade through all the data from German dialectology and make sense of *anything*.

The system of noun pluralization, on the other hand, offers important evidence about origins. No High German dialect forms plurals by adding *-s* or *-im*. That of course would not be expected. But if we leave aside those two categories of plural formation we are left with four:

1. Plural marked by *-n*.

2. Plural marked by umlaut alone.

3. Plural marked by *-er* (with obligatory umlaut if the noun has a back vowel).

4. Plural marked by 'zero' (no change, i.e. singular identical with plural).

Almost the identical system for forming noun plurals is found in Upper Austrian, which is a major representative of the Bavarian–Austrian dialect. Keller (1961: 218–220) describes one of the Upper Austrian dialects in great morphological detail, and he lists five ways of forming the plural of nouns in this dialect (his informants were from Linz and Gmünden). Four of those, adjusted for the phonetic differences in the dialect, are identical with those reconstructed above for Proto Yiddish. The fifth is a plural marked by change of lenis to fortis in a small group of masculine nouns where the plural is indicated by a change of final consonant only. In the conventional orthography of the dialect, *Grif/Griff* 'grip', *Fiisch/Fisch* 'fish', *Tiisch/Tisch* 'table', *Fleg/Fleck* 'spot' (Keller 1961: 219–220). This relic category of plural formation is a consequence of a specifically Bavarian innovation, the 'Middle–Bavarian Lenition' (Keller 1961: 214–215).

Keller (1961: 218–219) attributes the other four forms of pluralization in this Upper Austrian dialect to two historical processes—the loss of a former final *-e* (apocope), and the preservation of the Middle High German ending *-en* and its extension as a plural suffix; and both are precisely the major factors in the emergence of the Proto Yiddish system of plural formation, as we saw. Also umlaut has pushed past its historical domain in this dialect, just as it did in Yiddish—and for the same reason, the need to preserve a morphological distinction at the phonetic level.

In short, the system of noun plural formation we are required to reconstruct for Proto Yiddish is found to parallel almost exactly the situation in a major dialect area of Bavarian. As far as I have been able to determine, no other German dialect family has precisely the same system.

The questions that I am asking are basically ones of genetic affiliation and degree of closeness. Where does Yiddish fit in the context of German dialectology? Where does Yiddish fit in terms of its historical relationship to German (see Althaus 1972)? What kinds of evidence do we look at when we are trying to determine which German dialects played leading roles in the formation of Yiddish?

I think it is high time we began to pay closer attention to morphology in addressing questions of the origins. I say this partly because morphology has been neglected. But more importantly I say this because a number of serious linguistic scholars from different times and of different persuasions have argued that morphology is more resistant to change than are the other components of a grammar (see for example Dauzat 1927: 49–55 and Uriel Weinreich 1953: 67, both citations taken from Markey 1978: 61). The way the argument goes is that the lexicon is most subject to change, then phonology, then syntax, and finally morphology. This hierarchy seems about right to me based on my experience of languages and historical change, and if true then it means that morphology is precisely the area we ought to be looking at first in trying to establish genetic relationships in general and genetic relationships of the various German dialects to Yiddish in particular. (And, again assuming the hierarchy is correct, it means that relatively little weight should be given to lexical correspondences—or the absence of them: which is the reason why it has never bothered me that a typically Bavarian word like *Ertag* 'Tuesday' is completely absent from Yiddish). It is significant, I think, that Edward Sapir, in most of his writings, placed the greatest weight on morphological similarities in establishing genetic relationships (see almost any of Sapir's papers in Mandelbaum 1963).

The theme of this conference is the origins of the Yiddish language, a theme that continues a venerable and noble tradition of inquiry in Yiddish linguistics. As Bin-Nun says: 'Die

Frage nach dem Ursprung beschäftigt die jiddische Sprachforschung von Anfang an'. There are many legitimate ways to approach the question of origins, and I claim no primacy for my own. But I do not think we can get to the heart of the matter without settling the question of the German 'foundation dialect' from which Yiddish is derived. And on this question all the linguistic instruments so far agree: Bavarian matters most.

REFERENCES

ALTHAUS, H. P. 1972 Yiddish. In Sebeok, 1972, 1347–1382.

BIN-NUN, J. 1973 *Jiddisch und die deutschen Mundarten unter besonderer Berücksichtigung des ostgalizischen Jiddisch*. Max Niemeyer, Tübingen.

BIRNBAUM, S. A. 1954 Two problems of Yiddish linguistics. In Weinreich, U., 1954, pp. 63–72.

BIRNBAUM, S. A. 1979 *Yiddish: A Survey and a Grammar*. University of Toronto Press, Toronto and Buffalo.

CATALAN, D. (ed.) 1958 *Miscelánea Homenaje André Martinet*, Vol. II. Universidad de la Laguna, Tenerife.

DAUZAT, A. 1927 *Les patois: évolution-classification-étude*. Delgrave, Paris.

FABER, A. and KING, R. D. 1984 Yiddish and the settlement history of Ashkenazic Jewry. *The Mankind Quarterly*, **24**, 393–425.

FISCHER, J. 1936 *Das Jiddische und sein Verhältnis zu den deutschen Mundarten unter besonderer Berücksichtigung der ostgalizischen Mundart*. Oswald Schmidt, Leipzig.

FUKS, L. 1957 *The Oldest Known Literary Documents of Yiddish Literature (ca. 1382)*. E. J. Brill, Leiden.

HALL, R. A., Jr. 1950 The reconstruction of proto-romance. *Language, **26**, 6–27.

HALL, R. A., Jr. 1960 On realism in reconstruction. *Language, **36**, 203–206.

HALL, R. A. Jr. 1983 *Proto-Romance Morphology* [= *Amsterdam Studies in the Theory and History of Linguistic Science, IV: Current Issues in Linguistic Theory, 30*]. Benjamins, Amsterdam and Philadelphia.

HERZOG, M. I. 1965 *The Yiddish Language in Northern Poland: Its Geography and History* [= *International Journal of American Linguistics*, III. Vol. 31, No. 2], Mouton, The Hague.

HERZOG, M. I. 1978 Yiddish. In Paper, 1978, pp. 47–58.

HERZOG, M. KIRSCHENBLATT-GIMBLETT, B., MIRON, D. and WISSE, R. 1980 *The Field of Yiddish*, Vol. IV. Institute for the Study of Human Issues, Philadelphia.

HERZOG, M., RAVID, W. and WEINREICH, U. (eds) 1969 *The Field of Yiddish*, Vol III. Mouton, The Hague.

KELLER, R. E. 1961 *German Dialects*. Manchester University Press, Manchester.

KING, R. D. 1980 The history of final devoicing in Yiddish. In Herzog, Kirschenblatt-Gimblett, Miron and Wisse, 1980, pp. 371–430.

KRANZMAYER, E. 1956 *Historische Lautgeographie des gesamtbairischen Sprachraumes*. Hermann Böhlaus Nachf., Vienna.

LLOYD, P. M. 1985 [Review of Hall 1983]. *Language* **61**, 881–884.

MANDELBAUM, D. G. (ed.) 1963 *Selected Writings of Edward Sapir in Language, Culture and Personality*. University of California Press, Berkeley and Los Angeles.

MARCHAND, J. W. 1959 [Review of Fuks 1957]. *Word* **15**, 383–394.

MARCHAND, J. W. 1960 Three basic problems in the investigation of early Yiddish, *Orbis* **9**, 34–41.

MARKEY, T. L. 1978 [Response to Herzog 1978]. In Paper, 1978, pp. 59–63.

MIESES, M. 1924 *Die jiddische Sprache. Eine historische Grammatik des Idioms der integralen Juden Ost- und Mitteleuropas*. Benjamin Harz, Berlin and Vienna.

PAPER, H. H. (ed.) 1978 *Jewish Languages. Theme and Variations*. Association for Jewish Studies, Cambridge, Massachusetts.

PAUL, H. and MITZKA, W. 1960 *Mittelhochdeutsche Grammatik,* 18th ed. Max Niemeyer, Tübingen.

PULGRAM, E. 1961 The nature and use of proto-languages, *Lingua* **10**, 18–37.

SCHAECHTER, M. 1969 The 'hidden standard': a study of competing influences in standardization. In Herzog, Ravid and Weinreich, 1969, pp. 284–304.

SCHIRMUNSKI, V. M. 1962 *Deutsche Mundartkunde. Vergleichende Laut- und Formenlehre der deutschen Mundarten.* (Deutsche Akademie der Wissenschaften zu Berlin, *Veröffentlichungen des Instituts für deutsche Sprache und Literatur,* Vol. 25.) Akademie, Berlin.

SEBEOK, T. A. (ed.) 1972 *Current Trends in Linguistics,* Vol. IX. Mouton, The Hague.

WEINREICH, M. 1954 Prehistory and early history of Yiddish: facts and conceptual framework. In Weinreich, U., 1954, 73–101.

WEINREICH, M. 1960a Di sistem yidishe kadmen-vokaln. *Yidishe shprakh,* **20,** 65–71.

WEINREICH, M. 1960b Old Yiddish poetry in linguistic-literary research. *Word,* **16,** 100–118.

WEINREICH, M. 1980 *History of the Yiddish Language.* The University of Chicago Press, Chicago and London.

WEINREICH, U. 1953 *Languages in Contact. Findings and Problems.* Mouton, The Hague.

WEINREICH, U. (ed.) 1954 *The Field of Yiddish,* Vol. I. Linguistic Circle of New York: New York.

WEINREICH, U. (ed.) 1958 A retrograde sound shift in the guise of a survival: an aspect of Yiddish vowel development. In Catalan, D. 1958, 221–267.

WEINREICH, U. (ed.) 1960 *Noz, nezer, nez:* a kapitl gramatishe geografie. *Yidishe shprakh* **20,** 81–90.

WOLF, M. 1969 The geography of Yiddish case and gender variation. In Herzog, Ravid and Weinreich, 1969, 102–215.

ZUCKERMAN, R. 1969 Alsace: an outpost of western Yiddish. In Herzog, Ravid and Weinreich, 1969, pp. 36–57.

Language & Communication, Vol. 7, Supplement, pp. 83–94, 1987.
Printed in Great Britain.

0271-5309/87 $3.00 + .00
Pergamon Journals Ltd.

PROTO YIDDISH AND THE GLOSSES: CAN WE RECONSTRUCT PROTO YIDDISH?

JAMES W. MARCHAND

University of Illinois at Urbana

I was somewhat surprised and, I must admit, gratified to receive an invitation from Dr Katz to speak on a subject I last wrote on 25 years ago, and I was reminded of the words of Bernard Bloch, who used to tell us, whenever he was shown to be wrong on a point: "That was a younger and less wise Bloch." Today you will hear an older and less wise Marchand. It is a great honour and pleasure for me to be able to address you today on a subject on which my ideas have not changed in essence since I wrote "Origins of Yiddish" in 1960 (published in 1965). The arguments which you will hear are those of 1960; unfortunately, the field has progressed little in these matters since then. I had intended to discuss the merits and failings of the Yivo approach and that of *Die Wissenschaft des Judentums,* but I have heard little defence of either, so I can, with Shakespeare, invoke a pax on both their houses.

To set the stage: There may be said to be, *grosso modo,* two points of view on the origin of Yiddish. The first was expressed already in 1832 by the father of *Die Wissenschaft des Judentums,* Leopold Zunz (1966: 452 f.):

Allen bis gegen dem Schluß des Mittelalters verfaßten Dokumenten zufolge standen die deutschen Juden in der Sprache bis auf einzelne Redeweisen und hier und da die Aussprache den deutschen Christen gleich.

It was further assumed that the origin of Yiddish was probably to be sought in the enclosing of Jews in ghettos, which followed upon their return to Germany in the 1360s after the Black Death, with its persecution and slaughter of Jews. This point of view was accepted, both tacitly and openly, by almost all of the workers in *Die Wissenschaft des Judentums* (Falk, 1908, 79 ff.):

Aber aus allen diesen Dokumenten ergibt sich immerhin die wichtige Tatsache, daß die deutschen Juden des Mittelalters keine andere Sprache gesprochen als die ihrer christlichen Landsleute, also die deutsche Sprache, und diese ebenso korrekt und rein wie die Nichtjuden, mit Ausnahme vereinzelter Redeweisen, Archaismen oder bisweilen etwas mundartlicher Färbung. Eine besondere jüdisch-deutsche Sprache bildete sich wohl erst im Laufe des XVI. und XVII. Jahrhunderts aus, wenn, man mit Zunz einen ungefähren Zeitpunkt annehmen will; wahrscheinlich infolge der Rückwanderung deutscher Juden von Polen nach Deutschland, wo sie seit den Tagen des schwarzen Todes keinen dauernden, gastlichen Herd mehr fanden, während sie das Deutsche, die Sprache eines Landes, das so unväterlich an ihnen gehandelt, als ihre Muttersprache in fremden Landen beibehielten und weiterbildeten.

This point of view, and the Black Death/Ghetto theory, was accepted, both openly and tacitly, by most workers in the field until about 1940: Güdemann 1880: 148; Sainéan 1902: 92; Karpeles 1963: II, 1002: *inter alios.* This notion was strengthened by their feeling that the Jews in the Middle Ages had simply copied Latin letter works (Steinschneider 1865)

. . . Romane und Lieder zunächst einfach mit hebräischen Lettern umschrieb.
Ich erwähne beispielsweise nur die Hss. Münch. 100 (Lil. 99), worin *Eulenspiegel (Serapeum* 1848, n. 388), *Sieben Weise Meister* (n. 399), *Kaiser Oktavianus* (413) und Münch. 100, wo das *Buch der Weisheit (Kalila und Dimna,* n. 392), sämmtlich aus deutschen alten Drucken.

One pointed to numerous works (such as Christian prayers) which because of their matter

and mode of treatment seemed to be non-Jewish and therefore non-Yiddish (Grünbaum, 1882, 561):

> Der Verfasser der jüdischen Theriak erwähnt an mehreren Stellen eine deutsche Bearbeitung desselben Gegenstandes—d. h. also auch in deutscher Schrift—die er für Christen verfaßt und bestimmt habe.

(Balaban 1912; 301):

> Es ist schade, daß die sogenannte jüdisch-deutsche Übersetzung des Neuen Testaments von Paul Helic (einem getauften Krakauer Juden) aus dem Jahre 1540 (Druck von ihm selbst, Krakau 1540-41 . . .) rein deutsch ist, sonst könnten wir die Fortenwickelung der jüdisch-deutschen Sprache in Krakau von 1540-1595 studieren. Das einzige uns bekannte Exemplar befindet sich in der Jagellonischen Bibliothek in Krakau.

(Steinschneider 1938: 81):

> Um so merkwürdiger ist es, daß im 16. Jahrhundert die ersten Drucke solcher Sagen, der 'Eulenspiegel' nicht ausgenommen, einfach in hebräischen Lettern abgeschrieben wurden.

Even N. Shtif (1926, 100, 112) saw that his materials were contaminated by the fact that some of them were simply copied from Latin-letter *Vorlagen,* although Mieses (1924) never realized this.

This, then, was the picture drawn, not only by *Die Wissenschaft des Judentums:* (1) Until the mid-14th century, Jews and Germans lived together, although not always in harmony, and Jews spoke the same language as the Germans around them. Güdemann (1880: 148) found even other reasons to believe this:

> Die Juden dieses Zeitalters führen die bei den Christen geläufigen Namen, selbst mythologische, sie sprechen die deutsche Sprache, und zwar ohne Jargon.
> Dies scheint mit daraus hervorzugehen, daß, so viel mir bekannt, in den gehässigen Liedern und Schriften dieser Zeit den Juden der Jargon nicht vorgeworfen wird, was der Fall gewesen wäre, wenn sie einen solchen gesprochen hätten.

He goes on to offer the usual Black Death/Ghetto explanation, but his point as to the fact that one finds no medieval references to the Jews' strange speech shows that they spoke no differently than other Germans is, I think, telling. [I should point out that it is not unusual to find in medieval German literature reference to others' speech patterns.] Birnbaum (1979: 46) does quote a work of 1451, by the way: "he . . . is also en jode geschapen unde spricket also."

(2) After the persecutions during the Black Death (1349-1350), during which Jews were either slaughtered or forced to leave Germany, they found upon their return to Germany in the 1360's and 70's that their property had been confiscated, and they were enclosed in ghettos for the first time in Germany. The ensuing separatism and close communication caused them to develop a separate speech community, with each area developing its own Yiddish at first. I hope I shall not be accused of too great a *prolepsis* if I point out that this scheme accounts for the origin of Western Yiddish, but makes no reference to Eastern Yiddish.

The contrary point of view, championed most strongly by Max Weinreich, holds (M. Weinreich 1954: 79):

> There was NO period in history before the 19th century in which any jewish GROUP had spoken anything approximately 'pure German'.

Yiddish was a *fusion language,* not based on German, but on an amalgamation of many languages. Words of Romance origin, such as *piltsl, tsholnt, bentshn, antshpozn, fatsheyle,* pointed to a pre-Yiddish component, based on the fact that German Jewry came in the main from LOTER (M. Weinreich 1953: 487):

> The Jews who formed the nucleus of Ashkenazic Jewry came to *Loter* from eastern France and, in smaller numbers, from northern Italy.

Of course, he had immediately to admit (1953: 487):

> This statement is more definite than the ones usually encountered on the subject. I am reserving proof for a further occasion.

Weinreich's views were shared by many workers in the field, notably L. Fuks and Solomon Birnbaum (1979: 58):

> The immediate predecessor of Yiddish was Zarphatic, which the Jews had brought from Northern France. From this the new language which was born in Germany inherited an element of Semitic origin. Zarphatic, of course, did not disappear without a trace. Thus it may be said that Yiddish at its birth consisted of three elements: Semitic, Romance and Germanic.

Yiddish arose around the year 1000 [Birnbaum (1979: 57) carries the point of origin back to the 9th century], and it is only by accident and the vicissitudes of time that we have so few documents from this period. Because of the desire to carry Yiddish back as far as possible, there have been a number of candidates for "the earliest Yiddish document", "the earliest Yiddish sentence": the Cologne medical fragment (Birnbaum 1931–32; Dünner 1904): the so-called Codex C. Y. (Fuks 1957); a sentence in the Worms Machzor (M. Weinreich 1963); the Berlin Aruch (Timm 1977). In fact in recent work the tendency has been, at least tacitly, but occasionally *expressis verbis,* to take anything written in "German" in Hebrew script in the Middle Ages to be Yiddish. Since we are lacking to a great extent in materials before 1350, the glosses and the onomastic material have come in for a close scrutiny, and there have been numerous attempts to reconstruct a Proto Yiddish along the lines of other "Proto" languages.

Although it does not seem that the differences between these two points of view are reconcilable, it is undoubtedly worthwhile to discuss and to reveal if possible their motivations. In order to do this today, I shall look at the question of the Origin of Yiddish and Proto Yiddish from four different vantage points: 1. Linguistic-Theoretical. 2. The Sociology of Knowledge. 3. The Stance of the Investigator. 4. The Facts and their Interpretation.

I. Linguistic-theoretical

I must begin by pointing out that our field is plagued by terminological inexactitude to an extreme: 1. The terms *Yiddish,* and *Eastern Yiddish* are frequently used as if they were synonymous, just as an earlier generation used the term *Yiddish* (or *Jüdisch-Deutsch*) as if it could only mean *Western Yiddish.* 2. Notions such as *Proto Yiddish* are used without regard to standard linguistic usage. 3. Middle High German, a convenient catchcall invented by linguists, is used as if it were an actually existing entity rather than a convenient fiction, and dictionaries of it are perused to find terms. Max Weinreich, for one, clearly saw that Middle High German was "a linguistic entity thrice removed from the actual German language of the Middle Ages" (1954: 74 f.), but his views had little effect, even in his own practice. 4. Terms found in the glosses, such as *loshn ashkenaz* and *galkhes* are often given meanings more specific than the evidence will bear. Our field could benefit from a careful scrutiny of its linguistic, literary and sociological usage, particularly from the point of view of concept formation. Solomon Birnbaum hit the nail on the head when he said (1932: 112): "Die Beantwortung der Frage, ob Jiddisch Sprache oder Dialekt sei, hängt von der Begriffsbestimmung ab."

Perhaps one ought to turn to the linguists for aid in this matter of "Begriffsbestimmung"; Max Weinreich once said concerning linguists (M. Weinreich 1955: 16): "men ken zikh af zey farlozn." Unfortunately, linguists are no more trustworthy than others. When it comes to the definition of language and dialect, linguistic terminology breaks down

(Marchand 1973), and the "definitions" given by Yiddish specialists are no better. Steinschneider (1848: 313) defines Yiddish as "etwas modificirte deutsche Sprache, jedoch mit hebräischen Lettern," and most people seem to have followed him in seeing the alphabet as a defining characteristic of the language, although it is obvious that a language can be spoken without being written and that it is possible to write any language in Hebrew characters—we even have examples of Latin in Hebrew characters in the Middle Ages (Schum 1887: 116). The definition proposed by Birnbaum (1979: 8), although I like it, will not hold water any better than that of other linguists: "The definition of a language we have arrived at is: the oral and written means of communication and expression of a clearly defined cultural group," for it leaves us with the added task of defining "a clearly defined cultural group," surely as hard as the task of defining a language or a dialect. The argumentative nature of such definitions is clearly shown by Fuks' circular discussion of the language of the Codex C. Y. (Fuks 1957: I, 26):

> It is customary to approach and answer the question 'what is the Yiddish language' from the linguistic point of view. . . . If one applies the linguistic criteria to the literary works of the first two periods (i.e. before 1500), works either with Jewish or adopted subjects, the answer to the question 'What is Yiddish' could not be given. The answer in the case of our manuscript could easily be given: the language used in the Codex C. Y. is neither primitive nor middle Yiddish, but Middle High German, written in Hebrew characters. It would be justified to doubt my definition of the language of the Codex C. Y. as Old Yiddish.

> Therefore, I have to assume that it is completely inadequate, if not correct to approach the problem only from the linguistic angle.

At least this is honest circularity.

In another connection, I discussed the problem of the definition of dialect and language on the basis of Max Weber's concept of the *ideal type* (Hempel, 1965, 155 ff.):

> In particular, many of the studies devoted to the logic of typological concepts use only the concepts and principles of classical logic, which is essentially a logic of properties or classes, and cannot deal adequately with relations and with quantitative concepts . . . Weber . . . makes a clear negative statement about their logical status: they cannot be defined by *genus proximum* and *differentia specifica,* and concrete cases cannot be subsumed under them as instances; i.e. they are not simply class, or property concepts. . . . An ideal type, according to Weber, is a mental construct formed by the synthesis of many diffuse, more or less present and occasionally absent, concrete individual phenomena, which are arranged, according to certain one-sidedly accentuated points of view, into a unified analytical construct, which in its conceptual purity cannot be found in reality; it is a utopia, a limiting concept, with which concrete phenomena can only be compared for the purpose of explicating some of their significant components.

As I pointed out on that occasion (Marchand 1973: 125), there is no reason for linguists to be ashamed of using such "fuzzy" concepts, we just need to avoid using *dialect* and *language* as if they were not simply ideal types, and we need to realize that it is quite difficult if not impossible to assign a document to a dialect; indeed the whole question of attribution and assignment in both language and literary studies needs a thorough discussion (Kraft 1979). The last half of Hempel's definition of Weber's usage is sufficently close to the manner in which linguists use such concepts as *language, dialect,* and *stage of the language* that it shows that these are indeed ideal types. If this is true, then taking a document and assigning it to a particular language or dialect without further ado is logically wrong. The problem of delimiting languages, of determining when language split has taken place, has, so far as I know, never even been discussed from a general and theoretical standpoint (but cf. Hartig 1984). The sociological criterion, that is, what language speakers feel they are using, is particularly unsatisfactory (Ziskind 1941: 161 f.):

> Zu der Frage von 'deutscher' Lautung für hebräische Namen, besonders "a" für "å" sei noch auf Eryk, 56 ff., besonders aber 128 hingewiesen, wo er mehrere Beispiele von jiddischen Bibelumdichtungen bringt, die die Namen jüdischer Heiliger und Bibelhelden in ihrer deutschen Form gebrauchen. Eryk verdammt diese Nachahmung des Deutschen etwas entrüstet als 'Daitshmerism' und verkennt dabei doch die Bedeutung dieses systematischen Vorgehens, nämlich, daß die aj. Dichter nicht mit demselben Gefühl dem Jiddischen gegenüber

standen wie der jiddisch sprechende Dichter von heute. Denn gerade diese Schreibeweise ist der schlagendste Beweis dafür, daß der altjiddische Dichter 'deutsch' und nur deutsch schreiben wollte und selbst wenn er besondere Formen, die nur dem Jiddischen eigen waren, gebrauchte, meinte er mindestens doch 'deutsch' zu schreiben und strebte darnach. Es war ihm gar nicht um eine besondere 'jüdische' Sprache zu tun. Deswegen vermeidet er auch die hebräischen Lautungen der jüdischen Namen und, wie es sich Eryk ausdrückt, 'operiert geradezu mit Ausdrücken aus der christlich-religiösen Begriffswelt.' Daraus geht hervor, daß unser Dichter unbedingt glaubte, nur Deutsch zu schreiben und keinerlei besonderen gefühlsmäßigen Beziehungen für eine spezifisch jüdische oder jüdisch-deutsche Sprache hatte.

Native speakers are notoriously bad informants as to the language or dialect being spoken. Linguists call the speech of Vienna *Middle Bavarian,* for example, but no Viennese would accept that or the fact that his speech in any real way resembled that of Bavaria.

The definition of the terms *Proto* and *Pre* is no better off than is that of *language* (Marchand 1973b), particularly when it comes to the discussion of the possibility of the attestation of a proto language (so important for our treatment of the early glosses and the dating of stages of Yiddish!) or of the existence of unified proto-languages (also of great importance to the reconstruction of Proto Yiddish). To give an example of the question of unified proto languages (Marchand 1955):

(Kent 1948: 194): 'This . . . view . . . removes the basis for scientific linguistics. Our Proto-IE must be only *one* of these slightly differing dialects (set up by Pisani); that it is itself the product of dialect mixture of an earlier date is irrelevant to the problem. But even if one grant that several different dialects are IE, that only means that one has not gone far enough back . . . In this, I think, lies the fundamental error of those who refuse to accept *Ursprachen* as a part of our linguistic science.'
(Twaddell 1948: 139): 'A successful reconstruction transcends the several changes; it antedates dialect differences which appear in the sequel languages . . . The fruitfulness of such reconstruction is attested by a century of scholarship, the punctuation (*) is firmly established, and the terms *Proto-, Ur-, Primitive* are firmly attached to formulate which are timeless, non-dialectal and non-phonetic.'

It seems then that the attempt to reconstruct Proto Yiddish will require a gathering of witnesses, which requires a definition of Yiddish, or at least criteria to determine when we have a Yiddish document before us, which requires a careful discussion of the nature of dialect and language. Given the statements of Kent, Twaddell and Hempel, one wonders if it is possible. Max Weinreich has already accepted the fact that we cannot arrive at a unified Proto Yiddish (1955: 12): "Do iz ort ayntsushtimen mit aza tezis bay Fraynd Ziskindn: 'Ur-Yiddish—vi an eynheytlekher dyalekt fun ale yidish-reyders—*hot keyn mol nit eksistirt* un nit gekont eksistirn.' Di shpatsirung iz getsilt kegn Fishers an aroyszogung un ikh shtim ayn durkhoys mit Fraynd Ziskind. Ikh hob in mayn artikl fun 1940 untergeshtrokhen az breyshes-yidish iz *nit* geven keyn eynheytlekher dyalekt." [As an aside, we may note that Weinreich maintains (1954: 77) that *he* 'he' does not appear in Yiddish at all; its existence in Codex C. Y. would either show that that document was not Yiddish or necessitate the assumption of competing forms in Proto Yiddish.].

As I said above, Birnbaum was right when he said that the problem of dialect or language in the case of Yiddish was a question of concept formation. We need to discuss Yiddish from a spatial, temporal and stratal point of view. It is important, it seems to me, to distinguish between Western Yiddish and Eastern Yiddish, since these are obviously based on a different raw material. Just on the morphological level alone, it would be necessary to include preterites and progressive tenses in Proto Western Yiddish, but not in Proto Eastern Yiddish. There are numerous dialects in Western Yiddish, based to a great extent on the coterritorial German dialects; there is a constant ebb and flow in these dialects; as one would expect, during the 16th and 17th centuries. The various Eastern Yiddishes operate as typical colonial dialects, and one needs close observation of the colonial German dialects before sweeping statements as to differences can be made. Balaban (1912: 301) feels that "dieses *Deutsch* der Juden war in Wirklichkeit nicht viel verschieden von dem

Deutsch der Krakauer Bürgerschaft.'' One might be able to reconstruct, e.g. Proto Galitsyaner, although I doubt it.

Also, the question used to be much debated as to whether Yiddish did not really come from Middle High German and not from Modern German. I must agree with Max Weinreich that there is really no such animal as Middle High German. What we have are written documents which we have come to attach to dialects which we have used as convenient fictions. To accept such labels as meaning anything other than convenient fictions is to take the label for the contents. It is wrong to look in a Middle High German dictionary such as Lexer [one even sees, *horresco referens,* Lexer's *Taschenwörterbuch* referred to] to see whether or not Middle High German possessed this or that word. Lexer does not even have all the known words of Middle High German, and our documents do not attest all of them. In the matter of *bentshn,* for example, I remember that Wolfram says (*Parzival* 94.1 "als der bendiz wart getan", thus supplying the missing *-d-* that bothers everyone so much. A MHG word *bendizen* would not be at all surprising. [If I may be permitted a small anecdote: A colleague of mine once took exception to my using the word *athetization,* although *athetize is* in the dictionary. I say, if athetize, *kal vekhoymer* athetization.] I am not fond of using dictionaries, so I cannot say whether *bendizen* is to be found in a dictionary or not. Comparison with German, for whatever reason, has to be done with great care, for it is certain that the "pure" German invoked by Weinreich is also a myth. Waldman is right in pointing out that there are many documents in "German" which, if written in Hebrew script, would be taken to be Yiddish, and the further back one goes the more likely this is (Waldman 1940: 122):

[speaking of Mais' *Bürgercapitain,* Anzengruber's *Pfarrer von Kirchfeld,* Hauptmann's *Rose Bernd* and Thoma's *Gelähmte Schwingen*] "Were these works to be reprinted with Hebrew characters, and were they to be viewed by a Judaeo-German speaking individual, who has no knowledge of German, he would feel quite at home therein and very likely consider the dialet a peculiar kind of Judaeo-German.''

He points to a number of "Judaeo-German" features in various German works, words such as: *Erbel* (Y. *arbel* 'sleeve'), *Arbeis* 'peas', *Lekkuchen* (y. *lekkach* 'spice cake') *Schuch* 'shoe', *Gorgel* 'throat' *nächten* 'to stay overnight', *darfst* 'needest', *finnen* (Y. *gefinnen* 'find'), *frägen* 'ask', *zerunnen* 'melted away', *zuloffen* 'dispersed', etc. etc. In Mais' *Bürgercapitain,* written in the "Frankfurt dialect", he notes: *losst es, hot recht, hobs gesogt, du host mich beruhigt* (Y. *baruhigt*), *hot wos mitgenumme(n), wos ist do, heint, ebbes,* etc. He notes also the following Hebrew words in the Frankfurt dialect: *acheln, ganfen, tsores, dalles, schawesschmus, mis, khale, ksaires* (<*gseres*).

Now that we are on the subject, if we are interested in naïve statements about language, we have Heine's word (reported by Waldman (1940: 122; cf. Marchand 1958):

Was wir Norddeutschland Mauscheln nennen ist nichts Anderes als die Frankfurter Landessprache, und sie wird von der unbeschnittenen Population ebenso vortrefflich gesprochen, wie von der beschnittenen, Boerne sprach diesen Jargon sehr schlecht, obgleich der, ebenso wie Goethe, den heimatlichen Dialekt nie ganz verleugnen konnte.

Should we take this to mean that Goethe spoke Yiddish (he certainly studied it)?

The point of this whole discussion is that, from a linguistic and theoretical standpoint, a decision on the Yiddish or German nature of a document in Hebrew script is difficult, if not impossible, yet that is exactly what we need before we can embark on the reconstruction of Proto Yiddish if we are to take into consideration early documents and the glosses. It will certainly not do to assume that anything in Hebrew script is Yiddish.

We need to develop criteria, if we wish to be at all objective, and if we do not wish to accept Marchand's admittedly rather positivistic criteria (Marchand 1959).

II. Sociology of knowledge

(Merton 1973: 23 [quoting Scheler]):

The sociological character of all knowledge, of all forms of thought, intuition and cognition is unquestionable. Although the *content* and even less the objective validity of all knowledge is not determined by the *controlling perspectives of social interests,* nevertheless this is the case with the selection of the objects of knowledge. Moreover, the 'forms' of the mental process by means of which knowledge is acquired are always and necessarily codetermined sociologically, i.e. by the social structure.

It is difficult for us as scholars to realize that we are social animals, and that our ambience influences us to such an extent.

To quote myself (Marchand 1975: 1 f.):

Here, I must pause and point out what is meant by *sociological; ecological* might be a better term. The society or culture in which we live is only one aspect, one part of what is meant by *sociology* in the term *sociology of knowledge.* The ambience in which ideas exist conditions them totally. 1. This means that the metalanguage operates upon the scientist as Whorf conjectured that the Hopi language did upon the Hopi: We find it extremely difficult to think thoughts not given by the metalanguage, so that he who controls it will control the field. 2. This means that the channels of the dissemination of knowledge contaminate it. Conferences such as this one, by their very organization, location, etc., mold linguistic thought. 3. This means that the structure and the reward system of the university taught in, the classes taught, etc. influence the linguist as a college teacher, as does the fact that most linguists are in universities. 4. This means that the interconnections of linguistics and other disciplines form a part of its vicinage, *ergo* its world view. I could continue, but the point is that we linguists are not the free thinkers we wish to be and frequently present ourselves as. Our thought is 'socially' conditioned.

Thus, the fact that many of the scholars of *Die Wissenschaft des Judentums* were not native speakers of Yiddish and were German coloured their scholarly opinions. [For a sensitive appreciation of *Die Wissenschaft des Judentums,* see Wallach 1938.] But it is nonetheless true that the opinions of the Yivo group, writing as they did in Yiddish and as passionate lovers of their native language and Eastern Jewish culture, were also biased, and sought to create an "ethical distance" as Uriel Weinreich used to call it, between their culture and German. As Augustine said: "Quis egeat auctoritatem in re tam perspicua", but the following words of Max Weinreich would not have been written in *galkhes,* as I now write them, nor in any Western language (M. Weinreich 1955: 13 f.):

Geto—Fakt un fiktsye. . . Vi zogt Hayne: ikh ken dem nign, ikh ken dem tekst, ikh ken di mekhabrim oykhet. Fraynd Ziskind vet mir moykhl zayn, der shablon vakst vider a mol fun yene daytsh-yidishe historikers, vos mit zey hobn mir shoyn eyn mol bagegnt bam boydek zayn dem termin 'yudendoytsh'. Vaksn vakst der shablon fun a konkreter historisher konstelatsye, bshas yidn in mayrev- un tsentraleyrope hobn zikh gerisn tsu emantsipatsye.

Do hobn es yene historiker in der bekhine fun publitsistn ufgeboyt di teorye, az yidn zaynen fartsaytns geven daytshn . . ., di opzunderung iz gekumen durkh dem vos men hot farshpart yidn in getos; nemt nor arop di khumres, vet ir zen, vi yidn veln tsurik vern fule daytshn.

Hert zikh nokh ayn: 'Men hot dem yidn oysgeshlosn fun intelektueln lebn; hot er zikh opgeshlosn fun der arumiker velt . . .'Ikh volt geven a baln tsu visn, vos far an intelektueln lebn Fraynd Ziskind hot in zinen. Teaters? Kontsertn? Visnshaftlekhe gezelshaftn? Universitetn? Dos alts, veysn mir dokh, iz biz 1350 oder in gantsn nit geven, oder s'hot ersht genumen shprotsn. Geven iz der kloyster un di intelektuele funktsyes vos hobn aroysgeshtralt fun em. Ober zogn, az men hot yidn fun dem 'oysgeshlosn' iz punkt vi men volt gezogt, az men hot mikh oysgeshlosn fun dem kloyster vos gefint zikh in mayn gegnt, hob ikh zikh deriber nokh shtarker tsugetulyet tsu yidishkayt. Ir megt mir gleybn, ikh rays zikh nit mit aza impet in kloyster arayn, az men zol mikh azh darfn oysshlisn. Un fun vanen nemt zikh Fraynd Ziskinds svore, az der shakets teshaktsenu hot zikh geshafn in 'geto' nokhn ershtn kraytstsug? Er hot zikh geshafn nokh frier vi bizn ershtn krayts.

We need to discuss our problems in a quiet, scholarly manner, and not as "publitsistn", although (Marchand 1975: 1):

I cannot resist adding here (*mutatis mutandis*) a famous quote by Thoreau, who saw clearly the nature of 'scientific' truth: 'All men lead lives of quiet desperation, and what passes for truth is only compromise.'

III. Stance

This naturally brings me to the problem of stance. I am not a positivist and as a scholar in the humanities I have adopted Terence's motto *homo sum, nihil humani a me alienum puto.* I find myself siding with Max Weinreich in his dislike for documents and compelling proofs in human discussion. M. Weinreich 1955: 15 f.:

DOKUMENTALE RAYES UN DRINGDERVAYZN

Di shprakh fun undzer dor kenen mir forshn afn bazis fun geherte oder fartseykhnte lebedike reyd. Vi azoy dergeyen mir tsu der shprakh vos iz *elter* vi di letste zibetsik-akhtsik yor? Der entfer iz: dokumentn, un ikh shrayb zikh unter Fraynd Ziskinds entuziazm far dokumentn. Ober reyshes darf men visn, vu der khamer shteyt (dokumentn kenen oykh farfirn, saydn men analizirt zey mitn geherikn filologishn metod); tsveytns darf men gedenken, az der filologisher metod iz nit der eyntsiker bam lingvist.

Di eltste geshriftsn in italyenish zaynen fun 12tn yorhundert; di eltste geshriftsn in rumenish oder letish—fun 16tn yorhundert, ober di lingvistn hobn undz tsu dertseyln a sakh vegn der geshikhte fun di dozike shprakhn mit yorhunderter frier, un men ken zikh af zey farlozn.

As I mentioned above, I cannot share his enthusiasm for linguistics or linguists. We need to decide whether we are going to argue with our reason or with our hearts. It is certain, for example, that Fuks in the above circular quote (Fuks 1957: 26) is making a fundamental logical error, a *circulus vitiosus.* Shall we, for sake of our desire to have the Codex C.Y. be Yiddish, let him get away with it? The answer, it seems to me, is to label our discourse as to whether it is cognitive or affective, scientific or persuasive, but perhaps I am being too idealistic.

IV. Facts

This brings me to my fourth category. In discussing the glosses and Old Yiddish in general, many facts are twisted and ignored. Here are some:

1. *galkhes,* as Max Weinreich (1953: 489) points out, refers to the Latin alphabet, the alphabet of the *galokhim* "the tonsured ones"; it does not refer to German *per se,* as numerous authorities assume (e.g. Shtif 1926: 116).

2. *bloshn ashkenaz* in a gloss does not mean "in Yiddish", as everyone (e.g. Timm 1977: 23) seems to assume. In one of the Pfefferkorn documents published by Kracauer (1900: 170), the Emperor Maximilian addresses the Archbishop *bloshn ashkenaz,* and in one of the glosses published by Rubashov (1929: II, No. 13) a gentile *hegmen* speaks *bloshn ashkenaz.* The term meant to the persons writing here "in the language of Germany". Who knows what it meant every time it was used, but it did not necessarily mean "in Yiddish".

3. We need to use the word "some" more frequently in our discourse. It is often maintained that Jews did this or that in the Middle Ages; we cannot read from one instance a custom of a whole group. Weinreich 1953: 489:

Even if there had been in the Middle Ages a German literature in the modern sense of the word, the Jews would have been unable to read it. The Latin alphabet was practically unknown among them and its very name in the Hebrew and Yiddish of the period, *galkhes,* reveals the reason; literally, the word signifies something belonging to the *galokhim* 'the tonsured ones', i.e. the Catholic priests. The barrier between the alphabets, then, just as between the languages was of a religious nature, and until the emancipation the Jewish alphabet was practically the only one the Jews knew and used, including the signing of official (non-Jewish) documents."

Some Jews obviously read *galkhes* quite well, as the Pfefferkorn letters show. I have been at some pains to demonstrate that at least some of the works in the Codex C.Y. had Latin-letter *Vorlagen,* as is demonstrated by the writing of geminate consonants, errors such as *t* for *c, g* for *j,* etc. (Marchand 1959). And some gentiles read Hebrew, as evidenced by the example of Roger Bacon, by the interest in Christian scholars in the *hebraica veritas,*

and even by the fact that some prescriptions for Jewry oaths contained the Hebrew alphabet and instructions as to how to use it.

4. We need to find some way to offer a neutral transliteration of the Hebrew alphabet used in our manuscripts, particularly when writing for a gentile audience which may not be familiar with the Hebrew alphabet and its use in the Middle Ages. This is particularly important in the case of *alef* (Joffe 1954: 104–107). To transliterate it as 'o' in every case is to argue by transliteration. The same may be said of Birnbaum's method in his transliteration of the Abraham poem from Codex C. Y. (1979: 146, as elsewhere), where he transliterates *alef vov* as 'oo', and then transliterates *vov* also as 'oo'. MHG *verwâzen* probably had a long stressed [ǣ], which in many dialects, including Yiddish, became /o/, but who knows what it was in the Codex C. Y.?

Revenons a nos moutons. There used to be a custom, in Dutch dissertations, to append a set of *stellingen,* or positions taken. I should like to end my talk with a few:

(1) From my point of view, all Yiddishes are dialects of German. If we used the same methods used to prove that medieval documents are not German in dealing with "German" dialects, we could show that most of them are not German.

(2) The scheme of Zarphat, Loez, Loter, etc. is a false one. Jews came into Germany from all over. We know of Charlemagne's importation of at least one Jew into Carolingian Germany, and there has been no lack of studies showing that St. Guillaume and his son, Bernard of Septimania, were Jews (Zuckerman 1972), and, although I am unable to subscribe to most of Zuckerman's theories (Marchand 1984), I must admit that some are plausible. Max Weinreich's admission (1953: 487) that he had no proof for his *Loter* statements ought to be listened to, as should also his call for help from historians.

(3) We must not expect Western Yiddish and Eastern Yiddish to have the same point or type of origin: they are two different animals. I suspect that each of the three major Eastern Yiddish dialects needs also separate treatment.

(4) Many of our early (Pre-1500) documents, even when written by Jews, are simply German. Certainly, the Codex C.Y. does not show the same admixture of Hebrew as do the glosses.

(5) The first work of *Yiddish* literature is the *Bovo-Bukh* of 1507. It is a great work of literature and is wrongly neglected by German specialists, who think that the first work in "German" in *ottava rima* is more than a century later.

(6) Western Yiddish, as usually defined, with its collapse of MHG *ei, ou* into *a,* betrays its Hessian origins. The language of the Wetterauer congregation, strong as that group seems to have been in the late Middle Ages, seems to have become an extra-territorial *lingua franca*. The Yiddish of Levita has none of the dialect characteristics of his Bavaro-Franconian homeland.

(7) The various Eastern Yiddishes operate like colonial dialects of German. Of course, they differ by the fact that they have an admixture of Hebrew words, particularly those peculiar to the Jewish religion and its practices, but that is the nature of group dialects, such as *Weidmannssprache*.

(8) The responsa project of Bar-Ilan University, in the work of Bar-El (1977), Choueka (1980), Slae, Schreiber and their colleagues, has made by use of the computer the vast literature of the responsa, including Yiddish responsa, truly available.

(9) Conferences such as this one, where we have a chance to come together and discuss problems such as *Origins of the Yiddish Language,* are a sign of the health of our discipline. *So eine Arbeit wird nie fertig.*

REFERENCES

BALABAN, M. 1912 Die Krakauer Juden-Gemeinde Ordnung von 1595. *Jahrbuch der Jüdisch-Literarischen Gesellschaft,* **10**, 298–350.

BAR-EL, 1977 *A Dictionary of Yiddish in the Responsa of Ashkenaz Rabbis in the 13th–15th Centuries* (Hebrew) Publication of the Bar Ilan University, Ramat-Gan.

BEST, O. F. 1973 *Mameloschen Jiddisch—Eine Sprache und ihre Literatur.* Insel, Frankfurt.

BICKEL, S. and LEHRER, L. 1958 *Shmuel Niger-Bukh.* Yivo, New York.

BIN-NUN, J. 1973 *Jiddisch und die deutschen Mundarten unter besonderer Berücksichtigung des ostgalizischen Jiddisch.* Max Niemeyer, Tübingen.

BIRNBAUM, S. A. 1929 Jiddische Sprache. *Jüdisches Lexikon* **3**, 269–278.

BIRNBAUM, S. A. 1931–32 Umschrift des ältesten datierten jiddischen Schriftstückes. *Teutonista,* **8**, 197–207.

BIRNBUAM, S. A. 1932 Jiddisch. *Encyclopedia Judaica* **9**, 112–127.

BIRNBAUM, S. A. 1939 The Age of the Yiddish Language. *Transactions of the Philological Society,* 31–43.

BIRNBAUM, S. A. 1979 *Yiddish. A Survey and a Grammar.* University of Toronto Press, Toronto.

BOROKHOV, B. 1913 Di ufgabn fun der yidisher filologye. In Niger, S., 1913, 1–22. Also in Borokhov, 1966.

BOROKHOV, B. 1966 *Shprakh-forshung un literatur-geshikhte.* Gezamlt un tzunoyfgeshtelt: N. Mayzel. I. L. Peretz Publishing House, Tel-Aviv.

CHOUEKA, Y. 1980 Computerized Full-Text Retrieval Systems and Research in the Humanities: the Responsa Project. *Computer in the Humanities* **14**, 153–170.

DINSE, H. 1974 *Die Entwicklung des jiddischen Schrifttums im deutschen Sprachgebiet,* Metzler, Stuttgart.

DÜNNER, L. 1904 Die hebräischen Handschriften-Fragmente im Archiv der Stadt Cöln. *Zeitschrift für hebräische Bibliographie* **8**, 84–90; 113–117.

FALK, F. 1908 Die Bücher Samuelis in deutschen Nibelungenstrophen des XV. Jahrhunderts. *Mitteilungen der Gessellschaft für jüdische Volkskunde* **28**, 79–116, 129–150.

FISCHER, J. 1936 *Das Jiddische und sein Verhältnis zu den deutschen Mundarten unter besonderer Berücksichtigung der ostgalizischen Mundart. Erster Teil. Erste Hälfte. Allgemeiner Teil. Inauguraldissertation zur Erlangung der Doktorwürde einer hohen philosophischen Fakultät der Ruprecht-Karls-Universität Heidelberg.* Oswald Schmidt, Leipzig.

FUKS, L. 1957 *The Oldest Known Literary Documents of Yiddish Literature (c. 1382).* II vols. E. J. Brill, Leiden.

GRÜNBAUM, M. 1882 *Jüdischdeutsche Chrestomathie.* Brockhaus, Leipzig.

GÜDEMANN, M. 1880 *Geschichte des Erziehungswesens und der Cultur der Juden in Frankreich und Deutschland.* Alfred Hölder, Vienna.

GUGGENHEIM-GRÜNBERG, F. 1977 Sprachen und schrieben die Zürcher Juden jiddisch zu Ende des 14. Jahrhunderts? In Müller and Röll, 1977, 2–3.

HARTIG, M. 1984 Sociolinguistics and the Description of Language Change and Language Ecology or: Language Splitting versus Language Contact. *Zeitschrift für Dialektologie und Linguistik.* Beiheft **45**, 237–246.

HEIDE, M. G. 1974 *Graphematisch-phonematische Untersuchungen zum Altjiddischen. Der Vokalismus. Europäische Hochschulschriften.* Lang, Berna and Frankfurt.

HEMPEL, C. G. 1965 *Aspects of Scientific Explanation.* Free Press, New York.

HERZOG, M. I., KIRSHENBLATT-GIMBLETT, B., MIRON, D. and WISSE, R. 1980 *The Field of Yiddish.* Fourth Collection. Institute for the Study of Human Issues, Philadelphia.

JOFFE, J. A. 1954 Dating the Origin of Yiddish Dialects. In Weinreich, U., 1954, pp. 102–121.

KACHRU, B. B., LEES, R. B., MALKIEL, Y., PIETRANGELI, A. and SAPPORTA, S. (eds) 1973 *Issues in Linguistics. Papers in Honor of Henry and Renée Kahane.* University of Illinois Press, Urbana.

KARPELES, G. 1963 *Geschichte der jüdischen Literatur*. 4th edn. Akademischer Druck und Verlagsanstalt, Graz.

KENT, R. G. 1948 [Review of Pisani's *Linguistica generale e indeuropea*]. *Language* **24**, 194–195.

KRACAUER, I. 1900 Actenstücke zur Geschichte der Confiscation der hebräischen Schriften in Frankfurt a.M. *Monatsschrift für Geschichte und Wissenschaft des Judenthums* **24**, 114–126, 167–177, 220–234.

LANDAU, L. 1912 *Hebrew-German Romances and Tales*. Teutonia 21. Avenarius, Leipzig.

LANDAU, L. 1928 Der jiddische Midrasch Wajoscha. *Monatsschrift für Geschichte und Wissenschaft des Judenthums* **72**, 601-621.

LUNSKI, K. 1924 Iserlins yidish. *Yidishe filologye* **1**, 288–297. With a supplement by Weinreich, pp. 297–302.

MARCHAND, J. W. 1955 Was There Ever a Uniform Proto-Indo-European? *Orbis* **4**, 428–431.

MARCHAND, J. W. 1958 Goethe's *Judenpredigt*. *Monatshefte* **50**, 305–310.

MARCHAND, J. W. 1959 [Review of Fuks 1957]. *Word* **15**, 383–394.

MARCHAND, J. W. 1960a Three basic problems in the investigation of early Yiddish. **9**, 34–41.

MARCHAND, J. W. 1960b Einiges zur sogenannten 'jiddischen Kudrun'. *Neophilologus* 56–63.

MARCHAND, J. W. 1965 The Origin of Yiddish. *Communications et Rapports du Premier Congrès International de Dialectologie générale*. pp. 248–252. Centre international de Dialectologie générale, Louvain, pp. 248–252.

MARCHAND, J. W. 1973a Observations on the use of dialect evidence in historical linguistics. In Scholler and Reidy, 1973, pp. 122–133.

MARCHAND, J. W. 1973b Proto-, pre- and common: a problem in definition. In Kachru *et al.*, 1973, pp. 644–657.

MARCHAND, J. W. 1975 Towards a sociology of linguistics. ERIC ED 107 146.

MARCHAND, J. W. 1984 The Frankish Mother: Dhuoda. In Wilson, J. M. (ed.) *Medieval Women Writers*, pp. 1–29.

MARK, Y. (ed.) 1958 *Yuda A. Yofe-Bukh*. Yivo, New York.

MERTON, R. K. 1973 *The Sociology of Science*. University of Chicago Press, Chicago.

MIESES, M. 1915 *Die Entstehungsursache der jüdischen Dialekte*. R. Löwit, Vienna.

MIESES, M. 1924 *Die jiddische Sprache*. Benjamin Harz, Berlin, Vienna.

MÜLLER, H.-J. and RÖLL, W. (eds) 1977 *Fragen des älteren Jiddisch. Trierer Beiträge. Aus Forschung und Lehre an der Universität*. Sonderheft 2.

NIGER, S. (ed.) 1913 *Der pinkes. Yorbukh far der geshikhte fun der yidisher literatur un shprakh, far folklor, kritik un biblyografye*. B. A. Kletskin, Vilna.

PERLES, J. 1876 Bibliographische Mitteilungen aus München. *Monatsschrift für Geschichte und Wissenschaft des Judenthums* **25**, 350–375.

PRILUTSKI, N. and LEHMAN, S. (eds) 1933 *Arkhiv far yidisher shprakh-visnshaft, literatur-forshung un etnologye*, Vol. I. Nayer farlag, Warsaw.

REYZEN, Z. 1920 *Gramatik fun der yidisher shprakh. Ershter teyl*. Sh. Shreberk, Vilna.

RUBASHOV, Z. 1929 Yidishe gvies-eydes in di shayles-tshuves fun onheyb XV bizn suf XVII y'h. *Historishe shriftn fun Yivo* **1**, 115–196.

SAINÉAN, L. 1902 Essai sur le judéo-allemand. *Société de Linguistique de Paris* **12**, 90–196.

SCHOLLER, H. AND REIDY, J. (eds) 1973 *Lexicography and Dialect Geography. Festgabe für Hans Kurath. Zeitschrift für Dialektologie und Linguistik*. Beiheft 9. Steiner, Wiesbaden.

SCHUM, W. 1887 *Beschreibendes Verzeichnis der Amplonischen Handschriftensammlung zu Erfurt*. Weidmannsche Buchhandlung, Berlin.

SHIPER, Y. 1924 Der onheyb fun 'loshn ashkenaz' in der balaykhtung fun onomatishe kveln. *Yidishe filologye* **1**, 101–112, 272–287.

SHIPER, F. 1933 Loshn ashkenaz beeysn fertsetn un fuftsetn yorhundert. In Prilutski and Lehman, 1933, pp. 79–90.

SHTIF, N. 1926 Ven-den (bindverter in der yidisher shprakh. Dos XV, XVI yorhundert). *Filologishe shriftn fun Yivo* **1**, 95–128.

STEINSCHNEIDER, M. 1848 Jüdisch-Deutsche Literatur. *Serapeum* 1848, 313–384.

STEINSCHNEIDER, M. 1865 [Review of Avé-Lallemant]. *Hebräische Bibliographie* **8** No. 741.

STERN, M. 1931–32 Aus Regensburg. Urkundliche Mitteilungen. *Jahrbuch der jüdisch-literarischen Gesellschaft* **22**, 1-124.

TIMM, E. 1977 Jiddische Sprachmaterialien aus dem Jahre 1290: Die Glossen des Berner kleinen Aruch—Edition und Kommentar. In Müller and Röll, 1977, pp. 16–34.

TWADDELL, W. F. 1948 The Prehistoric Germanic Short Syllabics. *Language* **24**, 139–151.

WALDMAN, M. 1940 Origin and development of Judeo-German and the old German legends. *Philological Quarterly* **19**, 114–122.

WALLACH, L. 1938 *Leopold Zunz und die Grundlegung der Wissenschaft des Judentums.* J. Kauffmann, Frankfurt.

WEINREICH, M. 1951 Ashkenaz: di yidish-tkufe in der yidisher geshikhte. *Yivo bleter* **35**, 7–17.

WEINREICH, M. 1953 *Yidishkayt* and Yidish. In *Mordecai M. Kaplan Jubilee Volume,* pp. 481–514, The Jewish Theological Seminary of America, New York.

WEINREICH, M. 1954 Prehistory and early history of Yiddish facts and conceptual framework, in Weinreich, U. 1954, pp. 73–101.

WEINREICH, M. 1954–1955 Ikrim in der geshikhte fun yidish. *Yidishe shprakh* **14**, 97–110, **15**, 12–19.

WEINREICH, M. 1956 The Jewish languages of romance stock and their relation to earliest Yiddish. *Romance Philology* **9**, 403–428.

WEINREICH, M. 1960 Old Yiddish poetry in linguistic-literary research. *Word* **16**, 100–118.

WEINREICH, M. 1960b Di sistem yidishe kadmen-vokaln. *Yidishe shprakh* **20**, 65–71.

WEINREICH, M. 1963 A yidisher zats fun far zibn hundert yor. *Yidishe Shprakh* **23**, 87–92. Note also the corrections, **24**, 61–62.

WEINREICH, M. 1973 *Geshikhte fun der yidisher shprakh,* 4 vols. Yivo, New York.

WEINREICH, M. 1977 *History of the Yiddish Language* (Trans. Shlomo Noble, with the assistance of Joshua A. Fishman). University of Chicago Press, Chicago.

WEINREICH, U. (ed.) 1954 *The Field of Yiddish.* Linguistic Circle of New York, New York.

WEINREICH, U. (ed.) 1965 *The Field of Yiddish,* Second Collection. Mouton, The Hague.

WILLEMYNS, R. 1976 Historische grammatica en dialectologie. *Verslagen en mededelingen van de Koninklijke Academie voor Nederlandse taal- en letterkunde* (Gent), pp. 45–59.

ZISKIND, N. 1941 Das Shmuel-Buch. Dissertation, New York University.

ZISKIND, N. 1953 Batrakhtungen vegn der geshikhte fun yidish. *Yidishe shprakh* **13**, 97–108. Reprinted in Mark, 1958, pp. 146–157.

ZISKIND, N. 1969 Altyidish un mitl-yidish. A kurtser araynfir. *Yidishe shprakh* **29**, 43–64.

ZUKERMAN, A. 1972 *A Jewish Princedom in Feudal France 768–900.* Columbia University Press, New York.

ZUNZ, L. 1966 *Die gottesdienstlichen Vorträge der Juden.* Reprint of 2nd edn., Frankfurt 1892. G. Olms, Hildesheim. Original edition, 1832.

Language & Communication, Vol. 7, Supplement, pp. 95–103, 1987.
Printed in Great Britain.

0271-5309/87 $3.00 + .00
Pergamon Journals Ltd.

TRANSGRESSING THE BOUNDS: ON THE ORIGINS OF YIDDISH LITERATURE

DAVID NEAL MILLER

Ohio State University at Columbus

Indeed I think that we have to give a very complex account of hegemony if we are talking about any real social formation. . . . We have to emphasize that . . . its own internal structures are highly complex, and have continually to be renewed, recreated and defended; and by the same token, that they can be continually challenged and in certain respects modified.
Raymond Williams (1973: 8).

The primacy of Hebrew in principle was not questioned. It had to be that way in a universe where scripture ruled. This was the theory; in practice the balance was bound to be upset. Sometimes Hebrew broke into the domain of Yiddish. . . . Yiddish transgressed its bounds much more frequently. . . .
Max Weinreich (1972: 283–84).

These boundaries, however, existed only to be circumvented.
David G. Roskies (1979: 276).

I

Imagine a language sufficiently old to warrant a conference at Oxford University to consider its origins that has had no stable name for itself (Weinreich 1973, I: 321–333). Imagine, too, a body of texts in that language spanning some six centuries and the broadest of generic ranges—chivalric romance, *Volksbuch* narrative, biblical translation, homiletic verse, chapbook fiction, belles-lettres in the European manner. Imagine, finally, that the speakers of this language (and, to no appreciably greater extent, the authors of these texts) would not think to assert that these texts together map a literary tradition—to say nothing of constituting a national literature.

This was precisely the situation of Yiddish letters through the mid-nineteenth century.

Indeed, this was necessarily the case: how else could the People of the Book have remained so determinedly oblivious to books of their own making? And, considering the immodest expenditure of psychic energy which this collective decision to ignore the bibliographically obvious must have entailed, we might reasonably conclude that the stakes were seen as worthy of the effort. The stakes were, I would suggest, nothing less than the protection of a central Book from the claims of all books which followed it—a textual *seyag la-Torah* [fence around the Torah] arguably more durable than other such fences of a more tangible nature (Mishna Avot, I: 1; see now Bloom 1975: 45). The product of a single revelatory moment (Scholem 1963: 19, the Torah was independent of prior texts for precedence and authority. Thus it could define, but not participate in, literary tradition, for to enter into tradition is to admit of retrospective change. "The past," Eliot reminds us, "is altered by the present as much as the present is altered by the past (1972: 5)."

Strict construction would have precluded successor texts: syllogistic rigour purchased at the expense of textual silence. In its stead developed a notion of semantic implication

whereby newly-produced texts are either rejected as post-canonic (that is, new) or projected backward as part of original revelation:

> Die Leistung jeder Generation in ihrem Beitrag zur Tradition wird in die ewige Gegenwart der Offenbarung am Sinai zurück projiziert . . . Nach dieser . . . Auffassung der Offenbarung schliesst sie nun schon alles in sich, was je legitim über ihren Sinn vorgebracht werden kann. . . . Im Grunde braucht [die Wahrheit] nur überliefert zu werden. [Der Forschende] entwickelt und erklärt das, was vom Sinai her überliefert ist; sei es, dass es stets bekannt war, sei es, dass es in Vergessenheit geraten und wieder aufgestellt werden muss. Die Anstrengung des Wahrheit Suchenden besteht nicht darin, sich etwas auszudenken, sondern vielmehr darin, sich in die Kontinuität der Tradition des göttlichen Wortes einzuschalten und das, was ihm von dorther zukommt, in seiner Beziehung auf sein Zeitalter zu entfalten. . . . Für die Art der Produktivität, die wir in der jüdischen Literatur antreffen, ist dies in der Tat ein überaus wichtiger Satz. *Die Wahrheit muss an einem Text entfaltet werden, in dem sie vorgegeben ist* (Scholem 1963: 28–29; my emphasis).

> [The achievement of every generation, its contribution to tradition, was projected back into the eternal present of the revelation at Sinai. . . . According to this . . . doctrine, revelation comprises within it everything that will ever be legitimately offered to interpret its meaning . . . Fundamentally, truth merely needs to be transmitted. The [exploring scholar] develops and explains that which was transmitted at Sinai, no matter whether it was always known or whether it was forgotten and had to be rediscovered. The effort of the seeker after truth consists not in having new ideas but rather in subordinating himself to the continuity of the tradition of the Divine word and in laying open what he receives from it in the context of his own time. . . . This is a most important principle indeed for the kind of productivity we encounter in Jewish literature. *Truth must be laid bare in a text in which it already preexists* (Scholem 1966: 14–15; my emphasis; compare Nohrnberg 1974: 16–17).]

Even where the metaphysics of textual assumption had been supplanted by the rhetoric of textual authority, newly-authored works were constrained to derive such authority from the single, central, preextant text (Weinreich 1972, I: 215). This exigency was unequally congenial. While, say, a (Hebrew-language) biblical commentary would welcome whatever authority the status of its referent might convey, a (Yiddish-language) chivalric romance in terza rima might find a similar claim more difficult to stake.

Yet just such a text managed to remain available in successive editions from the time of its initial appearance in 1541 through the early decades of the present century (Prilutski 1932: 354–370; on the *Bove-bukh* in general, see Joffe 1949: 7–32.) Though I propose to survey only those strategies arising from the yiddophone realm, it is important to remember that the problematics of writing in Yiddish is only a subset of the issue of post-Scriptural literary creation *schlechthin* (see, for example, Spitzer 1948: 18 et passim and Curtius 1948: 219).

A number of texts—surprisingly few, considering the sizeable corpus of pre-modern Yiddish literature—claim to derive their authority from Scripture. Thus, for example, tales of the most unmistakably secular cast in the early seventeenth-century *Maysebukh* announce themselves as exempla on Biblical themes. "Der rebe vos iz gevorn a vervolf" is typical: though utterly Germanic in form and temper, it nonetheless purports to engender Solomonic virtues and concludes with a quotation from the Book of Psalms. Indeed, well into the nineteenth century, works of imaginative literature in Yiddish typically cast themselves as twice-told tales from Scripture, as translation of sacred text or quasi-sacred commentary, or, at the very least, as works inspired by and inspiring of scriptural virtues.

What critical tradition there is has treated the matter of vertical legitimation with deadly earnest; and, to be sure, the stakes—nothing less than the possibility of a national literature in the Jewish vernacular—were high enough. What the tradition has generally failed to acknowledge (for ideological more than methodological reasons) is that these subversive claims were, in very large measure, subversively offered. Though it may set those who view Yiddish historically as a language as Caliban (Miron 1973: 34) to howling, I suggest that the great majority of hebraically-derived attempts at vertical legitimation were made with

a wink and a smirk: the consumers of Yiddish literature had, I would maintain, mastered a semiotic code nowhere published but widely understood; if the gullible were mollified or taken in, so much the better. Postmodern rereadings of pre-modern Yiddish texts are urgent desiderata.

Nor, incidentally, should one conclude from the near-absence of explicit appeals to the authority of texts in the non-Jewish coterritorial vernaculars that such texts did not serve important legitimating functions. Weinreich is not inaccurate in remarking that "in Ashkenaz biz der emantsipatsye zet zikh nit keyn eyn kentiker pruv fun horizontaler legitimirung" (1973: 215). I suspect, however, that Weinreich seriously underestimates both the existence and—more importantly—the theoretical import of unmistakable Jewish-Gentile intertextualities. Is it reasonable to suspect that a yiddophone reader of, say, *Ditrikh fun Bern* would remain inattentive to the work's scarcely-concealed gentile referents? Indeed, the primacy of a foreign antecedent is expressly acknowledged in the end matter to the Kraków edition of 1597, which mentions [boasts?] that the work was "oysgenumen fun galkhes un oyf yidish fartaytsht." The non-Jewish origin or *Ditrikh fun Bern* would appear, in this instance at least, rather to legitimate (horizontally!) the Yiddish text than to lessen its stature (compare Shtif 1924: 1–11, 112–122). The hostility with which such texts were greeted by the (hebraophone) rabbinate argues no less for their perceived legitimacy than for their undisputed popularity among the yiddophone readership. One should bear in mind who writes the history books, and to what ideological ends.

Weinreich, Roskies, and others have pointed out the central role of what I have elsewhere termed the packaging of Yiddish literature (Miller 1974). The related matters of titling and typography are instructive. Both title and front matter of pre-nineteenth-century Yiddish belles-lettres tend to display a decidedly hebraic cast. As Weinreich writes in his *Geshikhte:*

> Yidish-sforim, afile originel geshribene af yidish, geyen aroys mit loshn-koydeshe titlen: *Tsene-urene, Matsl-mimoves, Derekh hayosher looulem habe, Simkhes hanefesh,* un nokh un nokh. An andersh mol kumt khotsh an alternativer loshn-koydesher titl: *Seyfer hamare* oder *Brantshpigl, Seyfer hamuser* oder *Tsukhtshpigl, Rouzngortn* oder *Seyfer hagan; Kokhve deshovit* oder *Shternshus,* un nokh un nokh. In a sakh sforim iz faran tsum onheyb a haskome fun a barsamkhe, bederekh-klal a rov, az s'iz a vikhtik verk; iz afile in yidishe sforim di haskome alemol af loshn-koydesh. A mekhaber gufe shraybt tsaytnvayz tsu zayn yidish seyfer a loshn-koydesh hakdome (1973: I, 279).

A clearer case of vertical legitimation would appear to be difficult to find: Yiddish books took on an hebraic cast in order to partake of the putatively higher regard in which such texts were held. Deferring the matter of Hebrew's prestige vis-à-vis Yiddish for the moment, I should like to point out that these claims (titles, rabbinical assents, introductions) were asserted, if asserted they were, in a form and format *a priori* self-discrediting—namely, in a distinctive typeface reserved for Yiddish-language texts:

> Afn ershtn ort tsvishn di ale opsheyd-simonim tsvishn yidishe un loshn-koydeshe drukn volt men efsher gedarft dermonen dem fakt, vos biz in nayntsetn yorhundert arayn hot men gedrukt yidish mit an ander shrift vi loshn-koydesh. . . . Afile eyntsike yidishe frazes un verter in a loshn-koydeshn tekst hot men gezetst mit ot dem spetsyeln shrift . . . (1973: I, 280).

If clothing determines character (Baumgarten 1980: 32–55), typeface determines textual ontology. Is it outlandish to propose that Yiddish authors quite consciously undermined— once again, with a wink and a smirk—the ever-so-earnest rabbinical assents which so facilitated the distribution and public display of their literary artifacts? Since Yiddish texts have, by and large, been published for profit (by their authors or by printer-publishers often enough anxious to subsidize their less saleable sacred wares), surely the choice of typeface was also commercially motivated. Why, then, not appropriate Hebrew typographic norms for Yiddish rhetorical ends? The answer, I believe, is clear: Yiddish did not seek

to legitimate itself vertically, but only to placate the powers that be until it was sufficiently self-aware to invent itself.

II

This act of autogenesis was prolonged, though not invariably painful. It might, perhaps, prove instructive to glance briefly at the metaphors used by historians of Yiddish literature to describe the growth (itself a metaphor!) of collective authorial awareness before the latter nineteenth century. In contrast to the largely organicist metaphors invoked in the discussion of modern Yiddish literature—*The Flowering of Yiddish Literature* (Liptzin 1963), *The Maturing of Yiddish Literature* (Liptzin 1970), and the like—the controlling metaphors in studies of pre-modern Yiddish literature are customarily of a rather more bellicose turn. Notions of *kamf* and *gerangl* so predominate (Tsinberg 1928 stands in critical synecdoche for critics pre-nineteenth-century Yiddish literature, as does Reminik 1938 for those of modern Yiddish literature) that Max Weinreich felt called upon to note his own predisposition to such terminology (Weinreich 1973: I, 262).

I would not want to deny that Yiddish and Hebrew engaged in a *Kulturkampf* of sorts; and, to be sure, much ink and energy was devoted in the latter decades of the nineteenth century to the Jewish version of this pan-European problematic. Yet the military metaphor both catches and misses the point: in the battle for autolegitimation, Yiddish was Jackson to Hebrew's Bakenham. Lacking the conceptual armor for direct combat with the sacred language, advocates of Yiddish waged centuries-long guerrilla warfare with the dominant culture, eschewing direct confrontation and developing instead a remarkable—and remarkably consistent—strategy of claiming and enlarging areas of sociotextual no man's land.

A diachronic mapping of skirmishes won and lost would, no doubt, be of interest, though the present corpus of extant texts could not, I fear, successfully sustain such an effort (see, however Pyekazh 1964, Goldsmith 1976: 27–43, and, especially, Tsinberg 1928). More to my point, however, is the synchronicity of surviving defenses of the use of Yiddish as a literary medium. By this I mean not that these texts date from a single locus of aggressive reflexivity but rather that authors of the most disparate geographical and chronological provenance engage in what appears to be simultaneous colloquy with colleagues whom they have surely never met and, more likely than not, with whose writings they are but slightly acquainted. What develops, in short, is both a mode of argumentation and a common rhetorical stance.

Let us consider as object case the use of Yiddish in sacramental and liturgical contexts. Less interesting than the local waxings and wanings of actual praxis is the collective-progressive nature of theoretical debate. At stake was the legitimacy of sacred texts written in or translated into Yiddish. Early advocacy of Yiddish reveals an umistakably instrumentalist turn of mind. Texts exist, the argument runs, to elicit desired behaviors; the more accessible the text, the more likely its injunctions of being fulfilled. Initially applied to self-help manuals with scant claim to canonic status (guides to ritual purity, festival observance, and the like), instrumentalist arguments appear to be language-neutral.

This stance of language-neutrality is all the more evident in Yiddish-language translations of sacred texts. Thus, for example, the preface to Khayim ben Nosn of Prague's *Esrim vearbe* (1674), a Yiddish translation of the Hebrew Scriptures, states that "Es gilt nun glaykh er lernt es ouf loshn-koudesh oder ouf taytsh. . . . Drum hengt es nayert das men es gor

voul farshteyt'' (cited by Tsinberg 1928: 98). One probably does best to construe this apologia uncomplicatedly and at face value. Note, however, how Khayim ben Nosn's preface serves as subtext to Yekhiyel-Mikhl Epshteyn's considerably more subversive paraphrase:

> Azou shraybn etlekhe sforim: eyn vort dos men farshteyt tut mer pule als hundert verter di men nit farshteyt. . . . Drum, mayne gute fraynt, zekht dos undzere foreltern hobn ale undzere tfiles oder tilim oder andere bekoshes un alts ouf taytsh gemakht. . . . oukh a teyl makhzourim gedrukt, oukh . . . ale tkhines un bekoshes, afile bay di tfiles hot men far lange yorn dos taytsh derbay gedrukt (cited by Weinreich 1973 I: 265).

Epshteyn begins unthreateningly with a restatement of the familiar argument of intelligibility (''one word which one understands. . . .''). The argument from traditional practice (''see how our ancestors . . .''), a comprehensive consideration of which would lead us unacceptably—though not unpleasantly—far afield, would have been no less familiar to Epshteyn's readership. Though his is a relatively benign recapitulation of statements dating back at least to the first half of the thirteenth century, one does well to bear in mind the normative force of historical precedent in traditional Jewish society. Moreover, such arguments are doubly textual, if only implicitly so: our knowledge of, say, the historical authority of Aramaic language texts is itself textually mediated—via Hebrew language commentary. The tone of the passage, at once familiar and conciliatory, all but conceals Epshteyn's third and extraordinarily radical gambit: the privileging of *Yiddish* textual precedent. Quite aside from the instrumental value of Yiddish as *davn-shprakh* [language of prayer], aside even from non-Yiddish precedents and parallels, the sizeable corpus of sacred texts in approbated Yiddish editions itself warrants further production. The rather tedious catalogue of sacred genres with Yiddish publication histories serves both to camouflage and buttress Epshteyn's position.

That such texts did indeed continue to be produced, and in growing number, testifies to the efficacy of this and other subversive modes of textual legitimation; that the language nonetheless failed to gain a name for itself, and the aggregate of texts an awareness of self as corpus, testifies to the limitations of legitimation by indirection.

III

The logic of diachrony would now carry us to the eve of the period which is the primary focus of the present study—the latter decades of the nineteenth century and the first decade of the present one. But, for reasons which are both obvious and beyond the scope of the present study, we have reentered a period of hebraic hegemony, if not over Jewish intellectual life *tout court,* at least over those aspects which are still conducted in one or another of the Jewish languages. Perhaps, then, it should not surprise us to see (as one says in Yiddish) the same widow in a different veil. Not that the producers and consumers of Yiddish literature have any need for this particular garb: so well did Yiddish literature invent itself that demographic inevitabilities have had little measurable effect on its collective sense of self. The problem, rather, lies in an hebraophone academy ideologically embarrassed by the national literature to which it is heir, yet unable—at times unwilling—fully to part with it.

The resulting process—a reclaiming of a yiddophone tradition made harmless by assigning it a subsidiary function in an intranational polysystem (Even-Zohar and Shmeruk 1981; Even-Zohar 1978a, 1978b)—more properly belongs to a study of *Hebrew* literary legitimation. What, on the other hand, should interest us here is the application of polysystem theory and, more generally, of recent literature on diglossia and internal bilingualism (e.g. Fishman 1966, Fertig and Fishman 1969, Herzfeld 1982, Macaulay 1965, Pool 1972) to the study of pre-modern Yiddish literature. While hebraophone criticism

of twentieth-century Yiddish literature tends to be of a theoretical piece with that pursued by the broader academic community (conceding, in effect, the mutual autonomy of both Jewish national literatures), studies of earlier literary periods have developed a prefatory convention hardly less prevalent than the earlier rabbinic *haskomes*—namely, an assertion that Yiddish literature is characterized by, indeed predicated upon, an awareness by its authors (if not necessarily its readers) of its subsidiary position in the literary polysystem. Some versions of this historical fiction (e.g. Yudkin 1982: 11–12) are cruder than others. Of no less interest, and somewhat greater relevance to the present agenda, is the reappearance of Epshteynian argumentation in modern critical garb. Even the subversive rhetorical stance is familiar.

It might prove helpful briefly to recapitulate that rhetorical stance in somewhat schematic fashion:

(a) the hegemony of the sacred tongue is immediately acknowledged;

(b) possible objections to the use of Yiddish are sympathetically enumerated;

(c) a local exception is identified and advocated, often on transparently disingenuous grounds;

(d) a defense is modestly cast, framed as digression or aside, embedded in an irrelevant passage of text or thrown off in a relative clause;

(e) the apparently minimalist argument reveals itself to be a subversively maximalist one.

With this in mind, let us examine the opening subsection of an important history of Yiddish literature, published by Tel Aviv University in 1978. It, too, begins with a concession of Hebraic hegemony:

> Yiddish literature, in all its development and growth in traditional Jewish society, did not originally have . . . the ability to answer the aesthetic and spiritual needs of the bilingual society from which it sprang.

> If, in our context, one can use terms of functional division in its linguistic-literary sense, it seems clear that most of the areas of possible literary activity in the Jewish community were already occupied by its traditional Hebrew-Aramaic language, or Loshn-koydesh (Holy Tongue), its more accurate designation in terms of its status, its makeup, its tradition, its uses, and its aims (Shmeruk 1978: 12).

The author concedes even more: areas of social and intellectual activity routinely conducted in Yiddish (scriptural commentary, theological inquiry, matrimonial agreements, financial dealings and personal correspondence) were nonetheless recorded in Hebrew (Shmeruk 1978: 11). That Yiddish serves as verbal subtext to subsequent canonic renderings simply bespeaks its function in the polysystem; that it also serves as stylistic and even lexical model for such renderings provides a rather less tractable challenge to the notion of functional division.

Several pages later, a local exception of rather nonthreatening cast—the use of Yiddish in private correspondence—is identified and briefly discusssed. Note, however, how the author assumes the point of view of an hebraophone correspondent who, in imaginative reconstruction, limits his use of Yiddish to those addressees insufficiently sophisticated to understand the Holy Tongue:

> In private correspondence . . . we see evidence of overlap between the two languages: part of the community uses only Yiddish, while for the other part we should postulate bilingualism . . . conditioned upon the addressee and an estimation of his ability to understand a letter in the Holy Tongue (Shmeruk 1978: 21).

The cited passage is rather subtly crafted, inasmuch as it acknowledges demographic realities without foregrounding them. If a segment of the community enjoys elective recourse to Hebrew while the community as a whole shares a common language of private correspondence, which *shraybshprakh* constitutes the linguistic base line, and which the local exception? Withal, the stakes here are relatively low, since correspondence in whatever

language constitutes a genre only recently retrieved from the margins of literary discourse (a felicitous term itself retrieved from Herrnstein Smith 1978).

The author expands his argument cautiously, and by analogy: much as Yiddish serves the (primarily practical) needs of private correspondence among those without access to Loshn-koydesh, so, too, it serves the (primarily aesthetic) needs of that same population:

> In a not inconsequential portion of Yiddish literature through the end of the eighteenth century, one can see . . . a response . . . to the needs deriving from the traditional way of life for those parts of the society for whom direct access to the sources in the Holy Tongue was blocked (Shmeruk 1978: 20).

Though no mention is made of the specific genres constituting this "not inconsequential portion" of pre-eighteenth-century Yiddish literature, the passage would appear to refer to works of sacred provenance, inasmuch as these would most likely be seen as answering "the needs deriving from the traditional way of life." The point is important to the author's general apologetic: at least within the frame of post-Enlightenment aesthetics, instrumentally-induced compromises with the received tradition are more easily forgiven than are aesthetically-motivated challenges to it.

In the course of a more general discussion of the dynamics of Yiddish literary production and consumption, the author makes casual but significant mention of the "possibilities," as well as the "limitations," engendered by "the intellectual level of those strata of society who were solely dependent upon reading Yiddish" (Shmeruk 1978: 20). This is not, however, generalized to a notion of singing in one's chains or a defense of the rewards of working within formal constraints, though either is available to the contemporary student of literature. And yet antipathy is channeled away from the texts and toward their intellectually-wanting readership—that is, away from the still-present and toward the long-dead, a clever if ungenerous rhetorical ploy.

After a final preliminary gambit—the suggestion that areas of overlap between Hebrew and Yiddish literatures be further explored, if only the better to delineate the functional differences among texts superficially similar in all but language—the author advances his principal thesis: Yiddish is a literature of the interstices. What cannot be written in Hebrew, whether for lack of potential audience or absence of canonic paradigm, falls to Yiddish:

> The independent literature in Yiddish . . . fulfilled a complementary role for the literary types that in fact did not exist in the Holy Tongue, or whose development was prevented or limited because of the character of the Ashkenazi Jewish intellectual elite who did not evince a particular interest in them (Shmeruk 1978: 23).

Which, precisely, were these literary types cast off by the hebraophone intellectual elite? The author teases us with an apparent digression on the life and works of one Elye Bokher, sixteenth-century Hebrew grammarian and author of such long-forgotten works as *Seyfer habokher* (1517) and *Masoyres hamasoyres* (1538). Almost in passing, we are told that this same Elye Bokher also penned Yiddish romances in ottava rima, one of which continued to circulate in revised form well into the present century. Of course,

> It would not have occurred to Elye Bokher to compose his poetic novels in the Holy Tongue, because in the sixteenth century there were no processes in Hebrew for literary forms such as these (Shmeruk 1978: 22).

By default, as it were, Yiddish inherits the entire domain of secular poetry and bellestristic narrative!

Shmeruk's smile and wink were long in coming: with barely a lapse in decorum, he unmasks his argument (if not himself) in all its subversive maximalism. Yiddish literature only fills the gap in the Jewish intralinguistic polysystem; that gap is Literature in any modern sense of the word.

IV

From Yekhiyel-Mikhl Epshteyn to Chone Shmeruk would not appear to be so very great a distance, at least as regards strategies of vertical legitimation. As I have attempted to demonstrate, both the substance and—especially—the disingenuousness of their arguments bear more than casual resemblance to one another. Yet one must not mistake the persistence of the past for its presence, or what appears to be cultural continuity for the absence of change. "A synchronic state of culture," Juri Lotman reminds us, "may include its diachrony and the active reproduction of 'old' texts" (1975: 14). For what must have been central in late seventeenth century Frankfurt is, without a doubt, peripheral in late twentieth century North America: the producers and consumers of Yiddish literature take its existence as a nonproblematic given.

REFERENCES

BAUMGARTEN, M. 1980 *City Scriptures: Modern Jewish Writing.* Harvard University Press, Cambridge, MA.

BOKHER, E. 1949 *Poetishe shafungen in yidish.* Vol I, *Bove dantona* (Isny, 1541). Joffe, A. (ed.) Judah A. Joffe Publication Committee, New York.

BLOOM, H. 1975 *A Map of Misreading.* Oxford University Press, Oxford.

CURTIUS, E. R. 1948 *Europäische Literatur and lateinisches Mittelalter.* Francke, Bern.

ELIOT, T. S. 1972 Tradition and the individual talent [1919]. In *Selected Essays.* Faber and Faber: London.

EVEN-ZOHAR, I. 1978a The function of the polysystem in the history of literature. *Papers in Historical Poetics.* Porter Institute for Poetics and Semiotics, Tel Aviv. 11–13.

EVEN-ZOHAR, I. 1978b The polysystem hypothesis revisited. *Papers in Historical Poetics.* Porter Institute for Poetics and Semiotics, Tel Aviv. 28–35.

EVEN-ZOHAR, I. and SHMERUK, C. 1981 Lashon 'otentit, mesirat dibur 'otentit: ivrit veyidish. *Hasifrut* **30–31**, 82–97.

FERTIG, S. and FISHMAN, J. A. 1969 Some Measures of the Interaction between Language, Domain, and Semantic Dimension in Bilinguals. *Modern Language Journal* **52**, 244–249.

FISHMAN, J. A. 1966 Bilingualism with and without diglossia; diglossia with and without bilingualism. *Journal of Social Issues* **2**, 29–38.

FISHMAN, J. A. (ed.) 1972 *Advances in the Sociology of Language.* Vol. II. Mouton, The Hague.

GOLDSMITH, E. S. 1976 *Architects of Yiddishism at the Beginning of the Twentieth Century: A Study in Jewish Cultural History.* Fairleigh Dickinson University Press, Rutherford, NJ.

HERRNSTEIN SMITH, B. 1978 *On the Margins of Discourse: The Relation of Literature to Language.* University of Chicago Press, Chicago.

HERZFELD, M. 1982 *Ours Once More: Folklore, Ideology, and the Making of Modern Greece.* University of Texas Press, Austin.

HOWE, I. and GREENBERG, E. (eds.) 1972 *Voices from the Yiddish: Essays, Memoirs, Diaries.* University of Michigan Press, Ann Arbor.

JOFFE, J. A. 1949 Elye Bokher: Der mentsh un der kinstler. In Elye Bokher, 1949, 7–32.

LIPTZIN, S. 1963 *The Flowering of Yiddish Literature.* Yoseloff, New York.

LIPTZIN, S. 1970 *The Maturing of Yiddish Literature.* Jonathan David, New York.

MACAULAY, R. K. S. 1965 Negative Prestige, Linguistic Insecurity and Linguistic Self-Hatred In *Lingua* **36**, 147–61.

MILLER, D. N. 1974 *Di yunge:* The Education of An Audience. Paper presented to the 1974 annual meeting of the Modern Language Association of America.

MIRON, D. 1973 *A Traveler Disguised: The Rise of Yiddish Literature.* Schocken, New York.

NOHRNBERG, J. 1974 On literature and the Bible. *Centrum* **2**, 16–17.

POOL, J. 1972 National development and language diversity. In Fishman, 1972, pp. 213–230.

PRILUTSKI, N. 1932 Vi azoy di rusishe tsenzur hot gebalbatevet in der 'Bobe-mayse'. *Yivo-bleter* **4–5**, 354–370.

PYEKAZH, M. 1964 Vegn yidishizm in sof fun 17tn yorhundert un der ershter helft fun 18tn yorhundert. *Di goldene keyt* **49**, 168–180.

REMINIK, H. 1938 Sholem-Aleykhem in kamf far realizm in di 80er yorn. *Shtern: Literarish-kinstlerisher un politish-visnshaftlekher khoydesh-zhurnal* **5–6**, 122–148.

ROSKIES, D. G. 1979 The medium and message of the Maskilic Chapbook. *Jewish Social Studies* **41**, 275–290.

SCHOLEM, G. 1963 Tradition und Kommentar als religiöse Kategorien im Judentum. *Der Mensch, Führer und Geführter im Werk* [= *Eranos-Jahrbuch, 1962*]. Rhein-Verlag, Zürich.

SCHOLEM, G. 1966 Tradition and commentary as religious categories in Judaism. *Judaism* **1**, 26–27. [Trans. (rev.) by Henry Schwarzschild of Scholem 1963.]

SHMERUK, C. 1978 *Sifrut yidish: Prakim le-toldoteha.* Porter Institute for Poetics and Semiotics, Tel Aviv.

SHTIF, N. 1924 Ditrikh fun Bern: Yidishkayt un veltlekhkayt in der alter yidisher literatur. *Yidishe filologye* **1**, 1–11, 112–122.

SPITZER, L. 1948 Muttersprache und Muttererziehung. In *Essays in Historical Semantics.* Vanni, New York.

TSINBERG, Y. 1928 Der kamf far yidish in der altyidisher literatur. *Filologishe shriftn* **2**, cols. 69–106.

WEINREICH, M. 1972 Internal bilingualism in Ashkenaz. Dawidowicz, L. S. (trans), in Howe, 1972, pp. 279–288.

WEINREICH, M. 1973 Der nomen yidish. In *Geshikhte fun der yidisher shprakh: bagrifn, faktn, metodn.* Vol. I, pp. 321–333. Yivo Institute for Jewish Research, New York.

WILLIAMS, R. 1973 Base and superstructure in Marxist critical theory. *New Left Review* **82**, 8.

YUDKIN, L. I. 1982 *Jewish Writing and Identity in the Twentieth Century.* Croom Helm, London.

Language & Communication, Vol. 7, Supplement, pp. 105–109, 1987.
Printed in Great Britain.

0271-5309/87 $3.00 + .00
Pergamon Journals Ltd.

POSTWAR SOVIET THEORIES ON THE ORIGINS OF YIDDISH

WOLF MOSKOVICH

Hebrew University of Jerusalem

Soviet sociolinguistics recently turned its attention to the origins of Yiddish with paradoxical results. It made the "discovery" that Yiddish is neither a Jewish language, nor a language at all, but a "judaized jargon of German". This "discovery" has been voiced by a number of authors in different places and is connected with attempts to prove that Jews do not constitute a separate nation. Some of these authors are well known researchers and their "discovery" has been published in books in many thousands of copies. The paradox is that Yiddish is a politically recognized language in the USSR, and a Yiddish periodical *Sovetish heymland* as well as books in Yiddish are published in the USSR; moreover, though the Yiddish language has not been researched recently in mainstream Soviet linguistic publications, it has status in Soviet linguistic circles. In fact, a comprehensive Russian-Yiddish dictionary prepared forty years ago was published in an updated version in Moscow in 1984 (see Moskovich 1984).

The first modern Soviet "discoverer" of the non-Jewish character of Yiddish was apparently Professor I. Shmidt, who noticed in 1970 that French historian Joseph Ernest Renan (1887-93) had considered Yiddish to be a ghetto language, i.e. a non-Jewish language (citations from Shmidt's article, which appeared in the provincial Far Eastern *Sovetskij Saxalin,* are given in Shapiro 1970).

Developing the idea, Shmidt regards modern Yiddish as "a jargon of the German language . . . an undeveloped German of the 10–12th centuries". Trying to prove that Soviet Jews have nothing in common with the rest of the Jewish people. Shmidt writes that "the mother tongue of the Russian Jews is Russian. Our parents, we ourselves, our children and grandchildren were educated, spoke and worked in Russian". Shmidt's "discovery" elicited a protest from J. Grinshteyn, an ordinary Soviet Jew (a labourer, not a professor of philology like Shmidt)—who reminds Shmidt that the mother tongue of their parents is Yiddish and not Russian. In his turn, Shmidt accuses Grinshteyn of denying the irrefutable fact that Russian is the only mother tongue of Russian Jews and thereby defending the idea that "a jargon borrowed in Germany in the 12th century is dearer to Russian Jews than the Russian language: it is false and it is an offence to the patriotic honour of Russian Jews". This discussion came to light after the Soviet Yiddish magazine *Sovetish heymland* published a rejoinder by Soviet Yiddish linguist M. Shapiro, who sides with Grinshteyn. Shapiro asks Shmidt the following questions: (1) Had he ever read German texts of the 10–12th centuries? (2) Had he ever read Yiddish texts? (3) Did he know that in addition to the German component Yiddish also a had a Slavic and a Hebrew component? (4) Did he realize that Yiddish phonetics was different from German? (5) Did he know that Yiddish morphology developed in a way different from German,

i.e. by losing a number of forms and by creating new ones? (6) Did he realize that from the middle of the 19th century Yiddish had become a highly developed literary language in which world famous works were written? (Shapiro 1970: 138–140).

Subsequent protagonists of Shmidt's views who did not read Shmidt's revelations published in the Soviet provincial press in Russian and who could not read the Yiddish article in *Sovetish heymland,* apparently had to rely on some older sources. For example, in 1977 Begun in his widely publicized book on Zionism called Yiddish "this Jewish-German jargon which appeared in the Middle Ages", with the following footnote: "Calling the Yiddish vernacular a jargon does not imply any contempt. It only reflects such characteristic features as the distortion of the German word stock, germanicization of Hebrew words, numerous loan words from Slavic and other languages, instability of grammar, existence of various dialects, etc." (1977: 87). An important turning point in the further development of this idea was the publication of the book *The Class Essence of Zionism* by L. A. Korneev in 1982. Korneev is a bona fide Soviet orientalist. He is a senior research worker at the Institute of Asia and Africa at the Academy of Sciences of the USSR, a corresponding member of the Malagasy Academy of Sciences and author of over one hundred publications. The most prominent of his linguistic works are the Malagasy-Russian and Russian-Malagasy dictionaries (Milliband 1975: 272). When Malagasy studies appeared to be too narrow a field for him, he started moonlighting as a specialist on the Jewish question. Korneev has now become one of the leading Soviet experts on the subject by producing dozens of papers for the Soviet mass media based on an extensive file of "facts" about Jews and Zionism.

Korneev has no doubt that Yiddish is a German jargon and in no case a Jewish national language. As proof, he notes that Engels considered Yiddish to be "German distorted beyond recognition" and Lenin always called Yiddish a jargon. Modern Soviet scholars, Jews by origin, allegedly call Yiddish a jargon too (Korneev 1982: 35). Korneev's "unique" contribution is his theory of the conspiratorial origin of Yiddish as a secret jargon. He writes: "The origin of 'Jewish languages', such as Yiddish, Ladino, the jargon of the Bukharian Jews, through borrowing and altering the language of the country of residence, can be explained first of all by the inclination of the Jewish ruling circle to achieve maximal isolation from the local population; moreover, speaking a jargon (in additon to the national language of the country of residence) could impart additional advantages in commerce and machinations of all kinds" (Korneev 1982: 36).

Korneev's viewpoint is hardly original. It finds expression in a collection of documents on the early history of the Soviet KGB from which Korneev cites the following passage: "In the organization of economic sabotage against the young Soviet state the big Jewish businessmen used the ancient Bukharian Jewish language 'Reshi' [sic!] as a specific secret code" (Iz istorii 1958: 22). As an orientalist, Korneev should have known that no such language ever existed, and that Jews wrote Judeo-Tadjik in a type of Hebrew script called Rashi. The use of this script was a normal practice in various Jewish communities and there was nothing secret about it. In order to explain how the Jewish ruling circle could succeed in implanting Yiddish as a secret jargon without the participation of the whole Jewish community Korneev puts forward the following suggestions. Though the majority of the Jewish community consisted of exploited poor people, craftsmen, servants, etc., a great part of them, he maintains, participated in auxiliary roles in the execution of trade, usury and other illicit operations of the Jewish ruling circle. "The mercenary element considerably increased in the Jewish communities of the Middle Ages" (Korneev 1982:

9–10). He proceeds to argue that bound together by their thirst for profit, the Jews as a community of tradesmen, middlemen and moneylenders, created Yiddish as a secret jargon. Korneev explains that "similar practices (or creating secret jargons) are characteristic of mercenary and middlemen organizations among other ethnic groups" (Korneev 1982: 36).

Korneev is unhappy that publications in Yiddish still appear in the USSR. In his afterword to a book on Jewish emigration from the USSR he writes: "The great attention given by the Soviet authorities to the publishing of works in Yiddish is remarkable, given that only a negligible part of the Jewish population of our country (only 17.7%) read and speak it. Yiddish, a Judaized dialect of the German language, which was called by Engels and Lenin a jargon, did not spread widely in foreign countries. Nevertheless, a daily newspaper, *Birobidzhaner shtern* is published in the USSR . . ." (Korneev 1982: 257).

Korneev's views have gained wide currency and acclaim among Soviet colleagues who write on the Jewish question. The following citation from Doev (1983: 26) shows this clearly: "Researchers explain the origin of jargon languages thorough borrowing and changing the language of the country or residence, first, by the desire of the Jewish ruling circle to be maximally isolated from the local population, and second, by the desire to acquire additional advantages in commerce and illicit machinations of all kinds" (citing Korneev 1982: 36).

The recent wave of Soviet publications depicting Yiddish as a jargon of German is an atavistic revival of some ideas prevalent in the nineteenth century. The hostile attitude toward Yiddish was initiated by the Haskalah (Jewish Enlightenment) movement of the eighteenth and nineteenth centuries which advocated the assimilation of Jews. It was taken up afterwards by the champions of modern Hebrew nationalism. S. A. Birnbaum gives the following concise description of this attitude: "Many of the contentions and criticisms that had been levelled against the great European languages before they received recognition and acceptance among their own peoples were now flung against Yiddish by its antagonists from both camps, assimilationists and Hebrew nationalists. Let us enumerate some of them. Yiddish was referred to comtemptuously as 'jargon', as a patchwork of various languages. Critics said that it is no language at all, since it has no grammar; it is only corrupt German; it is merely a dialect of German; it is not the language of education and scholarship; it is incapable of expressing the high flight of thought; it sounds ugly; it is doomed to extinction; it is a symbol of national slavery; it is basically un-Jewish; it is not a language for there is not one nation on earth speaking Yiddish" (Birnbaum 1979: 37). In addition, the diametrically opposed camps of Jewish assimilationists and Hebrew nationalists both grounded their hostility to Yiddish on the fact that the Yiddish language lacked the political recognition that the German language enjoyed, and hence had little prestige both among native speakers and non-native observers. Neither group attempted to explore the reasons why Yiddish had developed important features distinguishing it (in its native component) from German (see on this Wexler 1981: 103).

A negative attitude to Yiddish was expressed even by those non-Jews who worked for the emancipation and assimilation of Jews. Gregoire, an active proponent of the emancipation of the Jews during the period of the French Revolution, called in 1789 for the eradication of "that type of slang, that Teutonic-Hebraic-rabbinic jargon used by German Jews, which only serves to deepen ignorance and to mask trickery" (1789: 160–1). Many Russian publications of the nineteenth century also espoused these negative views toward Yiddish. Begun and Korneev took their information from the first edition of the

encyclopedia of Brokgaus and Efron which in 1894 described Yiddish as a Jewish-German dialect (jargon) which constituted a distortion of German and has "an unstable intricate grammar which does not lend itself to scholarly study" (Brokgaus and Efron 1894, XIA: 485).

The negative attitude to Yiddish only changed at the beginning of the twentieth century when Yiddish became a universally accepted language of culture among Jews in Eastern Europe, following the appearance of the literary classics of Mendele Moykher Sforim, Y. L. Peretz and Sholem Aleichem. For example, the second edition of Brokgaus and Efron's encyclopedia gives an extremely well balanced description of the Yiddish language emphasizing its differences vis-à-vis German, the simplicity of its grammar in comparison with German, its richness, suppleness of expression and the progress of its scholarly study (1906–1916: XVII: 250–1). In fact, an objective characterization of Yiddish is given in all three editions of the *Great Soviet Encyclopedia* (*BSE* 1, XXIV: 160–3; XXVII: 477; *BSE* 2, XVII: 340; *BSE* 3, X: 114–5). The first edition of the *BSE* recommended not calling Yiddish a jargon at all (*BSE* 1, XXVII: 477), as "it is the language of the overwhelming majority of Jews which has long been a language of culture and literature" (*BSE* 1, XXIV: 160). Two excellent detailed essays on Yiddish were published in the last twenty years in Russian by the Soviet Jewish scholar Elye Falkovich (1966; 1984). In other Soviet publications, Yiddish is sometimes referred to as "a common European Jewish language" possessing a rich literature (Tokarev 1964: 903).

Alongside this objective Soviet scholarship, authors like Shmidt, Begun and Korneev continue to revive obsolete ideas about the origin and nature of Yiddish. Time alone will tell whether this recent trend in Soviet sociolinguistics will be a passing phenomenon (see also Moskovich 1986).

REFERENCES

BEGUN, V. 1977 *Vtorzhenie bez oruzhija*. Moscow.

BIRNBAUM, S. A. 1979 *Yiddish. A Survey and a Grammar*. University of Toronto, Toronto, and University of Manchester, Manchester.

BROKGAUS, R. A. and EFRON, A. I. 1894 *Enciklopedicheskij slovar'*, Vol. XIA. St. Petersburg.

BROKGAUS, R. A. and EFRON, A. I. 1906–16 *Novyj enciklopedicheskij slovar'*. St. Petersburg.

BSE 1 1932 *Bol'shaja sovetskaja enciklopedija*, XXIV ed, Vol. 1st. Moscow.

BSE 2 1952 *Bol'shaja sovetskaja enciklopedija*, 2nd ed, Vol. XVII. Moscow.

BSE 3 1972 *Bol'shaja sovetskaja enciklopedija*, 3rd ed, Vol. X. Moscow.

DOEV, A. B. 1983 *Sovremennyj iudaizm i sionizm*. Frunze.

FALKOVICH, E. M. 1966 Idish. *Jazyki narodov SSSR* I, 599–629.

FALKOVICH, E. M. 1984 O jazyke idish. *Russko-evrejskij (idish) slovar'*, Moscow, 666–720.

GREGOIRE, H. E. A. 1789 *Essai sur la régénération physique, morale et politique des Juifs*. Metz.

IZ ISTORII 1958 *Iz istorii Vserossijskoj Chrezvychajnoj Komissii 1917–1921. Sbornik dokumentov*. Moscow.

KORNEEV, L. A. 1981 Chad chuzhbiny. In Tarasov, V. N., *Posidi na kamne u dorogi . . .* Novosibirsk.

KORNEEV, L. A. 1982 *Klassovaja sushchnost' sioniszma*. Kiev.

MILLIBAND, S. D. 1975 *Bibliograficheskij slovar' sovetskix vostokovedov*. Moscow.

MOSKOVICH, W. 1984 An important event in Soviet Yiddish cultural life: the new Russian–Yiddish dictionary. *Soviet Jewish Affairs* **14**, (3), 31–49.

MOSKOVICH, W. 1986 Recent sociolinguistic theories on Yiddish in the USSR. In Wexler, P., Borg, A. and Somekh, S. (eds.) *Studia Linguistica et Orientalia Memorial Haim Blanc Dedicata*. Otto Harrassowitz, Wiesbaden.

RENAN, J. E. 1887–93 *Histoire du peuple d'Israël*. Vols. 1–5. Paris.

SHAPIRO, M. 1970 A por bamerkungen tsu eynem a shtrayt. *Soviet heymland* **9**, 138–140.

TOKAREV, S. A. (ed.) 1964 *Narody zarubezhoj Evropy,* Vol. I. Moscow.

WEXLER, P. 1981 Jewish Interlinguistics: Facts and Conceptual Framework. *Language* **57** (1), 99–149.

Language & Communication, Vol. 7, Supplement, pp. 111–126, 1987.
Printed in Great Britain.

0271-5309/87 $3.00 + .00
Pergamon Journals Ltd.

THE ORIGINS OF YIDDISH PRINTING

MOSHE N. ROSENFELD

Rose Chemicals Ltd. and Yesodey Hatorah School, London

Systematic printing of Jewish books began in Italy in the second half of the fifteenth century. It took another seventy years for Yiddish books to emerge from the press. This paper seeks to highlight the typographic and bibliographic aspects of these earliest Yiddish works— the Yiddish incunables. A concise bibliography of Yiddish printing until 1558 is presented.

To facilitate examination of the first Yiddish printed texts, a bibliographical listing must be prepared. Only recently have publications of this nature appeared (Shmeruk 1981 and 1982), which, though not complete, lay a foundation for cataloguing Yiddish prints in Poland and Italy until the middle of the seventeenth century. A similar list for Yiddish books produced in Germanic lands does not exist to my knowledge. I felt it would be beneficial to the Yiddish scholar to obtain a comprehensive presentation of the earliest stages of Yiddish printing and have incorporated recorded and unrecorded material in chronological order. This listing is split into two parts, the confirmed and the speculative issues.

It seems that it took a certain amount of courage to print Yiddish, the art of printing referred to as *Mlekhes hakoydesh* 'the Holy Task', whereas Yiddish remained the language for everyday purpose. Indeed, among the Hebrew prints of early times we find almost exclusively Bible editions, Halachic texts and Liturgy. A short Yiddish text was printed for the first time at the end of the 1526 Prague Passover Haggada, utilizing the same letters as some of the other texts in this book. We must assume, that this text, a song, had originally been composed in Yiddish and its popularity made its inclusion a natural addition to the Haggada.

The cradle of Yiddish printing was Cracow. Here three brothers, Samuel, Asher and Eljakim, the sons of Chaim Helic, made an appearance in the early 1530s. Their first Yiddish work must be seen as a compromise, being a Hebrew-Yiddish Lexicon of the Bible. This book, *Merkeves hamishne,* also known as *Seyfer Rebi Anshl* (= No. 1 in the appended Bibliography) is accepted as the earliest Yiddish book, though it bears no date (see Fig. 1). It became very popular among Gentiles, which accounts for its survival in reasonable numbers. This was not the fate of some ethical tracts which they printed in Yiddish (Nos. 2 & 3, see Fig. 2). Around the year 1536, however, the brothers split up, after converting to Christianity. The strongly religious community of Cracow banned all their books, a decision reinforced by the production of the New Testament in Yiddish (No. 4) by Paul (= Asher ?) Helic. It was he who published a pamphlet *Elemental oder Lesebüchlein* (No. 9) in the village Hundsfeld near Breslau. Then we lose his track. It is noteworthy that Samuel Helic returned to the faith of his fathers and showed his repentance on the title of a Bible he printed in Constantinople in 1553/4.

Fig. 1. First page of *Merkeves Hamishne* (No. 1) (reduced).

No further evidence of Yiddish printing in Poland has been recorded until the year 1571.

The next products of Yiddish printing we owe to the diligence and perseverance of a Gentile, the pastor Paulus Fagius. This man arrived in Isny in 1538 and seems to have been obsessed with the idea of establishing a Hebrew printing press. His object was the furthering of Hebrew as a language amongst his colleagues. Ambrosius Blaurer writes on October 28, 1539 to his brother Thomas:

> Fagius von Isny ist hier [Augsburg], er richtet mit Erfolg eine hebräische Druckerei ein mit Hilfe unseres Bufflers.

What was the purpose of Fagius' trip to Augsburg? The only person of interest to Fagius, who was present in Augsburg in late 1539, was Chaim Schachor, the only Jewish printer in Germany at the time (Rosenfeld 1985: 8). Did Fagius tempt Schachor with a job as Hebrew printer in Isny? We have no proof for this assumption, though we find in 'Biberacher Chronik' the following cynical note:

> Die Gebrüder Buffler hatten etliche gelehrte Juden aus *deutschen* und *welschen* Landen nach Isny beschrieben, ihnen drei Häuser eingeräumt, und von denselben die hebräische Bibel vertiren (verdeutschen ?) zu lassen vermeint . . . doch die Juden waren nicht kontent, sondern wollten mehr Geld haben (Giefel: 1884, 125–6).

לוטן דעת כֿל טוּוי הֿאָרֶץ ' וָּדְרִי נָֿדָר עֿווּדִי פרן '
רֵוּשׁיֵ לֿשַבַֿטִיֵ וּנְקִנָת קְדֵמִי דֿוד הַקָּטֿוּן וּמֿאֿחֿיו
הַכֿהֿנֵ הֿוּבְּאֵ שֵני סַפֿרִים הֿוּעֿתְקֿוּ הֿלֿשׁוּ עָֿבֿרִי
לֿשׁוּ וֵישׁוּכֿנֵ לֿתֿווֹת צֶֿהֿרֵת נשׁים נֿדֵה חֿלֵה הֿדֵיק'
והֿוּשׁמֵ לֿהֿזֵי שֶׁהֿווֹחֵד תֵיקַן הֿגָּאֿוֶ וֹנֵהֿדֵר יוֹדֵֵ
מֿינֵקֵ זֿל   והֿשׁיֵי תֵיקַן הֿגֿאֿוֶ וֹנֵהֿדֵר שֶׁתֿווֹאֵל מ ק' ק'
וֹוִרהֿס יֵ' וֹרֵיִתֵי בֿשׁנֵיהֿתֵ שֿוּה שֿגֵֿילֿה זֶה לֿז נֿוֹה
זֶה וֹהֶה שֶׁגֵֿילֿה זֶה לֿז נֿוֹלֿה זֶה אֿווֹרֵתֵי כֿדֵי וֹזֿכֿה בֿהֵ
רֿבֵיֵ לֿחֿבֿרֵת יֿחֵד לֿהֿיֿוֹת שֿנֵיהֿתֵ הֿלֿוֹיֵֵ בֿיד כֿל
אֿחֵד וֹאֿחֵד   וֹהֿתֿפֿלֿה לֿהֿשֵׁם יֿ' לֿהֿצֵילֿנֵי הֿשֵׁ וֹוֹת
                  וֹהֿהֿגֵֿה וֹהֿתֿחֿיֵל וֹהֿווֹוֵר '

יהֿי שֵׁם יֿ מֿבֿוֹרֵך מֿעֿתֿה וֹעֿד עֿוֹלֵם '   וֹאֿשֵׁר
קֿדֵֿשׁנֵ בֿמֿצֿווֹתֿיו ' וֹהֿבֵֿדֵילֿנֵ מֵן הֿעֿווֹיֵם ' וֹגֵֿוֹ שׁוֹן
לֿהֿטֿוֹז בֿשׁוֹם טֿוֹמֿאֵה   אֿך הֿיֿה בֿטֿהֿרֿה וֹבֿקֿדֵֿשׁה
שֿנֵֿוֹוֹר קֿדֵֿשׁיֵ תֿהֵיו כֿי קֿדֿוֹשׁ אֿנֵי י '   נֿט יֵת'
זֵי וֵיֿוֹבֵט אֿווֹוֵמֿר אֿוֹנֿ' אֵיבֵיק דֵשׁ מֿר הֿ:וֹ נֿ:ֿט נֿהֵיוֹיֵקֿט
אֿוֹנֵשׁ מֵיוֹ זֵייֵ נֿיבֿוֹטֵ   אֿוֹנֿ' הֿוֹט אֿב נֵ:שׁ:ֿיֵיֵד אֿוֹנ:ֿשׁ
בֵיֵ דֵעֵ בֿ:וֹיֿקֿרֵ   אֿוֹנֿ' הֿוֹט וֿבֿוֹטֵ אֿוֹנֵשׁ גֿוֹ נֵיטֵ וֵר
גֿוֹנֿדֵרֵינֵיֵֿ אֵיֵ קֵיֿנֵרֿלֿייֵ אֿ:גֿ:רֵיֿנֵיֵקֿייֵט גֿוֹרֵט גֿוֹ זֵיֵ
רֵיֵ אֿוֹנֿ' הֵיֵלֵיֵ ,   אֿ:נֵ דֿ:וֹ אֵיֵד גֿוֹוֹרֵ נֿ:וֹטֵ:וֹנ:ֿשׁ אֿ:יֵ דֵעֵר
תֿוֹרֿה הֿיֵיֵלֵיק גֿוֹוֹט אֿ:יֵר זֵייֵ וֹוֹטֵ
                  הֿיֵוֹוֹיֵק בֵיֵ אֵיֵֿ גֿ:וֹטֵיֿת' ,

Fig. 2. *Azhoras noshim* (No. 3) (reduced).

Fagius was not disheartened. It was no other than Elijah ben Asher Ha-Levi, better known as Elijah Levita among Christians and Elye Bokher among Jews, who heeded his call, and joined him in Isny.

Levita hailed from Neustadt an der Aisch and came to Italy sometime after 1496. He was keen on writing and publishing and from the introduction to his *Bovo bukh,* Isny 1541, we learn:

es is nun 34 yor, das ikh fun aanem velsh bukh hon gemakht.

This puts the date of composition (or rather translation) back to 1507, whilst he resided in Padua. A number of Yiddish works must have been prepared by him in this period, which had not yet been printed.

Das mir etlekhe frouen fir ibl habn, worum ikh nit aakh für zey druk, mayner taytsh bikher eyn shtik.

Thus sounds his apology for printing the *Bovo bukh.* A historic event is of importance here. Levita laments the loss of *all* his possessions (*Meturgemon,* Isny 1541), when the troops of Charles V capture Rome:

(translated) and in the year 1527 the city was conquered and all my books were taken from me, I was left penniless.

Is it therefore not a possibility that the *Bovo bukh* was reprinted from the questionable Pesaro 1518 edition, a copy of which was more likely to have survived than his original manuscript? Too little attention has been paid to the presence of Levita's grandsons in Isny in 1541. Joseph and Elijah were the sons of Rabbi Isaac Böhmen of Rome, whose wife Hanna was Levita's daughter. Both converted at an unknown date to Christianity, but stayed with the printing profession. There is no documented evidence of any activity on their part until their reappearance in Italy in 1559. No doubt, they were not in a hurry to leave Germany and indicated their plans to print further Yiddish works. They may have

been involved in the production of the *Seyfer mides* (No. 7), which was printed without mention of personnel. The omission of Fagius' name makes Isny as actual printing place somewhat dubious. The Yiddish type, however, is identical with the fount used in *Shemous devorim* (No. 6), which carries a Latin preface by Fagius. Another Yiddish work, *Shir hayikhud* (No. 8) was wrongly ascribed to Isny (Steinschneider p. 504/3314; Cowley 360; Yiddish Bib. Microfiche Catalogue), as is evident by types and watermark. A proper designation of this item will be the subject of further research.

The scene of activity now shifts to Konstanz, a small town forty miles from Isny. Levita had returned to Italy in 1541, plagued by the cold weather, the spreading of the pestilence and a general feeling of homesickness. There are indications that he did not see the *Bovo bukh* (No. 5) completed. Fagius had accepted a position in Strassburg, following the death of his colleague Wolfgang Capito, but was given leave in late 1542 to sort out matters in Konstanz. Here a Jewish convert, Michael Adam, assisted him with his printing venture. He translated the first four chapters of Genesis into Yiddish, and edited this book with the preface from Anshl's *Merkeves hamishne* (No. 10, see Fig 3). This work was then extended to comprise the complete Pentateuch, Megillot and Haftaroth in Yiddish only.

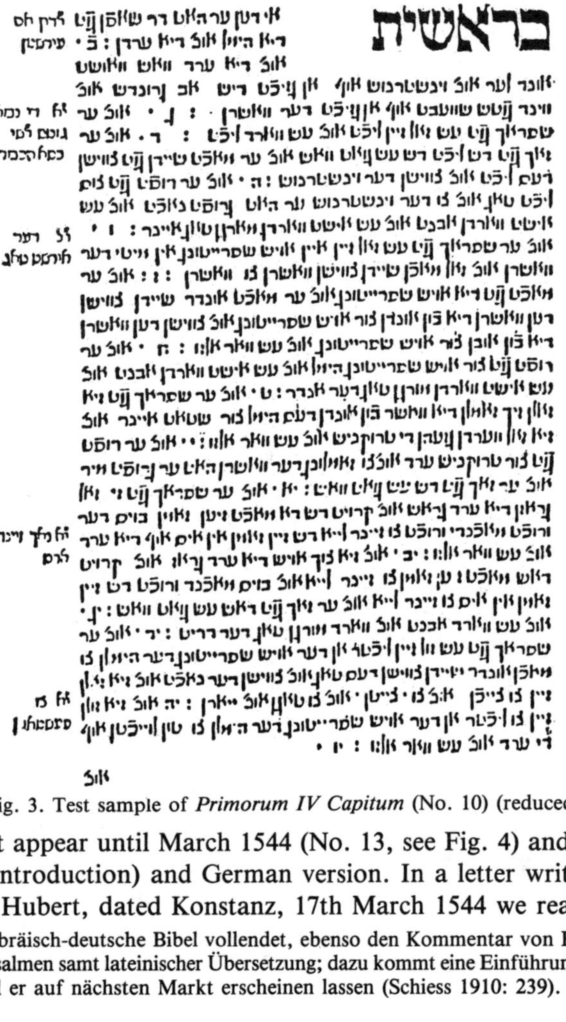

בראשית

Fig. 3. Test sample of *Primorum IV Capitum* (No. 10) (reduced).

The volume did not appear until March 1544 (No. 13, see Fig. 4) and exists in a Jewish (Hebrew title and introduction) and German version. In a letter written by Ambrosius Blaurer to Konrad Hubert, dated Konstanz, 17th March 1544 we read:

> Fagius hat die hebräisch-deutsche Bibel vollendet, ebenso den Kommentar von Rabbi David Kimchi zu den ersten zehn Psalmen samt lateinischer Übersetzung; dazu kommt eine Einführung in die heilige Sprache. Diese Bücher will er auf nächsten Markt erscheinen lassen (Schiess 1910: 239).

Fig. 4. Test sample of Pentateuch (No. 13) (reduced).

This clearly puts the printing date of Adam's Yiddish Pentateuch before that of Paulus Aemilius.

Aemilius was also a Jewish convert. He was active in Augsburg, where he printed the *Melokhim bukh* and *Shmuel bukh* (Nos. 11 & 12) and copied Fagius' venture of producing a Yiddish Pentateuch (Nos. 14 & 15, see Fig. 5) for the use of Jews and Gentiles (Rosenfeld 1985: 9 ff.). The fact that the market was able to absorb two editions in the same year speaks for the demand for Yiddish printed material.

Whether Adam or Aemilius were the only converts responsible for Bible translations is not certain. Another Swiss ex-Jew, Leo Jud by name, had been active in Zürich and later in Augsburg for some time. Perles (1884: 164–165) suspects he is identical with Adam. From a letter written in Konstanz by Ambrosius Blaurer, we know, however, that Leo Jud died June 19, 1542 (Schiess 1910: 129), whilst Michael Adam was still active in 1546. His activity as Bible translator is documented by Rosenfeld (1985: 30) and Schiess (1910: 83).

It is only now, towards the end of 1544, that Jewish printers begin to produce Yiddish works solely for consumption by Jews. Khayim ben Dovid Shokhor, after fifteen years of printing, finally turned to a Yiddish work. Having left Augsburg for Ichenhausen, a village on the way to Ulm, he printed a Yiddish prayer book jointly with his son Isaac and his son in law Yosef bar Yokor (No. 16, see Fig. 6). He justifies his project by the neccessity to understand the daily prayer:

. . . di in loshen hakoudesh veln orn, un farshteyn keyn vort . . .

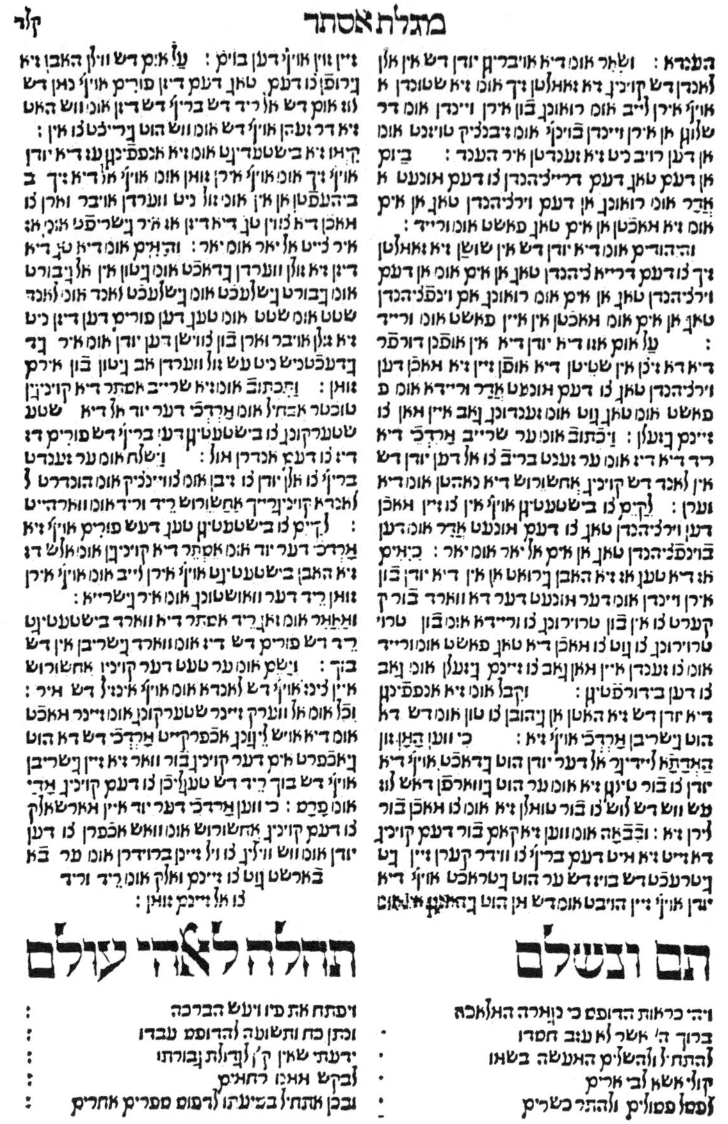

מגלת אסתר   קלו׳

[Two columns of Old Yiddish (Rashi script) text, here in reading order right-to-left:]

בגמרא : ושאר אומ דיא אויבריגן יודן דש אין אלן לאנדן דש קוניג אחשורוש זיך אלזו שטונדן א אונ׳ אירן לייב אום רואונג בון אירן וינדן אונ׳ דר שלוגן אן אירן וויגדן בויכן׳ אונ׳ בנבליק טויגנט אומ אן דען רויב ניט זיא זענדרטן איר העגד : ביום אן דעם טאג דער דרייצהנדן צו דעם אונעטס א אחר אונ׳ רואונ׳ אן דעם ויר צהנדן טאג אן אים אום זיא אויבר מאכטן אן אים טאן באשט אומוריד :

והיהודים אונ׳ דיא יודן דש אין שושן זיא זאמלטן זיך צו דעם דרייא צהנדן טאן אן אים אונ׳ אן דעם ויר צהנדן טאן אן אים אום רואונג אסר זינבצהנדן טאן אן אים אום מאכטן אין אין באשט אונ׳ וריד : על אום אונ׳ דיא יודן דיא אין אופן זין זיא אוכן דען ורלצהנדן טאן צו דעם אונגעט אחר ורידא אום ם באשט אונ׳ טאן ועט אונ׳ זענדרונג ואב אין אן לו זיגק בועלן : וכתוב אומ׳ אור שרייב מרדכי דיא ריד דיא אונ׳ ער זעגט בריב לו אל דען יודן דש אין לאנד דש קוניג אחשורוש דיא נאהטן אונ׳ ורן ערן : לקים לו בישטעטן אונ׳ אן לו זין אאכן דען זי ורלצהנדן טאן צו דעם אונגנט אחר אונ׳ דען בונבצהנדן טאן אן אים אל איר יאר אונ׳ יאר : כימים אז דיא טעג אן זיא האבן רואט אן אין דיא יודן בון אירן וינדן אונ׳ דער אונגנט דער דא ווארד בוריך קערט לו אין ורוידונג לו וריידא אונ׳ בון טרוירונג לו גוט לו אין מאכן דיא טאן באשט אומורידד אוגן לו זענדרן אין׳ אן לו זינק בועלן אונפ׳ ואב לו דען בדרולטיגן : וקבל אונ׳ זיא אנפשימן דיא יודן דש זיא האטן אן גהובן לו טון אונ׳רד דא הוט גשריבן מרדכי צו אין זיא : כי המן זון הגדתא לידרי׳ אל דער יודן הוט בדאכט אויף דיא יודן לו בור טיגן זיא אונ׳ ער הוט גוואלן זיא אונ׳ לו האבן בור לין זיא : ובבאה אונ׳ אום זיא ורקאם זיא צו דעם קעגן זין הוט גשאגט מיט דעם בויך דא אר ווידר קער לו וודי קעטן זיין׳ זין ועט בטרעגבטראש בויד דש ער הוט בטראכט אויף דיא יודן אויף זין היובט אומדש דא אין הוט גהאננא אובן אן בוים :

[Left column:]

זין זין אויף דען בוים : על אום דש וועון האבו זיא גרופין לו דעם טאן דען דען בורים אונ׳ נאן דש לו אום דש אל ויר דש בריף דש דין אונ׳וש האט ... זיא דר זעה׳ און׳ דש אומ׳וש הוט בריבטו׳ אן : קיאו זיא בישטעדיגט אומ זיא אנפם יגן עו דיא יודן אונ׳ זיך אונ׳ אויף אירן זוון אונ׳ אומ אויף אל דיא׳ ב ביהעלמאן אן אין אובר ניט ועדרי אויבר אונ׳ לו אאכן דיא אלזון טן דיא אז איר נשריפֿט׳ אומ אז איר ליט אל יאר אומ יאר : והאימ אומ דיא אומ׳ טן דיא דין זיא אונ׳ ועררן בדאכט אומ׳בטון אין אל ביבורט אונ׳ ורטרט נשלעכט אונ׳ נשלעכט ואנד אונ׳ לאנד שטט אומ שטט אומ טען דען בורים דען יודן דין נים כ זיא גון אויובר אומ אונ׳ לו נושן דען אומ׳ איר ני בדעולטאטיש ניט עו עש זול וועדרי אב נ׳יטון לו אירק גועל : וזכתום אומ׳זיא שרי׳ אסתר לו דיא אל דיא שטע טוברר אבתי׳ אומ׳ מרדב׳ דער יוד אל די׳ שטענ שטערקונג לו בישטעט׳ינן דע׳ בריף דש בורים דו ד׳יו לו דעג אנדרן אול : וישלח אומ ער זענדרט בריף לו אלן יודן לו דיבן אומ לוויונציק אונ׳ הוגדרט ל אהרק קוניג אחשורוש אומ׳ ר׳ד׳ אומ וארהיט דיא : לקים לו בישטעטן דעם בורים אונ׳ יזא אוכ מרדב דער יוד אומ׳ אסתר דיא קוניגן אונ אלש דז זיא האבן בישטעטונ׳יט אויף לייב אורן אויף אירן זוען ריד וואושטונג אונ ארי נשריייא : ואתאמר אומ אומ׳ר׳ד אוורד דיא ווארד בישטעט׳ינט רד דש בורים דש זי דיא אומ׳וארד נשריבן אין דש בוך : וישמ אומ אונ טעט דעל קוניג אחשורוש אין ליגו אויף׳ דש ל אנדרא אומ אויף אינזל אינו׳ דש אי איר : וכל אומ אל ווערק זיינר שטערקונג אומ זינ׳ר מאכט דיא דא הוט ני אבפערט׳ין עו׳גנ אלבפרי׳ט מרדב׳ דש דא הוט אויף דש בוך ר׳ד דש טענ׳לוכן לו דעם קוניג מדי : כ ווגן מרדב דער יוד אין אנרשאלק לו דעם קוניג אחשורוש אומ וואש אכפרן לו דען יודן אומ׳וש ולינ׳ לו ול זינן בדוודרן אומ ער בא באושט נט לו זיינק אומ ו׳רד לו אל זיינכן זאמן :

תחלה לאחד עולם   הב ונשלם

וישתח את פיו וישע הברכה   ויהי כראות הדפום כי כמירה המלאכה
וכתן כח ותשובה להדפוס עבדו   ברוך ה׳ אשר לא עזב חסדו
ידעתי שאני ק׳ לעדרות בבורתו   להתתי׳ ל והשלים האעשה בשאו
לבקש אאני רואים   קול אשא ובי אדיק
ובכן אתתי׳ל בסיעתו לדפוס ספרים אחרים   אסא׳ פטוליק ולהתר כשרים

Fig. 5. Colophon of Pentateuch (No. 15) reduced.

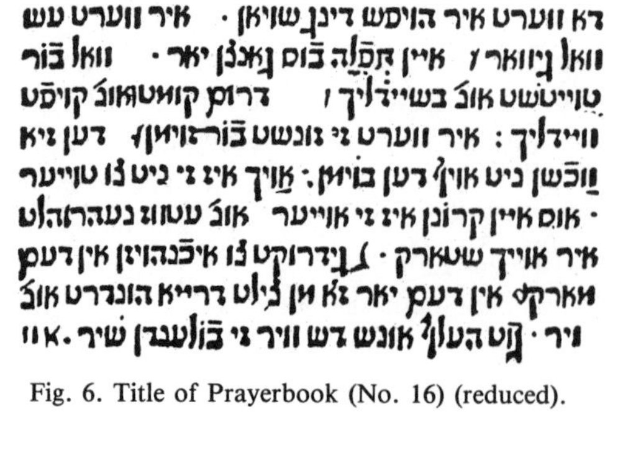

קומט הער איר ורומן ורויאן

דא ווערט איר הוישש דינג שויאן ·   איר ווערט עש
וואל נוואר ו · אין תפלה בום נאנן יאר ·   וואל בור
טווטשט אוב בשיידליך ו ·   דרוק קומטאוב קוסט
ווידליך :   איר ווערט זי זונשט בורזויאן ·   דען זיא
וואבשן ניט אוך דען בויאן · אוך איז זי ניט נו טוייער
· אום אין קרונן איז זי אויער ·   אוב עטוו נעהרהאלו
איר אויך שאארק ·   נעידרוקט נו איבנהויזן אין דעם
מארקש · אין דעם יאר זא אן גיטו דרייא הונדרט אוב
ניר · גט העלף אונש דש ווער זי בולועבן שיר · א...

Fig. 6. Title of Prayerbook (No. 16) (reduced).

יוסיפון פרק נ רעז

נאנן אונדר דעם היאל וואראוס אונ אום וויס וילן הוט ער ניט
לאסן טוברן נוט בון דעם היאל היראב אויך מיך אונ וואראוס הוט
ער ניט לאסן בלויבין אויך מיט איינם דובבשלאן אונ ער
הט נשטיט אויך וואן איך אלו נאוונדינט האב נאנן דיר אונ בוך
היא זיך בון איך בין נבארן אויבר דש מיר אונ וואראוס איז ניט
אויך נשטאנבדן וידר מיך איין אונבוויטר אונ הוט דר טרעבקט
אויך עליך אלו ער איז דר נראיט וואורהן דער נורן דיש מירס
אויבר דען וויס אנר יובה דא ער וליהן וואלט בון נו נור נוט :
אונ בוך מיא זיך נון איך בין נונאנן אויך דער ערדן אונ
וואראוס הוט דיא ערדן ניט אירן אובט אויך נשטאן בו ור שלינדן
אויך עליך ווא זיא אירן אובט הוט אויך נשטאן אונ זיא הט ור ש
שלובדן דען קרח דתן אונ אבירם דיא דא ווארן אויך נשטאנבדן
וידר משה רבינו דערדאבניט הט נטאן קיין בוים בו דען ישראל
אונ ער איז נוועין בו אינן אלו איין באטר אונ איין שטראבר :

ורא אבשלום דער ון דוד מיט וירבם באר אן איינם בוים בליבט
בעטנן אונ מיא דער יאב קואט אונ אין אן דעם ,ועלבין בוים טויט

Fig. 7. Text sample of Yousifn (No. 18).

The translation into Yiddish was the brainchild of others, as is stated in the introduction:

  . . . oukh hob ikh di tfile nikht fartaytsht ous mayn kop zondern hob mir eyne, di mikh hot gedakht,
zi zay di best gevezn . . .

Though plans existed to print the *Shmuel bukh* in Yiddish, no further Yiddish works are known by these printers.

When Paulus Fagius left Konstanz for Strassburg in 1544, he practically ceased to print. Michael Adam returned to his native Switzerland and, encouraged by his earlier success, contacted the long established printers Froschauer in Zürich. In line with the literary interest of those days, he translated Josephus from Hebrew into Yiddish, and produced the volume with pleasant woodcuts (No. 18, see Fig. 7). In the very same year, 1546, he presented *Seyfer hayiro* in a Yiddish version (No. 19, see Fig. 8). When twelve years later, in 1558,

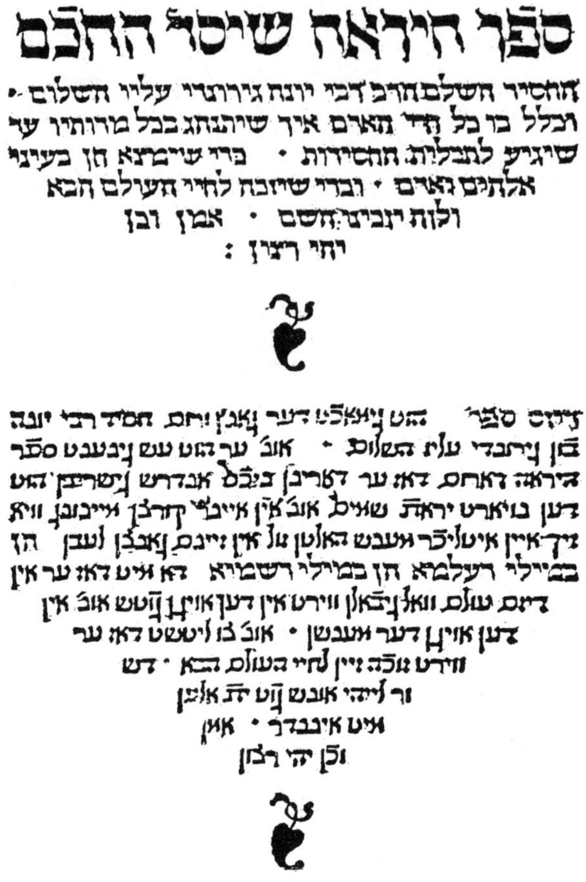

ספר חירא\ שיסי\ החכם

דזחסיר תשלם חרפ דבי יונה גירורתי עליו חשלום ·
ומלל בר כל \די חאים איך שיתנהג בכל מרוותיו ע\
שיגיע לתכליה החסירות · ברי שימצא חן בעיני
אלהים ואים · ובדי שיהיבה לחיי העילם הבא
ולות ינביר חשם · אמן ובן
יחי רצין :

זיזה ספ\   הט גיזאל\ דער וַאגן וחם חמד רבי יונה
בון ניהבדי על\ השלום · אונ ער הט עש גינעבט ספ\
היראה דאחם דא\ ער דאריג\ בצב\ אנדרש גישריב\ הט
דען בואיגרט ירא\ שויל\ אונ\ אק\ איב\ קרב\ ויינובג\ וו\
זיך אק\ איטליבר מענש האלטן על\ אק\ זיינמ\ גאבב\ לעבן הן
בחיל\ רעלמא חן בחיל\ רשמיא דא איט דא\ ער אק\
דחם עולם וואל גבאל\ ווירט אק\ דען אק\ גוַטש אוב\ אק\
דען אק\ גמ\ דער מענש\ · אונ\ בו ליטשט דא\ ער
ווירט גב\ זיק לחיי העולם הבא · דש
ור ליהי אנש גַט הַ אלהן
איט אינבדר\ · אמ\
וב\ יהי רבון

Fig. 8. Title of Seyfer hayiro (No. 19).

Zürich came up with a reproduction of the Venice 1545 *Tehilim* (No. 17 see Fig. 9), the Yiddish types were still the same (No. 24, see Fig. 10). With the disappearance of people like Fagius, Shakhor and Levita, Yiddish printing was only maintained in Basel, and by the print shop of Cornelius Adelkind in Venice, who provided the initiative for other Italian printers.

Summing up, we come to the conclusion that Yiddish printing was launched by Gentiles or Jewish converts to further the study of the language. Yiddish proved attractive. The words proved familiar enough, and the understanding of texts was in good measure a matter of learning the alphabet. Jewish printers yielded only slowly to the demands of the broad masses for literature. A compromise was sought, and Biblical texts as well as liturgy were presented in Yiddish.

ספר תהלים

דָּא הָאֵט אִיר דש תְּלִים אוֹישׁ לְשׁוֹן הַקּוֹדֶשׁ
נְּאַכְט אִין טוֹיטְשֵׁר שׁפְרוּך דוּרך דֶען
נְּלֶערנטן אָאן אֵלִיָה בָּחוּר אַשׁכְּנַזִי הַלֵּוִי

דש הוּט נְדרוּקְט: קוֹרנֵילִיו אדֵיל קִינד אוּם
מֵאִיר בַּר יַעֲקֹב אִישׁ שרעגן יִצוּ בְשׁוּתָּפוּת
אִיק יאָר דא אָן לֵילט דֵרִיי הוּנדרט אוּם בוּנְף
אִין דֶערקֶלאֵיינִי נָאל הֵי אִין דֶער נְּרוֹשַׁן שׁטָט

וינידיג

ליוסראשון

אשרי

וואל דעם מאן דער דא נִיט נֵיט אִין
רוֹט דער רְשָׁעִים אוּם אִין וועג
דער זוּנדֵינֶער נִיט עֶר שׁטִיט אוּם אִין נֶּעשׁ
דער שׁפַּיטֶר נִיט עֶר זִילט: נוּאֵרט אִין תּוֹרָה
נָּטְהַאשׁ זֵיין בִּנְעֶרוּנֶן · אוּם אִין זֵיינֶר תּוֹרָה
עֶר טִיבְּט בֵּיי טַהן אוּם בֵּיי נאכְטַוּו וועֶרט עֶר
זֵיין אַז אִין בָּאוּם נֶּפְפְלַאנְּט בֵּיא בעַלֵיך
וואַשֵׁיר · דער זֵיין ורוּכְט נֶּבְּט אִין זֵיינֵר צֵייט
אוּם זֵיין בְּלַאט נִיט עֶט וֶר וָאלְבֵּט אוּם אַלְשׁ דש
עֶר טוּט עֶר מאַכְּט בִּנְלוּיקן · נִיט אַזו זֵיין דִיא
רְשָׁעִים · נוּיאֵרט אַז אֵיין שפרַניֵאר דאַשׁ וֶר
טוֹושֵׁט אִין דֶער ווינְד · דרוּם נִיט זוֹ וועֶלן
הישׁטִין דִיא רְשָׁעִים אֵם נֶּרִיבְּט · אוּם דִיא
א ב

Fig. 9. Title and text sample of Psalms (No. 17) (reduced).

ספר תהלים

דא האט איר דש תלים איש לשון הקודש
ניאקלט אין טייטשר שפרוך דורך דען
גלערנטין מאן אליה בחור אשכנזי
הלוי

נדרוקט אין דער ליבליכן שטאט צוירך
אים יאר דא מן צילט דרײ הונדרט
אונ אכטציהן אין דער
קלײניגי צאל

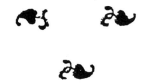

ליום ראשין

אשרי

וואל   דעם מאן דער דא ניט גֵיט אין
רוט דער רשעים אונ וועגן דר
זונדיגר ניטער שטיט אונ אונ
גֵזעש דער שפוטר ניט ער זיצט · נואָרט
אין תורה גָטאש זין בינערונגן · אונ אין זײנר
תורה ער טיכט בײ טאן אונ בײ נאכט · זו
ווערט ער זײן אז אין באוים גיפלאנצט בײא
בעכליך וואשיר · דער זײן ורוכט גֵבט אין
זײנר צײט אונ זײן בלאט ניט עש ור וואלבט
אונ אלש דש ער טוט ערואלגט בֵנֵליכן · ניט
אזו זײן דיא רשעים ·   נואָרט אז אין
שטרוייאר דאש ער שטושט אין דער וינד ·
דרום ניטזיא וערן בֵישטין דיא רשעים אם
גֵריכט ·   אונ דיא זונדינֵר אין גֵמײן דער
צֵדיקים · דרום דש ערוויש גָט וועג דער

A   ב

Fig. 10. Title and text sample of Psalms (No. 24).

BIBLIOGRAPHY

Note: Books are listed in chronological order. Book size includes margins. References to Steinschneider, Zedner and Cowley refer to Steinschneider 1852, Zedner 1867 and Cowley 1929.

1. [1530–1536] *Merkeves hamishne,* also known as *Seyfer Rebi Anshl.*
Cracow (Shmuel, Osher & Elyokim Helic), 16.5 x 20cm.
[88] pages, Yiddish-Hebrew concordance in 3 double columns in alphabetical order.
The title follows after the 2 leaves of introduction, which contain an acrostic of the name 'Anshl'.
The date is based on the fact that the 3 brothers named here as printers of the book, Shmuel, Osher and Elyokim, sons of Khayim Helic, split up in 1536.
An acrostic in the colophon gives the name *Yitskhok ben Menakhem,* who may have been a proofreader.
The Yiddish types are different from those used in other Yiddish works produced by the Helic brothers.
Steinschneider 4423/1, Shmeruk (1981: No. 1) (1534–35), Habermann (1978: 137) quotes 1535-6. Cowley 40.
Bodleiana Oxford.

2. [1535 or 1538] *Azhoras noshim* by Dovid Hakouheyn.
Cracow, Shmuel and Elyokim Helic, 11 x 16cm.
Completed Wednesday 24th Iyar. This combination suits the years 1535 (April 28) or 1538 (April 24).
[38] pages.
Shmeruk (1981: No. 2). Habermann (1978: 138). Friedberg (1950: 2) year: 1535.
On the title the author claims to have compiled his work from the books of R. Judah Mintz and R. Shmuel of Worms, which had been translated into Yiddish. These works may have only existed as manuscripts and not necessarily as prints.
The author may be identical with R. David b. Chaim Hacohen, who published *Tshuvot Haredach* (Constantinople 1538).
Schocken Library.

3. [1535–1540] *Den muser un hanhogo vi zikh eyn mensh haltn zol* [*Orkhous Khayim*].
Cracow, Elyokim b. Khayim Helic, 10 x 16cm.
[38] pages. The author is Rabbi Asher b. Jehiel, known as 'Rosh'.
Shmeruk (1981: No. 3). Habermann (1978: 139/140).
Schocken Library.

4. [1540–1541] *Dos naye testament.*
Cracow, Paul Helic. 'Gedruckt zu Krokau durch Paul Helic im Iar MDXXXX'.
Wolf IV: 204. Shmeruk (1981: No. 5), Habermann (1978: 142).
Cracow (Jagielonsk Library, Cim 8119).

5. [1541] *Bovo deantouno. Heyst dos bukh eyn hipsh getrakht. Man kent vol Elye Bokhers gemakht. Iz wordn gedrukt tsu Isni in der shtat* . . . Isny [Paulus Fagius], 9.5 x 15cm.
[alef—yud-dalet] *8 = [112] pages.
650 strophes in Yiddish rhyme of a popular story, based on the adventures of Sir Bevis of Southampton (Zedner 1863).
Personnel: Yosef and Elyohu, sons of Yitskhok Böhmen (the husband of Hanna, daughter of Elijah Levita, the translator).
At the end a register of *"Velshe Verter".*
I assume that the printing was completed after Elijah Levita had left Isny in June 1541, since only his grandsons are named as "printers".
According to the introduction, Levita adapted this book 34 years prior to publication, (i.e. 1507) from the Italian version. Deinhard (1915: 14) cites an edition Pesaro 1518, which would constitute the first Yiddish book ever printed (YIVO bleter III/3 p. 287).
Facsimile edition (enlarged): J. A. Joffe 1949.
Zürich Zentralbibliothek.

6. [1542, July] *Shemous devorim* . . . *Nomenclatura Hebraica Autore Helia Levita* . . .
Isny, [Paulus Fagius], 11 x 16.5cm.
[31] pages. Lexicon in Yiddish, Hebrew, Latin and German (in four columns). Watermark: K.
Wolf I: 159. Perles (1884: 131–140). Zedner 807. van Straalen 71.
Facsimile edition in preparation.
British Library, London.

7. [1542] *Seyfer mides.* Isny [Paulus Fagius or Paulus Aemilius], 15 x 21cm.
[99] + [1] p. [A–Z, a–b] *4 = [100] pages.
The book contains a dedication to "Frou Morada, Dokterin der frayen kunst der artsenay, vonhaftig tsu Günzburg". In my opinion, Lady Morada was not necessarily Jewish.

The Yiddish types are identical to Nos. 5 and 6.
Steinschneider 3412, Cowley 515. Perles (1884: 173–177).
Bodleiana Oxford.

8. [1542 ?] *Shir hayikhud.* (Isny, Paulus Fagius) 14.5 x 19cm.
[23] pages. [alef—he] *4, [vav] *3 + 1 blanc.
Steinschneider 3314, Cowley 360, 579.
This book has been ascribed to Isny. This is certainly wrong. The paper does not show the known Isny watermarks
(Rosenfeld 1985: 18). The ornamental frame for the words *Ashira* and *Anim* (the frame stands on its head) is
not found in any Isny book. The larger type seems to originate from the Khayim Shokhor printshop, and are
therefore also found in Lublin.
Further study is required to establish place and date of printing. This book must now be placed with Lublin
prints executed by Eliezer b. Yitskhok around the year 1562. No title page. Interlinear Yiddish translation. On
p. 21: Salik Shir Hajichud; p. 22: Anim Semiroth.

> Man zogt, Yude khosid hot den Shir hayikhud tun makhn . . . er hot in gemakht geraymt . . . der seykhl
> fun di gemeyne layt, kenen nit masig zayn azou vayt . . .

Bodleiana Oxford.

9. [1543] *Elemental oder Lesebüchlein . . . mit hebräischen und jüdischen Buchstaben geschrieben.*
Hundsfeld (bei Breslau), Paul Helic.
[8] pages. Facsimile: Verein Jüdisches Museum Breslau, 1929.
Wolf IV: 272 (1541!). Habermann (1978: 142). Shmeruk (1981: No. 7).
Soncino Blätter III, 1, p. 9.
Breslau Stadtbibliothek (?).

10. [1543] [Bible] (First four chapters of Genesis in Yiddish and Hebrew).
Prima Quatuor Capita Geneseos Hebraice, cum versione Germanica . . .
Konstanz, Paulus Fagius. 14 x 20cm.
[a–f] *4 = [24] pages. Watermark: bear.
Latin preface, followed by Hebrew text on the right and Yiddish translation on the left hand page. Marginal
notes give variations according to Rashi, Radak etc. . . .
Wolf II: 456 , IV: 193–4. Steinschneider 95, 1188. Cowley 78, 193.
Bodleiana Oxford; British Library, London.

11. [1543] [Bible, Melochim Buch]. *Das Seyfer melokhim in taytsher shprakh hipsh un besheydlikh oukh gar
kurtsvaylig . . .*
[Augsburg], [Paulus Aemilius], 14.5 x 20.5cm.
Completed Friday 14th Av 303 [15th July 1543].
The 15th July was Sunday. 9048 verses in 2262 stances in Yiddish prose.
[A–Z] 4, [a–g] 4, h3 = [123] pages.
The author of this Yiddish translation of the Book of Kings in poetry is assumed to be R. Moushe Esrim-Vearbe.
No printer is mentioned and the paper bears various watermarks including a letter "K", which is found with
the Hebrew prints of Isny. Steinschneider 185/1243 (Printer: Schachor). Zedner 121. Rosenfeld (1985: 40).
Facsimile edition: L. Fuks.
British Library, London. Schocken Library (defect.); UBJena.

12. [1544] [Bible, Shmuel Buch] *Das bukh Shmuel in taytsher shprakh hipsh un besheydlikh.*
[Augsburg], [Paulus Aemilius], 15 x 21cm.
[A–Z] 4, [a–b] 4, c2 = [102] pages. Collation also in Hebrew.
"Der Shmuel iz das ersht teyl fun dem Seyfer melokhim den es kert als tsueynander [tsu] for habt ir das Seyfer
melokhim un itsund hab ikh den Shmuel datsu gedrukt . . ."
The Book of Samuel, though printed in 1544 is the 'first part of the Book of Kings . . .'. Translator: Rabbi
Moushe Esrim Vearbe.
Editio Princeps. Steinschneider 184/1237. Zedner 121. Rosenfeld (1985: 41).
Facsimile edition: F. Falk.
British Library, London.

13. [1544, March] [Pentateuch, Megilloth and Haftaroth].
Konstanz, Paulus Fagius. 16 x 21cm.
[°] *4, [A–Z, Aa–Zz, aaa–zzz, a–f] *4 = [304] pages.
The Hebrew pagination is faulty.
The edition meant for sale to Gentiles has a German title page and introduction:

> Die fünff bücher Mosis sampt dem Hohen lied Salomonis
> Ruth/ Clag lied . . . auch der Juden Evangelien/ die sie
> Haphtaroth nennen . . . aus Hebräischer Sprach nach Jüdischer
> art von wort zu wort ins Teutsch schreiben . . .
> Gedruckt zu Constenz Anno M.D.XLIIII.

The "Jewish" edition has Hebrew title and 3 pages preface, taken from *Merkeves hamishne* (No. 1). The first four chapters of Genesis are essentially identical with the 1543 publication (No. 10).
Bass (1680: 86–No. 61) wrongly claims the translation was done by Elijah Levita. This error stems from the colophon which states: "So says Elijah Halevi". There follows, however, an excerpt from Levita's *Tishbi*, explaining the words *haftara*.
Wolf I: 159 & 758 (1545), II: 455, IV: 191–198. Steinschneider 1187, 4333/1. Zedner 107. Cowley 32, 115. Gesner C., Pandectis (1548): "Yiddish translation by Michael Adam".
Bodleiana Oxford; British Library, London (lacks title); Schocken (lacks title).

14. [1544, July]
[Pentateuch, Megilloth and Haftaroth].
Die fünff Bücher Mose/ aus dem Hebräischen von wort nach der yetzigen Juden art/ in die Teutsch Sprach gebracht/ un doch mit Hebräischen Buchstaben getruckt . . .
[Augsburg], Paulus Emilius, 22 x 28cm.
[2] + 134 pages.
Collation:
      First part: [0]2, [A–T]6, V4 = 120 leaves
      Second part: [0]1, [X–Y]6, Z2 = 15 leaves + 1 blanc
Edition for Gentiles.
Printed in 2 columns 46 lines per page. The watermark shows a bear, occurring in Isny prints (1542).
The introduction contains a letter addressed to Leonhard Beck and a dedication by Paulus Aemilius dated Sivan [July] 1544, in Latin and Hebrew (Yiddish type). He signs as "Buchdrucker bei St. Urstsil zu Augsburg", though his job was as a bookbinder in this Dominican Ladies' Convent.
Perles (1876: 361 ff.). Rosenfeld (1985: 41/42).
Bayerische Staatsbibliothek, München (Res. 2. A. heb. 9 (2)).

15. [1544]
[Pentateuch, Megilloth und Haftaroth].
Das als rekht un vartaytsht ous eynem altn khumesh for langn tsaytn geshribn un yetsund tsu ougsburg gedrukt.
Augsburg, [Paulus Emilius], 18.2 x 29.5cm.
[A–T] *6, [V] *4, [X–Y] *6, [Z] *4 = 133 pages + [1] blanc.
Title for the second part (Megillot) on page [119].
Jewish edition.
The following variations occur in this edition as compared with No. 15:
  1. The first title page is in Yiddish, naming the place of printing.
  2. This edition does not contain the Latin introduction. Neither date, nor the name of Paulus Aemilius are mentioned.
Cowley 115. Rosenfeld (1985: 42).
Cat. des livres imprimez de la bibl. du Roy: Theologie, I, p. 18 A 257 [Paris 1739]. REJ V, 142–4 [1882] and 315–6. Le Livre Hebraïque, Sorbonne 1962.
Bodleiana Oxford. Bibliotheque Nationale, Paris.

16. [1544] [Prayerbook] *Kumt her ir frumen frouen, da wird ir hipsh ding shouen. Ir werd es wol gevor, eyn tefile fum gantsn yor vol fartaytsht.*
Ichenhausen, Chaim b. David Shachor, ca. 12 x 16cm.
[167] pages.
Personnel: Yousef b. Yokor, Yitskhok b. Khayim.
Hebräische Bibliographie XII, 125–7. Israelit. Wochenschrift 1872, 241–2. Perles (1876: 355). Habermann (1978: 122–124).
Bay. Staatsbibliothek, München.

17. [1545] *Tehilim* Venice [Cornelio Adelkind], 11 x 15cm.
[17 Bogen] = [136] pages.
Personnel: Meir b. Yacob of France.
According to the introduction, Yiddish editions of Mishle, Hiob and Daniel were planned.
Literature: Zedner 126. Cowley 115, 173. Steinschneider 1268. Shmeruk (1982: No. 1). Habermann (1978: 173) and (1980: 30).
British Library, London; Bodleiana Oxford; Jewish Theol. Seminary, New York.

18. [1546] *Yousifn* Zürich, Christopher Froschauer, 12.5 x 19.5cm.
[12] + 501 + [2] pages. [alpha–gamma, a–z, A–Z, Aa–Zz, aa–zz, AA–ZZ] *4, [AAa–KKk] *4, [LL1] *3 = [515] pages.
This is the earliest illustrated Yiddish print known.
At the end we find an introduction into the laws of reading and writing Yiddish.
As stated in the colophon, the translation into Yiddish was prepared from the Hebrew version by Michael Adam, a Jewish convert.
Steinschneider 6033/11. Zedner 344. Cowley 32, 332.
British Library, London; Bodleiana Oxford.

19. [1546] *Seyfer hayiro*
. . . Dies seyfer hot gemakht der gants frum khosid rebi Youne fun Girondi . . .
Zürich, C. Froschauer, 14 x 19cm.
[27] pages.
The Mussar work of Rabbi Jonah Girondi, translated into Yiddish by Michael Adam.
Wolf I: 489. Friedberg (1937: 11).
UB Basel.

20. [1552] *Maasim di zenen geshehen etlekhe khasidim* . . .
Venice, Daniel Adelkind, 9 x 13cm.
[12] pages.
The colophon by Daniel's father Cornelio indicates the intention of printing further Yiddish tales from the Talmud.
It also includes an apology for the poor Yiddish translation.
Zedner 556. Habermann (1980: 89–90). Shmeruk (1982: No. 6).
British Library, London; Jewish Theolog. Seminary, New York.

21. [1552] *Mitsvas hanoshim. Frouenbikhlen* . . .
Venice, Daniel Adelkind, 9 x 13cm.
[52] pages. Index at beginning for 123 chapters.
The colophon by Cornelio Adelkind reads:
Libe frouen, nemt das bikhlen fir gut fun maynem zun Doniel der aykh es hot gedrukt . . .
This version is ascribed to Benjamin of Ordona.
Wolf III: 149. Steinschneider 3949. Cowley 227. Zedner 556. Habermann (1980: 90). Shmeruk (1982: No. 8).
British Library, London; Bodleiana Oxford; Schocken Library.

22. [1557 ?] *Di megile in taytsher shprakh.*
[Basel ?, Jakob Kundig ?], 6.5 x 12cm.
[36] pages. Prijs (1964: No. 101).
The types are identical to the Zürich editions of *Yosifn* or *Seyfer hayiro,* 1546 (No. 19), and since neither place nor date of printing are mentioned, it is possible that this booklet was printed in Zürich. The typographic material used by Eliezer Treves (see No. 24) was utilized in Thiengen in 1560, though no Yiddish books are recorded from this town.
University Library, Basel.

23. [1557] *Doniel bukh.*
Basel, Jakob Kundig, 10 x 15.5cm.
104 pages.
Personnel: Mordekhay b. Yosef, Shmuel b. Moushe Hakouhen.
Prijs (1964: No. 97).
University Library Basel; Schocken Library.

24. [1558] *Tehilim*
Zürich, Eliezer b. Naftoli Hirts Treves, Yosef b. Naftoli, 11 x 15cm.
[A–O] *8, [P] *7 = [119] pages.
Personnel: Yosef b. Naftoli.
This is a reprint of the Venice 1545 edition. The translation is by Elijah Levita. The colophon shows a woodcut of a deer.
Wolf III: 101. Steinschneider 1269. Zedner 126. Cowley 115, 173.
British Library, London; Bodleiana Oxford.

Unlocated or doubtful editions

25. [1518] *Bovo deantouno*
Pesaro, Soncino printers.
Deinhard (1915: 14).

26. [1535–1540] *Kearas kesef.*
Cracow, Helic brothers.
Shmeruk (1981: No. 4). Habermann (1978: 140).

27. [1541] *Seyder noshim.*
Cracow, Helic brothers.
Shmeruk (1981: No. 6).
This information stems from a Mantua censor's list. It is possible that this is identical with No. 2 above, the Shin alef referring to 's.a.' (without date).

28. [1544] [Bible]. *Doniel bukh.* In Yiddish prose.
Augsburg, Paulus Emilius.
Existence doubtful. The only reference is Friedberg (1951: Letter Dalet 894). Generally the Basel 1557 print is assumed to be the editio princeps.

29. [1541–1545] *Ditrikh fun bern.*
Mentioned by Cornelio Adelkind in the colophon of 'Tehilim', Venice 1545 (No. 17).

30. [1541–1545] *Bukh der sheynen glikn.*
Possibly printed in Isny 1541.
The intention to print this book is noted at the end of *Bovo bukh,* Isny 1541 (No. 5) and by Cornelio Adelkind in the colophon of *Tehilim,* Venice 1545 (No. 17).

31. [1544] *Iouv.*
In Yiddish prose by Elijah Levita.
Venice, Cornelio Adelkind.
Friedberg (1951: Letter Tav, 951).
The date seems suspicious. Adelkind writes in the colophon to his *Tehilim,* Venice 1545 (No. 17):

> Un dokh find man veynig Seforim in taytsher shprakh di do vol un rekht getaytsht zind, bin ikh gangen tsu reb Elye Bokher [= Levita] un hab mit im vertragen er zol mir etlekhe Seforim taytshn un tzum ersht das Tehilim nokh dem dikduk. Un bald viles got vil ikh druken das Mishle, Iouv un Doniel vol getaytsht.

Any possible editions of Mishle, Job and Daniel will have appeared after 1545.

32. [1548] *Megilas Matisyohu.*
Venice, Cornelio Adelkind.
Issachar Frenk used this edition for his reprint Vienna 1821.
Steinschneider 1390. Shmeruk (1982: No. 2) . Zfatman 1.

33. [1548] *Mitsvas hanoshim.* Venice.
Steinschneider (1848: No. 200).

34. [1552] *Merkeves hamishne.* Cracow.
Wolf I: 206. Steinschneider (1848: No. 376).
This edition certainly does not exist. There was no Hebrew or Yiddish printing in Cracow during the 1550s. The mistake stems from a typographical error by Bass (1680: 8—No. 168) who writes: *shin khes dalet,* seemingly making the year 1552. This should read *khes shin dalet = Khoser Shnas Dfus,* i.e.: s.a.

35. [1552] [Historye fun dray vayber].
Venice, Cornelio Adelkind.
Shmeruk (1982: No. 3), Zfatman 3.
A later edition: Prague s.a. (ca. 1650).
[Steinschneider (1852: 3891). Cowley 405].

36. [1552] [Zemer beloshn ashkenaz].
Venice, Cornelio Adelkind.
Shmeruk (1982: No. 4).

37. [1552] [Maase geshehen in Yerusholayim].
Venice, Cornelio Adelkind.
Shmeruk (1982: No. 7), Zfatman 4.

38. [1552] *Maase fun Rivke.*
Venice, Cornelio Adelkind.
Shmeruk (1982: No. 7), Zfatman 5.

39. [1552] [Tsvey historye].
Venice, Cornelio Adelkind.
Zfatman 6.

40. [1552] *Tefile* [Hebrew/Yiddish].
Venice, Cornelio Adelkind.
Shmeruk (1982: No. 9).

41. [1553] *Exodus, Joshua, (Jeremiah), Ezekiel, (Daniel), Song of Songs.*
Prague 1553.
Buxtorf (1651: 640). Wolf IV: 199. Friedberg (1935: 11).

42. [1555 (?)] *Ku bukh.* [Sabionetta ?]. I have discussed the possibility of the existence of this edition prior to the Verona 1595 edition (Rosenfeld 1984).

43. [1556 or before (not prior to 1551)].
Pariz un Viene.
Sabionetta, Cornelio Adelkind.
Shmeruk (1982: No. 33).
A fragment of the Verona 1594 edition is in Cambridge (Trinity College).

44. [1556] *Melokhim bukh.*
Prague.
Wolf II: 456.

45. [1558] *Maase khaneke.*
Mantua.
Shmeruk (1982: No. 10). Zfatman 7.

46. [1558] *Shoushane un Yehudis.*
Mantua.
Shmeruk (1982: No. 8). Zfatman 8.

47. [1558] *Kearas kesef.*
Mantua.
Possibly a reprint of the Cracow [1535–6] edition (No. 26).
Shmeruk (1982: No. 11).

REFERENCES

BASS, S. 1680 *Sifsey yesheynim* [First Hebrew bibliography of printed books]. D. Tartaz, Amsterdam.

BUXTORF, J. 1651 *Thesaurus Grammaticus Linguae Sanctae Hebraeae,* H. Ludovic, Basel.

COWLEY, A. E. 1929 *Catalogue of the Hebrew Printed Books in the Bodleian Library.* Oxford.

DEINHARD, E. 1915 *Atikot Yehuda* (Hebrew). A. M. Lunz, Jerusalem.

FALK, F. 1961 *Das Schmuel buch des Mosche Esrim Wearba.* Assen.

FRIEDBERG, B. 1935 *Geschichte der hebräischen Typographie der mitteleuropäischen Stadte . . ..* Antwerpen.

FRIEDBERG, B. 1937 *Geschichte der hebräischen Typographie der europäischen Stadte . . ..* Antwerpen.

FRIEDBERG, B. 1950 *History of Hebrew Typography in Poland.* Zvi Kaspi, Tel Aviv.

FRIEDBERG, B. 1951 *Bet Eked Sefarim—Bibliographical Lexicon.* Tel Aviv.

FUKS, L. 1965 *Das altjiddische Epos Melochimbuch.* Publ. Bibl. Rosenthaliana No. 2. Van Gorcum, Assen.

GIEFEL, 1884 Beiträge zur Geschichte der ehemaligen Reichsstadt Isny. In *Diozesan-Archiv, Blätter f. Kirchengeschichtliche Mitteilungen aus Schwaben.*

HABERMANN, A. M. 1978 *Perakim be-Toldoth ha-Madpissim ha-Ivrim we-Inyene Sefarim.* Rubin Mass, Jerusalem.

HABERMANN, A. M. 1980 *Hamadpiss Cornelio Adelkind ubeno Daniel.* Rubin Mass, Jerusalem.

PERLES, J. 1876 Bibliographische Mittheilungen aus München. *Monatschrift für Geschichte und Wissenschaft der Juden* **25,** 350–368.

PERLES, J. 1884 *Beiträge zur Geschichte der Hebräischen und Aramäischen Studien.* Theodor Ackermann, München.

PRIJS, J. 1964 *Die Basler Hebräischen Drucke,* Urs Graf Verlag, Olten u. Freiburg i. Br.

REJ *Revue des Etudes Juives.*

ROSENFELD, M. N. 1984 *The Book of Cows. A Facsimile Edition of the famed Kuhbuch.* Hebraica Books, London.

ROSENFELD, M. N. 1985 *Jewish Printing in Augsburg in the first half of the 16th Century.* Private Printing, London.

SCHIESS, T. 1910 *Briefwechsel der Brüder Ambrosius und Thomas Blaurer 1509–1548.* Band II. F. E. Fehsenfeld, Freiburg i. Br.

SHMERUK, C. 1981 *Yiddish Literature in Poland.* Magnes Press, Jerusalem.

SHMERUK, C. 1982 Yiddish Printing in Italy. *Italia* **3,** 112 ff.

STEINSCHNEIDER, M. 1848–9 Jüdisch-Deutsche Literatur. *Serapeum* **9,** 313–336, 344–352, 363–368, 375–384. **10,** 9–16, 25–32, 42–48, 74–80, 88–96, 107–112.

STEINSCHNEIDER, M. 1852–60 *Catalogus Librorum Hebraeorum* . . . Ad. Friedlaender.

VAN STRAALEN, S. 1894 *Catalogue of Hebrew Books in the British Museum* . . . *1868–1892.* London.

WOLF, J. C. 1715 *Bibliotheca Hebraica,* 4 parts. Hamburg & Leipzig 1715–33.

ZEDNER, J. 1863 Levita's Historie vom Ritter Baba. *Hebräische Bibliographie* **6,** 22–23.

ZEDNER, J. 1867 *Catalogue of Hebrew Books in the British Museum.* British Museum, London.

ZFATMAN, S. 1985 *Yiddish Narrative Prose.* The Hebrew University, Jerusalem.

ZfHB *Zeitschrift für Hebräische Bibliographie.*

Language & Communication, Vol. 7, Supplement, pp. 127–134, 1987.
Printed in Great Britain.

0271-5309/87 $3.00 + .00
Pergamon Journals Ltd.

A PARTISAN HISTORY OF YIDDISH

NATHAN SUSSKIND

City College in the City University of New York

If the Jews are the most outrageously maligned people ever, Yiddish is even more so.

Yiddish is maligned even by many Jews!

Libels—galore: based, as usual for libels, on ignorance and/or malice. For—the folksy saying does state: it ain't what we don't know that makes us so darn stupid, but what we do know, but ain't so!

And what *is* known about Yiddish mostly "ain't so". And that is true even of much that passes for "science". To point out that the latter would require volumes! God willing, we may return to it.

Misconceptions about LANGUAGE IN GENERAL are very common; about Yiddish they are just about universal. Therefore many will be shocked at the following claims, that: Yiddish is the most "Jewish" of all "Jewish languages", one of the most "natural" of modern languages generally; it has a most felicitous, organic grammar. The shock would give place to amusement at the next claim, that rather than dub Yiddish "spoiled German", German could, with equal "reason", be called "spoiled Yiddish"! But—no jokes: the claims are true. Here are some facts to prove them.

Laymen are generally unaware of the fact that Jews have more than a dozen languages that they can legitimately call their own. Even language historians and scientists have only recently discovered this truth. Mostly there still prevails the naive misconception of language as something static, properly the peculiar earmark of its own ethnic group FROM ETERNITY. Any change in the language is automatically considered an "improper" deviation from the "original", the "correct", and therefore—an error, a corruption. Any group changing to a language not "originally" its own is considered as speaking what is properly not their language legitimately—quasi they were wearing borrowed clothing, while their own was in hock.

Even the adoption of single foreign words into the native vocabulary is considered by "purists" to be a corrupting contamination. Due to a felicitous history, English has been so eclectic in its vocabulary that its speakers are generally blissfully unaware of the passion with which such self appointed guardians of "purity" in other languages have been trying to stem the tide of "foreign invasions". They engage in veritable orgies of excising from the quasi living body of the language every word of "foreign origin"—even such as had been naturalized, assimilated beyond recognition a long time ago, and it took the efforts of generations of scholars to work out their etymology; words of no readily available native equivalents; words for which neologic substitutes were artificially invented, meanings of which had first to be taught!

But in English too this linguistic chauvinism is expressed in a pedantry for a (supposed) "correctness". Pedants will resent deviation from *their* "standard" speech more vehemently than the "faithful" resent the "heresies" of the "infidel". Not to speak of the snobbish "elite", who self-indulgently enjoy and use this their "standard" as the symbol and proof of the intrinsic superiority, their higher "culture" vis-à-vis the "ungrammatical mob", the "uncouth murderers of the King's English". It has long become a universal human trait for people to poke fun at "dialect", i.e., nothing more serious than the normal, local "provincial" variation from their own speech peculiarities—which each dialect group considers exclusively "correct", "standard", and not at all "peculiar", or "dialect".

Much of what passes for "humour" in all literature is such snobbish sneering at the speech of "others"—even when these others are fellow nationals but of a different region or social class. When the "others" are foreigners, the mocking turns into malevolent jeering. Thus burlesquing the supposed "Jewish dialect" has been a cheap, easy, and sure way of entertaining the 'pit", of getting the audience to laugh. Jews themselves are subject to the same temptation and practice similar humour: consider the role "dialect" plays in Yiddish literature and on the stage, especially the exploitation of the *galitsyaner* and *litvak* dialects.

At its very best such humour can be generous and benevolent. Take Sheridan's *School for Scandal* or Shaw's *Pygmalion* or Sholem Aleichem's *Tevye* in Yiddish. But with all of its good nature the humour is still fundamentally the "laugh of superiority", a laughter that feels as solidly secure in that superiority as it is absolutely without any justification.

To return to: How Jewish is Yiddish?

Ask any well informed, educated person: what is the language of the Jews? He *may* answer that Jews have more than one language. But ask just anybody: what is the *original* language of the Jews?—and he will answer: Hebrew. And he will be wrong!

Hebrew was *not* the language of the first Hebrews. "Abraham the Hebrew" (Gen. 14, 13) spoke Aramaic! The language we call Hebrew today even the Bible calls Canaanite (Isaiah 19, 18). Abraham's clan spoke Aramaic (Gen. 13, 47).

Rebecca did prevent her son Jacob from marrying a Canaanite *shikse* by sending him off to her native land to marry his cousin (Gen. 27, 46), but she failed to prevent his assimilating to the *shikse's* language. When Jacob and Laban build a mound they swear not to pass with intent to hurt one another, they call the mound to witness: Laban in Aramaic (Abraham's tongue) *yegar sehaduta* and Jacob in Hebrew (i.e. Canaanite) *galed* (Gen. 31, 47).

The same language and even the very same words that the Jews have been using to glorifiy the One and Only God of the Universe, the Canaanites (and the Israelites!—of the Northern Kingdom) used, in the worship of Baal and other idols. Hebrew is holy in Jewish tradition only as the *leshon hakodesh* 'the tongue of holiness' (*not* the 'holy tongue' as such), but rather holy because of its content: it has been used for the Sancta of the civilization we call Judaism for over three thousand years—but not because of its origin.

Chaim Weitzman's "winged words" that Hebrew is *leshon kodesh* while Yiddish is *leshon hakedoshim* 'the tongue of the holy martyrs' is as well known as it is apt. But it is more than even that: as *spoken* language Yiddish rivals *all* other Jewish languages, including Hebrew. It has been spoken continuously for the longest period (about a thousand years) by the largest number of Jews (ca. 11,000,000 in 1933—before the Holocaust) and over

the largest area (all the five continents). Purely in terms of quantity it is also the most important *written* language: Before the rise of Israel there were more authors and more pages written for Jews in Yiddish than in all other Jewish languages *combined*. This quantity alone turns into a factor of quality as well—because of its dimension. But even purely on quality, independent of quantity, Yiddish has been second to none: the tragedies of which Jewish history is so full have "pushed" the Yiddish "tribe" to the highest pinnacle of achievement in culture and civilization, both Jewish and universal. In the last three hundred years there was not a single movement or development on the Jewish scene where Yiddish speakers were not in the lead: in Torah, in general scholarship, in philosophy, the sciences, the arts, political and social movements and even the reestablishment of the Jewish State and the revival of Hebrew. And this modern Hebrew, to the degree that it is innovative in its grammar, syntax and semantics, can be understood mostly as the reflex of Yiddish. Simply the character of this most productive of all Jewish tribes is best mirrored in Yiddish, the language in which its life in its totality found expression: its daily mundane cares; its holiday spirit; its insight and visions; its philosophies and humour; its hopes and despairs; its songs and its sorrows.

We hasten to add that modern Hebrew in the Jewish State is fast catching up with Yiddish—but it does have still some way to go!

But even as a *symbol* Yiddish is the most fitting to represent the Jew: like him it has been most maligned, libeled and despised—so undeservedly! Hebrew—unlike the Jew—has ever enjoyed due honour even from anti-Semites.

Hence it is Yiddish that it most characteristically Jewish of all Jewish languages.

Ask any scholars acquainted with the histories of most of modern languages and they *might* tell you of the baneful interference of would be "authorities", self appointed and government imposed guardians of "purity", pedantic "normativist", who succeeded in saddling their languages with all kinds of "correct" irregularities in grammar and spelling— dead wood they had picked up from past stages of the language, long after the living speech had discarded it—at best; at worst—from misconceived notions and imitations of "classic" models. Such interference succeeded to much higher degreees than is suspected by the layman. Yiddish was despised, so nobody before the advent of Yivo bothered to interfere in its natural growth, to "fix it up" and thereby spoil it.

On the other hand:

Modern standard literary German is a somewhat an artificial creation, its artificiality aggravated by the ignorance and snobbery of its creators. Around 1350 Kaiser Karl IV decided that he could control his imperial correspondence better if it were composed in his own vernacular, German, instead of Latin. He ordered his imperial chancellery to devise a uniform German writing style—called from its use—the *Kantzeleisprache*. The scribes who "got the job" were native Bohemians (the chancellery was situated in Prague!), who prided themselves on their Latin (acquired over decades of laborious study) and despised *all* vernaculars as being "vulgar" and common to the uneducated; but especially did they despise *German* as the language of the foreign enemy-conqueror. They *had* to learn this language of the oppressing masters—to a point. When the order came to create a writing medium in this hated "barbarity", they tried to create a language that was as similar to their precious Latin as possible—otherwise they would have lost their own professional self respect. Since the spoken "fused dialect" of the foreign colonizers looked too 'simple'', as it didn't have the wealth of inflexions with the multitude of rules and exceptions to

emulate Latin, the scribes tried hard and succeeded in digging up a German that had been dead for two to three hundred years. *That* they squeezed into the Sodom-bed of Latin syntax and word order, and came up with a *Kanzleisprache,* that in spite of being German was only slightly more intelligible to the average German than the Latin of which he was ignorant.

This horrible freak of language was imitated by other government offices, including the chancellery of the Dukes of Saxony at Meissen. By a fortunate accident Luther was a native of Meissen and when he was searching for a "uniform" German into which to translate the Bible, he decided on his native, Meissen dialect (because of its geographic centrality) and thought to enhance its "uniformity" by modifying it to conform with the usages of the ducal chancellery at Meissen. Luther happened to be a language genius, and he succeeded to transform by the sheer magic of his genius that Kanzlei scarecrow into a Venus—the thing of beauty ultimately of Goethe, Schiller, Heine, Nietzsche and Hesse. But the sin of its origin, the MACULATE CONCEPTION in the Kanzlei is still imprinted on its brow—in spite of all the genius and magic. In the words of Fred Bodmer, a descendant of Germans and a lover of German, Standard German, because of the peculiar history of its origin, carries a load of dead wood that makes it possible for people to seem profound when they have absolutely nothing to say—because the dead wood favours obscurantism. The "purists" of the seventeenth century, the "grammarians" of the eighteenth century and the government bureaucrats of the nineteenth and twentieth centuries did not improve German with their bungling interferences.

Yiddish was left to grow like an oak in adverse, hostile ground, and it did grow, struggle and survive as the best and "fittest" language of its kind!

Some have wondered why Yiddish deviated from German while still on German speech territory. All kinds of bizarre "causes" have been proposed by both friends and foes. Note the Khsam Soyfer's pious claim that the Jews *deliberately* changed their German so as not to commit the sin of trespassing the command of "You shall not follow their (the heathens') statutes" (Levit. 18, 3) expanded by the Talmud (Baba Kama 83a) to include barbering styles and further expanded by Deciders (*Poseksim*) to dressing customs (Yoreh Deah 178) and still further expanded by some pietists to include even *adopting* a non-Jewish language. Compare Schudt's libel that "Jews were accursed Christ-killers and were therefore incapable of speaking like human beings".

But it *is* a fact that even in the period of Old Yiddish (up to 1500) the "Judeo-German" (Jüdisch-deutsch) of the Jews in Germany differed from the speech of their neighbours— and not only in vocabulary-from-Hebrew, but in sounds and grammar as well.

And that does require a plausible explanation:

Jews came to what is Germany today with the armies of the Caesars. There is a Jewish tombstone in Cologne dating from the 4th century. However, conditions became too unsettled in the area for Jewish community life to persist there after the outbreak of the Barbaric Invasions. Official documents of Jews in "Germany" first begin to appear in the tenth century with the rise of the new Pax Romana of the Holy Roman Empire. Jews start coming from Romance speech territory in ever larger numbers. They speak variants of Judeo-French and Judeo-Italian one of which variants Z. Shaikovsky dubbed "Shuadit" (i.e. "Jewish" in their own tongue). Some three generations later they are creating Hebrew-*German* glossaries as an aid for teaching their children difficult Hebrew texts. Rashi (1040–1105) in the city of Worms, now German speaking, still explains difficult Hebrew

words for *realia* with French glosses. Later generations spoke German (with a French accent), but preserved a selected French vocabulary for purely Jewish realia, for which German had no terms anyway: e.g. *shalet-tsholnt* 'Saturday dinner meat stew, kept sealed hot in the oven from Friday to comply with the Sabbath work prohibition', *leyenen* 'chant, cantillate the Torah', and especially proper names (e.g. *Bela*), and some emotionally precious words (e.g. *piltsl* 'little girl').

The period from about 1100 to 1350 (and beyond) happens to be one of the most tragic in Jewish history so fraught with tragedies: The Crusades (nine in number from 1095 to 1272) destroyed most Jewish communities along their path down the Rhine and Danube—the very trade routes along which Jews had mostly settled; the Church kept issuing ever new decrees against Jews: prescribed Ghettoes, peculiar, special "Jewish" clothing, limitations on Jewish contacts with non-Jews, conversions, the Inquisition to decimate the converts, and frequent expulsions—total from England (1290) and France (1334), partial (but repeated!) from the many semi independent Jurisdictions of the Holy Roman Empire. The rash of malicious libels with their attendant massacres, culminated in the most monstrous, the allegation that Jews caused the Black Plague by poisoning the wells (1348–50). All these destabilizing conditions resulted in there not existing a single Jewish community or *Judengasse* in which the majority were NATIVE-SONS-OF-NATIVES. Every Ghetto consisted of a sorry collection of refugees from all German dialect territories—with those from nearer localities normally more numerous than from the more distant ones. In these refugee communities dialects "rubbed off" their sharp differences against one another and "fused", so that the resulting language patterns were not only a natural organic survival of competing forms, but they were also uniform and almost identical in every Ghetto, no matter how far apart. Since the component dialects were the same (even if not in identical proportions), and the process was the same—fusion, the resulting product everywhere tended to be relatively uniform.

There remained some differences between Yiddish dialects nevertheless from their very inception. They were and have remained relatively small in comparison with the almost mutual unintelligibility of the extreme dialects of German. Basically, what's identical is due to the dynamics of FUSION; what's different—to the inescapable, ever-present influence of each ENVIRONMENT: Thus for instance the first incisive division into Western Yiddish (= WY, on German speech territory) and Eastern Yiddish (= EY, on Balto-Slavic territory) was based on environmental influences. WY early monophthongized Middle High German (= MHG) diphthongs: MHG *koufe fleische* > WY *kāf flǎš* from a later variant *kaufe flaisch* (as in modern Standard German = SG) by lengthening the first element (*a*) of the diphthong, at the expense of the second (*u* or *i*); whereas EY continued the MHG diphthongs *ou* and *ei* and developed them further into new diphthongs: *ej* for both in Northeastern Yiddish (= NEY, "Lithuanian"), *ɔj* and *aj* in Mideastern Yiddish (= MEY, "Polish"), *ɔj* and *ej* in Southeastern Yiddish (= SEY, "Ukrainian") and there is every reason to believe that the different starting points for these developments in WY and EW (*au* and *aj* against *ou* and *ej*) must have crystalized on German soil and can only be accounted for by the influence of different German local dialects. Similarly, some of the other subdivisions, even of EY which underwent its greatest changes on Balto-Slavic soil, can be shown to be due to German local dialects: thus (MEY) *ets, enk, enker* for General Yiddish *ir, aykh* and *ayer* 'Ye', 'you' and 'yours' are clearly direct influences of Austro-Bavarian.

Thus the Jews, while still on German speech territory, achieved a fairly unified language, even in pronunciation and spelling, by 1350, centuries before German acquired a uniform

standard. It has already been mentioned that to this day Germans speaking different dialects are at times completely unintelligible to one another. The author has lost the reference to a World War I soldier's story of a Yiddish speaking native of New York who served as an interpreter in Germany, after a German-American speaker of Pennsylvania German failed at the task. His Yiddish may have been six hundred years apart in independent development from German and still closer to standard German than many a native German dialect.

In the sense of a naturally developed, efficient, most widely intelligible communication tool, Yiddish around 1350 was "more successful" than any then living German dialect!

Prof. Ephraim Cross of the Romance Department of the College of the City of New York once worsted one of us with a quiz on: what was the "lingua franca" of the Holy Roman Empire? The naive answer was Latin and/or Kanzlei-German. He corrected: Yiddish.

The only trouble is that even the Jews didn't realize that then, and most people still do not realize it now. The Jews had "builded better than they knew", but the sociolinguistic insights in 1350 were not equal to the task of understanding the organic evolution of Yiddish as an independent language. This "Ghetto speech" differed everywhere from the dialect of the surrounding neighbours, and it was derided by them with anger and hatred— *mauscheln: die schöne deutsche Sprache radebrechen* 'to speak like a Jew is to break the beautiful German language on the wheel'. All that made the Jew self conscious about his "Jüdisch-deutsch" and he "confessed" that he did change and hence "spoil" German; after all it was the Germans who "held the patent to German" and their speech must be the only legitimate and correct speech. This inferiority feeling with regard to Yiddish was so great that, in a bid at gaining Emancipation, the Jews of Germany in the second half of the eighteenth century deliberately abandoned Yiddish in favour of Standard German (= SG). Mendelssohn's SG translation of the Bible (1780-83) is the symbol for those strivings and marks the beginning of the end for Western Yiddish as a vehicle for serious literature. It was no longer "literaturfähig". It could only continue as a patois for humour or intimate use. Jospeh Herz typifies just such use.

There is a tragic irony in these efforts of German Jews to gain their neighbours' approval. David Friedländer, a coworker of Mendelssohn's, wrote an "Appeal to the German Jews" (*Sendschreiben an die deutsche* [sic!] *Juden,* 1786), pleading with them to give up their uncouth, irregular Jüdisch-deutsch that is (supposedly!) "so wild and lawless that it cripples the minds of their children to make them incapable even of thinking straight. How could they expect their neighbours to respect them, when they didn't even speak like human beings?"

Poor Friedländer! He could not have foreseen that the perfect SG of Jewish poets and thinkers would not save them from murder in the gas chambers of Hitler. And, in the very process of berating Yiddish for its "irregularities", poor Friedländer himself slips into these excellent "irregularities" unconsciously. Thus in the very title of his appeal there slipped in an error in German, but a precious improvement that SG would have done well to adopt, not from Yiddish (of course!), but from German living speech. In SG there are three adjective declensions—weak, strong and mixed. They are the bane of students: gut*er* Mann, d*er* gut*e* Mann, d*ie* gut*en* Männer, d*er* gut*en* Frau. In Yiddish the article and the adjective are analogically levelled: (d*er*) gut*er* man, d*i* (= [dɪ]) gut*e* (= [gútɪ]) mener, d*i* gut*e* froy, d*er* gut*er* froy. The different endings on articles and adjectives serve absolutely no useful purpose.

But the objectively more streamlined qualities of Yiddish could not be seen by friend or foe. The latter were blinded by hatred and bigotry, the former were dazed by the dazzling mirage of Emancipation and Enfranchisement. Between them it may therefore be truly said, Yiddish didn't just die in Germany, it was murdered deliberately.

Now to some details of Yiddish history proper:

Up to the First Crusade (1095) the speech of German Jews didn't differ much from the local German dialect of their nativity. It did differ *some:* in the specific vocabulary of Judaism (e.g. *toyre, kosher, khomets*); in calque—coinages via translating the Hebrew "literally", e.g. *kinign* 'be a king', 'be kinging' < Heb. *limlokh;* and finally in possible traces of Romance "accent" that may have persisted as an ancestral influence in an epoch of no common public schools and no "desegregation".

German Jews had to migrate perennially. On Slavic soil their language became their hallmark; hence they named it naturally: *Yidish* meaning 'Jewish' in Yiddish. Here special conditions (1500-1750) favoured its flourishing. These include and intensive independence (they were living in an Empire that had to tolerate multilingualism); compact masses (often constituting the majority in the small towns of Eastern Europe), an urban civilization that stood on a higher economic and cultural level than that of the feudal, rural environment (and people are reluctant to assimilate downward!); strong religious disciplines that limited contacts and favoured segregation by faith. Slavic influence now became paramount. It is obvious in phonology and lexicon (some 20% of the more than 200,000 words collected for the *Great Yiddish Dictionary*), less conspicuous in grammar and syntax, and most subtle yet pervasive, in semantics and the compound verb system. There is some evidence of a substratum of Slavic speaking Jews that merged with the more numerous immigrants from Germany.

As shown, from 1096 to 1348 "Jewish German" was in the process of evolving, independent of German *dialects,* but still participating in developments common to *all* German: the onset of New High German (= NHG) diphthongization ($\hat{\imath}, \hat{u}, iu > ei, au, eu$), monophthongizations (*ie, uo* $> \bar{\imath}, \bar{o}$), and lengthening of short vowels in open syllables (*săgen* > *sā-gen*). By 1350 MHG $\hat{a}$ was rounded to $\bar{o}$ in Yiddish. MHG *ou* and *ei* fell together into $\bar{a}$ in WY and became *oj* and *ej* respectively in EY, falling together into *ej* in NEY.

From 1350 to 1500 OLD YIDDISH became independent in sound and forms even of common German: e.g. MHG *ikh* (guttural) changed to *ich* (palatalized), but not in the bulk of Yiddish. In the MIDDLE YIDDISH period (1500–1750) MHG ă in open syllables (lengthened to $\bar{a}$ in NHG) became *o* throughout EY. It remained *o* only in NEY, gave *a* or *o* in WY, and became *u* in MEY by 1730. Both Yiddish and German reorganized their systems of plurals, future and conditional—independently of each other. Unstressed syllables were largely syncopated or apocopated: (*wartetet* > *wart*). Inflexions were reduced and simplified. By 1730 a most thorough going vowel shift transpired in MEY and SEY whereby $o > u$ and original $u > i$. In the NEW YIDDISH period (1750–today), the new sounds and forms evolved in EY emerge as a LITERARY NORM. New norms are established by Yiddish classic writers from Lefin (1749–1826) to Leyvik (1888–1962). They are the basis for the Standard Yiddish of today in which the vowels are based upon "Lithuanian" (NEY) while grammar is closer to "Polish" (MEY). On the stage "Ukranian" (SEY) predominates, because the founders of the Yiddish theatre were mostly from the Ukraine and Bessarabia.

By the nineteenth century Yiddish was carried the world over and became a world language. It then came again under a strong influence of modern German throught Secularist

and Labourist movements. There was even a conscious attempt to achieve "eloquence" by replacing forms with German (condemned now as *daytshmerish*) but national pride soon overcame this tendency.

In the first half of our century political ideologies stirred and divided the Jewish community, and Yiddish as an ideal became identified mostly with Autonomist, Secularist and Labourist parties, which generally rejected Zionism, Judaism and Hebrew. Zionism—because it was supposedly a romantic, superstitious delusion that diverted Jewish efforts from joining the common struggle for a just society right where they were. Judaism—because, according to Engels, Religion was "opium for the masses", used to lull them to submission to their oppressive masters with a promise of compensation in Eternity in Heaven. And Engels made no distinction between religions, and made no allowance for the clergy of oppressed minorities. So, Jewish radicals didn't either. Hebrew was dubbed by them the "croaked language" (*di gepeygerte shprakh*) which, in addition to being a corpse, was faulted for its association with Judaism and Zionism. The Yiddish language remained the only Jewish hallmark of the radicals and they became its champions and proclaimed it to be a national Jewish language (Tshernovits Conference 1908). Yiddish, in turn, was rejected by Assimilationists as a "jargon"; by Zionists, as an obstacle to the revival of Hebrew. The ultra orthodox, however, clung to Yiddish as a matter of "necessity": in their tradition Hebrew was considered too holy for profane use. From 1917 to 1948 Yiddish enjoyed the "special favour" of the Soviet government, which gave it official status as the only legitimate national language of the Jewish minority in the U.S.S.R., only to be cruelly liquidated together with all other Jewish identity elements and their champions (since 1948). In 1952 the leading Yiddish writers were murdered without trial in the Lubianka prison in Moscow at the behest of Stalin, and hundreds of Jewish artists and intellectuals, the total Jewish communal leadership (government-imposed though it was!) died a slow but horrible death in Soviet labour camps. The present Soviet policy continues Stalin's plan of forcing the Jews to give up their identity and assimilate: spiritual genocide.

Constant protests by the World P.E.N.C. as well as Communist groups outside of Russia resulted in the Soviet government's fostering a monthly journal in Yiddish (*Sovetish heymland*).

Elsewhere Yiddish networks of schools were established from kindergarten to postgraduate institutes. Yivo functions in part as a Yiddish language academy and has achieved wide recognition.

With Israel and Hebrew triumphing as the fulfillment of national Jewish aspirations, and with the consequent dwindling of the anti-Zionist and anti-Traditionalist ideologies, Yiddishism is no longer a militant rival of Hebrew. Now that the number of its speakers are declining there is a new nostalgia and love evidenced for it by Jews as well as non-Jews of all ideologies. They cherish it for its literary treasures and as a manifestation of the Jewish spirit.

Language & Communication, Vol. 7, Supplement, pp. 135–142, 1987.
Printed in Great Britain.

0271-5309/87 $3.00 + .00
Pergamon Journals Ltd.

RECONCEPTUALIZING THE GENESIS OF YIDDISH IN THE LIGHT OF ITS NON-NATIVE COMPONENTS

PAUL WEXLER

Tel Aviv University

It was Max Weinreich, more than any other linguist, who elaborated the theory that the Yiddish language was created around the 10th century by French and Italian Jews who settled in the Rhineland and secondarily in Regensburg (Weinreich 1940: 30, 35–6; 1954: 1956a,b; 1973). In Weinreich's view three to four centuries were to pass before Yiddish would begin its 700-year contact with the Slavic languages, first on the bilingual German-Slavic territory of Eastern Germany and shortly afterwards, in Bohemia. Weinreich credited the Judeo-Romance substratum in Yiddish with introducing a number of Judeo-Greek, Hebrew and Judeo-Aramaic components into the emerging Rhineland Yiddish dialects. Finally, Weinreich theorized that an influx of "Oriental" Jews in the 12th–13th centuries brought about a change in the Ashkenazic pronunciation norms of Hebrew (Weinreich 1: 1973: 30ff.). Weinreich's views on the genesis of Yiddish have enjoyed wide currency in Yiddish linguistic circles (see Joffe 1954: 121; Bin-Nun 1973: 26ff.; S. A. Birnbaum 1979: 16, 58; Fuks in this volume). The Romance theory finds its *raison d'être* in a number of facts: (1) First and foremost, there are a number of French and Italian elements in Yiddish, especially in the Western dialects, which differ radically from the surface cognates in German, or don't exist at all in German. (2) The Rhineland cities have the earliest mention of Jewish settlements in the German lands, while Jewish settlement in Bavaria and Franconia is attested only later, e.g. Augsburg in the mid-13th century (Weinreich 1940: 36). (3) The oldest monuments of Jewish settlement in Germany, e.g. ritual baths, synagogues, cemeteries, are found exclusively in the Rhineland and neighbouring Hessen (see Brann, *et al.,* 1934).

Today, the arguments for a Judeo-Romance substratum in Yiddish (as well as the claims of a post-natal contact with Slavic and an "Oriental" origin of the contemporary Ashkenazic pronunciation norms of Hebrew) look far less convincing. In this paper, I will show that the Judeo-Romance substratum is far less important than Weinreich and others imagined, while a (Judeo-) Slavic and (Judeo-) Greek substratum were also present at the birth of Yiddish. The genesis of the Ashkenazic pronunciation norms of Hebrew—both the merged and the whole variants—is omitted in the present discussion: see Faber and Katz in the present volume.

There are probably two reasons why Weinreich was inclined to posit a Judeo-Romance substratum on the basis of the handful of French and Italian elements unique to Yiddish (primarily in the dialects spoken between Holland and the Western Danubian lands). (1) First, Weinreich had disqualified the other non-native elements found in early Yiddish from participation in the birth of the language: Judeo-Greek elements were attributed either to the Judeo-Romance substratum or to indirect borrowing through Hebrew and Judeo-Aramaic texts, while the first Slavic contacts with Yiddish were localized in the Lusatian

and Bohemian lands where the first notice of Ashkenazic Jews dates only from the 12th century. (2) The absence of detailed information about the geography of the non-native components in German and other Western Yiddish dialects made it difficult for Weinreich to reconstruct relative chronologies and paths of diffusion. Yet, though the data from the *Language and Culture Atlas of Ashkenazic Jewry,* which were being collected in the early 1960s, would have given cause for re-thinking (see Herzog, ed., ms), the fields of colonial Judeo-Greek and Judeo-Slavic linguistics were too poorly developed to offer the Yiddishist much insight (see Wexler, 1985a, 1986 for a summation of achievements and challenges for the future).

Now, even if we leave linguistic geography and the other non-native substrata aside, the Judeo-Romance hypothesis has a number of shortcomings: (1) The age of most Romance elements in Western Yiddish has never been established. (The very fact that most of the components are now found in the Yiddish of southwest Germany and Switzerland suggests a rather recent dating—certainly several centuries after the reputed birth of Yiddish.) (2) Many Yiddish romanicisms are also shared by Middle High German and contemporary German dialects, and thus may have reached Yiddish via German and not via any Judeo-French community of speakers. A comparison of German Yiddish and German shows that the latter was far more receptive to Romance elements than Yiddish—a fact which seriously argues against a Judeo-Romance substratal hypothesis (see Müller and Frings 2: 1968). (3) The absence of mention of Jews in German archival materials outside the Rhineland for the 11-12th centuries may be due to chance (see also Faber's remarks in this volume). Weinreich also overlooked the evidence of a Jewish presence in Anhalt, Saxony and Bohemia in the pre-Ashkenazic period (see Wexler 1986). (4) Finally, Weinreich apparently failed to appreciate sufficiently the fact that northern Italy, one of the reputed homelands of the first Yiddish speakers, had been in large part Greek-speaking through the 8th century, and that parts of Bavaria and Franconia were still Slavic-speaking at the time of Jewish settlement (see Schwarz 1960).

In the discussion below I will examine the geographical parameters of the four major non-native Jewish substrata in Western Yiddish: Judeo-Romance, Judeo-Greek, Judeo-Slavic and Hebrew-Judeo-Aramaic. The emerging picture suggests very dramatically that the Bavarian-Franconian area played a significant role in shaping the pattern of isogloss diffusion within southern Germany as a whole in the first few centuries of the present millenium. Elements that find their way into Bavaria and Franconia across the Alps from northern Italy and along the Danube waterway from the Balkans are often diffused to Southwest German, Swiss, Alsatian and Dutch Yiddish—and sometimes, even beyond into Judeo-French territory—as well as into the Yiddish dialects that were to take shape in the Slavic lands. Conversely, Rhineland-Hessian features hardly penetrate to southwest Germany and beyond. The border between the two spheres of influence in Germany is difficult to define at this stage with any precision. The examples presented below constitute but a fraction of the data assembled (further examples and discussion are available in Wexler 1986). Finally, I will conclude with a list of research topics which immediately beg attention from Yiddish and German specialists.

The reader may well ask why the non-native Jewish components in Yiddish rather than the native Germanic component itself are being utilized to uncover the place of Yiddish genesis in Germany. Certainly a complete picture will require a consideration of all the facts. Yet, non-native components unique to Yiddish offer a distinct advantage at this preliminary stage of our investigations. While an analysis of contemporary Eastern Yiddish

dialects strongly suggests that these dialects are most closely connected with Bavarian German (see also King and Marchand in this volume), the "linkage" of Eastern Yiddish with Bavarian German would hardly enable us to recover the relationship between the two earliest centers of post-Roman Jewish settlement in the German lands—the Rhineland-Hessen and Franconian-Bavarian variants, and might even prove to be historically untenable. That is, features now associated with the Bavarian area (e.g. Yiddish *haynt*— Bavarian rural *haynt* vs. standard German *heute* 'today') might have enjoyed broader expanse in earlier periods. Moreover, the technique of matching cognates in German and Yiddish might well impel us to define the latter as a mosaic of bits and pieces of many dialects of the non-Jewish cognate language—a development that is hardly commensurate with the known facts of Jewish settlement history in the territory and with our knowledge of how mixed dialects arise (on the dangers of this approach, see Wexler 1977: 163ff.).

The existence of a Yiddish dialect atlas at Columbia University (now in press) and studies in Judeo-Slavic and Judeo-Greek linguistics put the Yiddishist in the enviable position of being able to reconstruct some elements of early Yiddish dialect makeup in the German lands. The sources and etyma of the examples cited below are discussed in detail in Wexler 1986 and thus need not be repeated here.

I. The Jewish linguistic substratum in the Rhineland appears to be limited almost exclusively to the area west of Franconia and Bavaria; only rarely do these elements appear east of the home area—and even more rarely, in Yiddish dialects spoken in the Slavic lands.

1. (Judeo-)French:
(a) elements limited to the area west of Franconia-Bavaria: *bafen* 'to drink'; *dormen* 'to sleep'; *piltsl* 'girl (servant)'; *praayen* 'beg'; *shpozering* 'wedding ring'.
(b) elements found to the west, and partly to the east of Franconia-Bavaria: *o(o)rn* 'to pray' (unless this is from Italian?); *porshn* 'remove the impurities from meat in order to render it kosher'.
(c) an element found extensively in both Southeastern and Southwestern Germany and in the Slavic lands: (newer) *shaalet ~ shoolet* (West) vs. (older) *tsholnt* (East) 'Sabbath food prepared on Friday'. I know of no other certain examples. The possibility that Eastern Yiddish *tsholnt* is derived from a Rheto-romance or northern Italian dialect rather than from French needs to be explored.

2. Judeo-French grecisms are found only in the Rhineland and adjoining areas: **tolme* 'wedding canopy' (see synonymous Judeo-Spanish *talamo*); *miniç* 'food that is neither meat nor dairy' (vs. Middle High German *münich* 'castrated horse').

3. Judeo-French hebraisms and pronunciation norms:
(a) primarily west of Franconia-Bavaria: *ħet* = /h, Ø/ as in *icik, sime* anthroponyms and *mekn* 'erase' (< Hebrew *jicħāq, śimħāh, māħaq* 'he erased'). The Hebrew component of German slang lexicons generally follows the geographical parameters of the Hebrew component in Yiddish, e.g. Hebrew *lɛħɛm* 'bread' > German *leem,* etc. in Basel (15th century-1733), Berne (1900), Luxembourg (1937), Karlsruhe (1820), Württemberg (18th-20th centuries), Konstanz (1791), Dutch (*Liber Vagatorum,* 1547); reflexes without *ħet* are also found sporadically east and north of this area, but only in recent lists, e.g. Regensburg (1900), Linz (1835), Vienna (1966), Madgeburg (1843), Berlin (1813) (see data in Wexler ms).

(b) *qaama(a)c* = /ˈaː/: *ba(a)kher* 'young seminary student; Jewish religious teacher'; *kʰaal* 'Jewish community'.

(c) lexical items: *nedunye* 'dowry' (< Aramaic); *mees* 'money' (< Hebrew *māʿōt*)

II. In contrast to the Jewish substrata in Southwestern Germany, the Jewish substrata in the Bavarian-Franconian area enjoy broad diffusion both to the west and to the east (including the Slavicized dialects of Yiddish).

1. (Judeo-) Italian: *bentshn* 'bless' (for the unlikelihood of a French etymology, see Berger 1899); *leyenen,* etc. 'read'; Eastern Yiddish (and Southeast German Yiddish?) *fatshayle* 'kerchief, shawl' < Venetian Italian *faziol,* etc., resembles Hungarian *fátyol,* Croatian *fačol,* etc., Byzantine Greek *fakiőlin,* Rumanian *fachiol,* Albanian *faqéll* 'veil' vs. Bavarian German *fazinetl,* etc. 'handkerchief'. I cannot date the age of the Yiddish form, but Hungarian *fátyol* is attested since 1250 (Benkő 1967-1984). The German borrowing, first attested in 1478–9, is clearly independent of the Yiddish form, i.e. < Italian *fazzoletto* (see discussion in Öhmann 1942:29; Wis 1955: 265–6; Skok 1971–4). On the spread of north Italian elements to Hungarian, see Muljačić 1983:246. On Bavarian Yiddish membership in the Danube Sprachbund, see below.

2. Judeo-Italian or Balkan grecisms: *trop* 'accent; cantillation of Hebrew texts' (also found as far west as Judeo-French in the 11th century but unknown in other Judeo-Romance communities); *katoves* 'jesting'; *dukes* 'duke' (ultimately from Latin *dux* 'leader' and also found on Judeo-Polish coins of the 12th-13th centuries); *kile* 'hernia' (unless a later borrowing from Western or Eastern Slavic): *sender* male anthroponym < *Alexander* (~ Hungarian *Sándor,* Italian *Sandro,* etc.); Old Franconian Yiddish **pinkosh* 'Christian Pentecost' (early 1400s) (see also Hungarian *pünkösd* 1138ff), Saxon German *pincoston* vs. standard German, Old German Yiddish [*Dukus Horant* 1382] *Pfingsten,* both < Greek *pentakostē.* It may be possible to define the area of Franconia-Bavaria as an area which preserved a knowledge of Greek longer than those German territories to the west, since in the former areas(?) and in slavicized Yiddish Greek anthroponyms may be translated into Slavic, while the preservation of Greek anthroponyms in southwestern Germany may attest to ignorance of Greek (see also Bavarian Yiddish **pinkosh* above, which is closer to the Greek etymon), e.g. *todres* male anthroponym (West) vs. *badane(s)* feminine, family name (now attested only in Lithuania; see Belorussian *Bahdana* feminine anthroponym). A problem both for Yiddish and German linguistics is to differentiate grecisms which entered across the Alps from grecisms which were diffused via the Danube (see Müller and Frings II: 1968: 100).

3. A Judeo-Italian Hebraism (of Judeo-Greek origin?): *tfile* 'prayerbook' (< Hebrew *tfillāh* 'prayer'). The hebraism with this innovative meaning is also found in Judeo-Provençal, Judeo-Italian and Balkan Judeo-Spanish—all areas historically in contact with Greek—vs. the use of Hebrew *maḥzōr* for 'prayerbook' in Judeo-French.

4. (Judeo-)West Slavic: *par(a)kh* 'skin disease; Jew (pejorative)'; *kowlech* 'festive bread' (also in 11th century Judeo-French); *krejn* 'horseradish' (surface cognates of *kowlech* and *krejn* only appear in Eastern German and Austrian German dialects); *nebič* unfortunate person'; *zlate ~ zlote* feminine anthroponym; *treyb(er)n* = Western Yiddish *porshn* cited in section I.1.b above (marginally attested in northwest Germany, and possibly of Balkan Slavic origin?). A number of Yiddish slavicisms which could plausibly be derived from Polish or an Eastern Slavic language may in fact prove to be of Sorbian or Czech origin.

Examples might be *blintse* 'pancake' (the term appears to be found only in Sorbian and Eastern Slavic); *yoykh* 'broth'.

5. Judeo-Slavic or Balkan Judeo-Greek iranianisms: *dav(e)nen* 'pray (of Jews)' < Iranian language? < Arabic *duwa* 'prayer'; according to Herzog, ed., ms (questionnaire #229018), the term is now attested at points quite far to the west, e.g. in the Rhineland and Luxembourg. *Shabash* 'tip paid to musicians by guests at a wedding' and *shibesh* 'trifle, small coin' < Iranian *shabash* 'tip at a wedding'. The term is first attested in a Rhineland Hebrew text from the 13th-14th century; surface cognates exist in German, Hungarian, Polish, Czech and Eastern Slavic slang lexicons in the meaning 'money' and in the standard Eastern Slavic languages in the meanings 'enough; stop work; wood fragments taken home by carpenters after the day's work'.

6. A Judeo-East and Judeo-West Slavic hebraism < (?) a Judeo-Turkic community: *peysekh* 'Passover', used as a male anthroponym. The name is attested in Turkic (including among 10th century Ukrainian Khazars), Iranian, Slavic, Hungarian and Eastern German lands but rare in the western German lands; the name is unknown in Judeo-Romance speech territory. In some German documents of the 16th century, the name appears with a final -*k*—which is reminiscent of Old South Polish phonological norms, but hardly required by German phonotactics, see e.g. Polish *Pessac* (Wrocław 1351–6); German *Petsak* (Wiener-Neustadt 1455), *Pessak* (15th century).

7. Judeo-West Slavic hebraisms. Compare with terms in section I.3. a-b-c above.
   (a) *ḥeṭ* = /x/
   (b) *qāmac* = /o/: *bokher* 'young seminary student'; *kool ~ kuul*
   (c) *nādān,* etc. (< Hebrew); *moos*
In Eastern Slavic languages and occasionally Polish, Hebrew loans with *qāmac* also appear with /a/, e.g. Belorussian *kahal* 'crowd of people; Jewish community organization'; *baxur* 'young unmarried (Jew); fat boy; child born out of wedlock' etc. The fact that Eastern Slavic- and Romance-speaking Jews apparently pronunced *qāmac* as /a/ suggests that the present-day Ashkenazic pronunciation of *qāmac* as /o/ ~ /u/ may have originated in the Bavarian-Franconian territory (among Judeo-West Slavic or Judeo-Greek speakers?) (see Wexler 1983 for further Slavic documentation).

8. Finally, in Southeast German and in part German Yiddish, there are two expressions found in both Judeo-Greek and Judeo-Aramaic which are shared with some languages of the Danube Sprachbund, e.g. Czech, Hungarian, Croatian and Rumanian:
(a) Greek *pinaks* 'board' > Judeo-Aramaic *pīnxā'* 'dish' > German *Pinke(-pinke),* Dutch slang *ping-ping* 'money', Czech, Hungarian *pinka* 'box for money paid to innkeeper by cardplayers', Bavarian German slang (Schopfloch) *pinkl* 'business record book' vs. Eastern (and Southeastern German?) Yiddish *pinkes* 'protocol' (< Hebrew *pinqās* < Greek *pinaks*). The original Greek term is still attested in Dalmatian and Bosnian Judeo-Spanish *pinak,* plural *pinakes* 'protocol'. The kernel of the Danube Sprachbund coincides with Roman Pannonia (Western Hungary, Northern Yugoslavia and Eastern Austria, bounded in the north and east by the Danube River). On the existence of the Danube Sprachbund, see H. Birnbaum (1984–5: 83).

(b) Judeo-Aramaic *yōmā' rabbā'* 'Yom Kippur' (literally 'the great day') > Judeo-Greek *hē megalē hēmera* > German *der lange Tag* (also described as Yiddish by Antoni Margaritha, a Yiddish speaker probably hailing from Regensburg, in 1530), Hungarian *hosszúnap,* Czech

dlouhý den. See also Balkan Judeo-Spanish *el dia grande* 'Tisha be'av; day of an important event, e.g. marriage'.

These examples are extremely important for establishing the possibility of a Greek (and Aramaic?) Jewry in areas where Yiddish was eventually to penetrate.

For an example of a Yiddish italianism shared with languages in the Danube Sprachbund, see section II. 1 above. For a discussion of where Greek and Aramaic inscriptions have been found along the Danube, see Wexler 1986, section 3.

On the strength of the above examples, I draw the following conclusions:

(1) The German lands in the beginning of the second millenium harboured two very different "Ashkenazic" Jewish communities: a slavicized (and monolingual Slavic?) and hellenized Yiddish community in the southeast and a romanicized Yiddish community in the southwest.

(2) Bavarian-Franconian Yiddish frequently lines up with languages in the Danube Sprachbund more systematically than Bavarian-Franconian German itself.

(3) The presence of Judeo-Italian, Slavic, Greek, Iranian and a possibly Turkic Hebrew anthroponym in both Southeast and Southwest German Yiddish—and on occasion even in Judeo-French of the 11th century (in Rashi's commentaries) vs. the relative absence of Judeo-French elements east of the Rhineland shows dramatically that Bavarian-Franconian Yiddish had a considerable impact on the Yiddish spoken in southwest Germany.

(4) The diffusion of linguistic elements from Southeast German Yiddish to Southwest German Yiddish (and Judeo-French) finds a parallel in German dialectology, with regard to Greek elements; see e.g. French *samedi* 'Saturday' < German *Samstag* < Balkan(?) Judeo-Greek *sambata* (see Müller and Frings 1: 1966: 30–1, 33, 39, 56, fn. 1 and map #3, and 2: 1968; 165–7, 318 for other examples).

(5) Modern Dutch and Southeast German Yiddish dialects often show close parallels vs. Southwest German Yiddish; e.g. Dutch, Southeast German Yiddish have reflexes of Hebrew *nādān* 'dowry' vs. Southwest German Yiddish *nedunye* < Aramaic (would this isogloss configuration also apply to West Slavicisms?). This phenomenon could be explained in three ways: (a) Rhineland and Southeast German Yiddish differed from one another as early as the 10th century due to the differential impact of Romance vs. Slavic-Greek substrata. (b) Rhineland Yiddish was originally similar in its non-native component makeup to non-Rhineland Yiddish but gradually came to deviate from the latter due to a strong Judeo-French superstratum, introduced after the expulsion of the Jews from France at the end of the 14th century. (c) Contemporary Rhineland Yiddish did not come into existence until after the 14th century with the settlement of French Jews. In keeping with the last explanation, present-day Rhineland Yiddish could be defined as historically more recent than all other forms of Western Yiddish. Now, if we accept the possibility of two cradles of Yiddish—separated chronologically as well as geographically—then we should also entertain the possibility that the process of judaizing non-Jewish languages in southwest and southeast Germany might have assumed radically different forms. This could account for the existence of Western Yiddish texts (from the southwest?) which bare an extremely close similarity to contemporaneous German; see also the striking difference in the use of the preterite in "Western" and "Eastern" Yiddish noted by King in this volume. In fact, Jewish linguistic creativity has often been known to assume heterogeneous forms in the same speech territory (see Wexler 1981: 104–8). In the case of Germany more recently,

note the co-existence of German Yiddish and Ashkenazes (a late 18th-early 19th century judaized standard German written in Yiddish characters but also differing marginally in lexicon from standard German). Future studies should attempt to determine whether two kinds of Yiddish developed in the German lands—a Southwest German Yiddish that developed on a Judeo-French substratum (between the 10th and 14th century) and a Southeast German Yiddish which developed on a Slavic-Greek (-Italian) (and other?) substratum as early as the 10th century.

(6) In the southeast German lands we may speak of a penetrating mixing of Slavic and Germanic in both the German and German Jewish communities—with the important difference that in the former speech community, German influenced Slavic more than it was influenced by Slavic, while among the Jews, Slavic had an important impact on the emerging German Yiddish (not to mention the Yiddish of the monolingual Slavic lands), before it became assimilated to the latter in Germany and in the Bohemian lands.

(7) If the Greek-Slavic (-Italian) substratum at the birth of Yiddish is correct, then the linguistic facts will have proven to have been far more revealing than historic documentation.

Problems for future research:

(1) Historians must assess the implications of the linguistic findings for the description of Jewish settlement history in northern Europe in the late first and early second millennium AD.

(2) It will be necessary to establish whether the putative isogloss configurations we have suggested here (separating the Rhineland-Hessen area from Bavaria-Franconia) are compatible with Max Weinreich's suggestion that the Upper Elbe River constituted a significant boundary between a slavicized and non-slavicized Ashkenazic community.

(3) What is the relative chronology of the diffusion of elements from Bavarian-Franconian (-Danubian) Yiddish to Southwest German Yiddish?

(4) What is the historical relationship between Southwest and Southeast German Yiddish in all periods (see also discussion above)?

(5) The age of the non-native components in Yiddish must be determined with greater precision. It may ultimately be necessary to regard a number of the examples cited above as ad- or even superstrata rather than substrata.

(6) Is it necessary to assume that Slavic and Oriental elements diffused progressively westward or might they have appeared first in Southwest German Yiddish territory and then spread to the southeast?

(7) What, if any, is the significance of the fact that west slavicisms appear as far west as Dutch and Alsatian Yiddish while iranianisms appear rather more sporadically in western German territory and not at all in Alsace, Switzerland and Holland?

To summarize, the facts of linguistic geography and substral components force us to conclude that Max Weinreich's model of the genesis of Yiddish is essentially wrong in most of its details. But Weinreich deserves no small credit for the reconceptualizing. After all, our conclusions were made possible largely because of the wealth of assiduously documented materials which Weinreich himself assembled and because of his insistence that Yiddish be studied in a comparative framework of Jewish linguistic creativity. Weinreich probably could not have suspected that when he put forward the notion of judaized dialects of Slavic in a systematic manner for the first time in his pioneering article of 1956b, he was defining

an area of study which was to hold the key to unraveling the mystery of where and when Yiddish was created. Thus, while the field of Judeo-Slavic was first defined by a Yiddishist, it is Judeo-Slavic that is helping Yiddishists to illuminate the genesis of Yiddish.

REFERENCES

BENKŐ, L. (ed.) 1967–84 *A magyar nyelv történeti-etimológiai szótára* Vol. 1–4. Akadémiai Kiadó, Budapest.

BERGER, H. 1899 *Die Lehnwörter in der französischen Sprache ältester Zeit.* O. R. Reisland, Leipzig.

BIN-NUN, J. 1973 *Jiddisch und die deutschen Mundarten unter besonderer Berücksichtigung des ostgalizischen Jiddisch.* Max Niemeyer, Tübingen.

BIRNBAUM, H. 1984–5 A typological view of Serbo-Croatian: some preliminary considerations. *Zbornik matice srpske za filologiju i lingvistiku* **27–8,** 72–84.

BIRNBAUM, S. A. 1979 *Yiddish. A Survey and a Grammar.* Manchester University, Manchester and University of Toronto, Toronto.

BRANN, M. *et al.* (eds) 1934 *Germania judaica* 1. Gesellschaft zur Förderung der Wissen. des Jundentums Breslau, J. C. B. Mohr, Tübingen, 1963.

HERZOG, M. (ed.) (in press) *Language and Culture Atlas of Ashkenazic Jewry,* Vol. 1.

JOFFE, J. A. 1954 Dating the origin of Yiddish dialects. In Weinreich, U. pp. 102–21.

JOFFE, J. A., MARK, Y. *et al.* (eds) 1961ff *Groyser verterbukh fun der yidisher shprakh* 1ff. New York, Jerusalem.

MULJAČIĆ, Ž. 1983 Sui venezianismi nello slavo balcanico occidentale (Aspetti storici—principi metodologici—compiti futuri). In Günter, H. and Metzeltin, M. (eds), *Linguistica e dialettologia veneta. Studi offerti a Manlio Cortelazzo dai colleghi stranieri,* pp. 243–51. Gunther Narr Tübingen.

MÜLLER, G. and FRINGS, T. 1966–68 *Germania romana* 1–2. VEB Max Niemeyer, Halle, Saale.

ÖHMANN, E. 1942 Zum sprachlichen Einfluss Italiens auf Deutschland VIII. *Neuphilologische Mitteilungen* **43,** 20–30.

SCHWARZ, E. 1960 *Sprache und Siedlung in Nordostbayern.* Hans Carl, Nürnberg.

SKOK, P. 1971–4 *Etimologijski rječnik hrvatskoga ili srpskoga jazika* Vol. 1–4. Jugoslavenska Akademija Znanosti i Umjetnosti, Zagreb.

WEINREICH, M. 1940 Yidish. In *Algemeyne entsiklopedye. Yidn B,* columns 23–90. Tsiko, Paris.

WEINREICH, M. 1954 Prehistory and early history of Yiddish: facts and conceptual framework. In Weinreich, U. pp. 73–101.

WEINREICH, M. 1956a The Jewish languages of Romance stock and their relation to earliest Yiddish. *Romance Philology* **9,** 403–428.

WEINREICH, M. 1956b Yiddish, Knaanic, Slavic: the basic relationships. Halle, M. *et al.* (ed.), *For Roman Jakobson: Essays on the occasion of his sixtieth birthday,* pp. 622–632. Mouton, The Hague.

WEINREICH, M. 1973 *Geshikhte fun der yidisher shprakh* Vol. 1–4. Yivo, New York.

WEINREICH, U. (ed.) 1954 *The Field of Yiddish.* [Publications of the Linguistic Circle of New York, 3]. New York.

WEXLER, P. 1977 Ascertaining the position of Judezmo within Ibero-Romance. *Vox romanica* **36,** 162–195.

WEXLER, P. 1981 Jewish interlinguistics: facts and conceptual framework. *Language* **57**(1), 99–149.

WEXLER, P. 1983 Hebräische und aramäische Elemente in den slavischen Sprachen: Wege, Chronologien, Diffusionsgebiete. *Zeitschrift für slavische Philologie* **43**(2), 229–279.

WEXLER, P. 1985a Recovering the dialects and sociology of Judeo-Greek in non-Hellenic Europe. In Fishman, J. A. (ed.), *Readings in the sociology of Jewish Languages,* Vol. 1, pp. 227–240. E. J. Brill, Leiden.

WEXLER, P. 1985b The role of Yiddish in the recovery of Slavic linguistic history. *Die Welt der Slaven* **30**(1), 1–23.

WEXLER, P. 1986 *Explorations in Judeo-Slavic linguistics.* E. J. Brill, Leiden.

WEXLER, P. ms. Three heirs to a Judeo-Latin legacy: Judeo-Ibero-Romance, Yiddish and Rotwelsch. To appear in the *Mediterranean Language and Culture Monograph Series.* Harrassowitz, Wiesbaden.

WIS, M. 1955 *Ricerche sopra gli italianismi nella lingua tedesca. Dalla metà del secolo XIV alla fine del secolo XVI.* Società Neofilologica, Helsinki.

Language & Communication, Vol. 7, Supplement, p. 143, 1987.
Printed in Great Britain.

0271-5309/87 $3.00+.00
Pergamon Journals Ltd.

SYMPOSIUM PROGRAMME

Sunday 15 December 1985

Welcoming Address by Dr Geza Vermes, Reader in Jewish Studies in the University of Oxford and Professorial Fellow at Wolfson College, Oxford.

Monday 16 December 1985

Morning Session—Chair: Professor Robert D. King
Paul Wexler, Reconceptualizing the Genesis of Yiddish in the Light of Non-Native Components.

David Neal Miller, Transgressing the Bounds: On the Origins of Yiddish Literature.

Christopher Hutton, Negation in Yiddish and Historical Reconstruction.

Solomon A. Birnbaum, Two Methods: 1. Paleography: Old Yiddish Manuscripts (in Yiddish; read by Shmuel Hiley); 2. Etymology: dávənən (read by Devra Asher).

Afternoon Session—Chair: Professor Wolf Moskovich
Jean Lowenstamm, Absolute Neutralization in Yiddish: Synchronic and Diachronic Consequences.

Leo Fuks, Reflections on the Romance Elements in Old Yiddish (read by Lindsay Levy).

Alice Faber, A Tangled Web: Whole Hebrew and Ashkenazic Origins.

Dovid Katz, The Proto Dialectology of Ashkenaz (in Yiddish).

Tuesday 17 December 1985

Morning Session—Chair: Professor F. E. Knowles and Professor Paul Wexler
Robert D. King, Proto Yiddish Morphology.

James W. Marchand, Proto Yiddish and the Glosses: Can We Reconstruct Proto Yiddish?

Hugh Denman, Comments on Professor Lowenstamm's Paper.

Nathan Susskind, A Partisan History of Yiddish (read by Elliot Gertel).

Afternoon Session—Chair: Professor James W. Marchand
Dov-Ber Kerler, Prewar Soviet Theories on the Origins of Yiddish (in Yiddish).

Wolf Moskovich, Postwar Soviet Theories on the Origins of Yiddish.

M. N. Rosenfeld, The Origins of Yiddish Printing.

Hermann Süss, The Oldest Yiddish Book.

Language & Communication, Vol. 7, Supplement, p. 144, 1987.
Printed in Great Britain.

0271-5309/87 $3.00 + .00
Pergamon Journals Ltd.

REGISTERED PARTICIPANTS

Ms Devra Asher, St Cross College, Oxford.

Ms Dafna Clifford, Oxford.

Mr Hugh Denman, Queen's University, Belfast.

Professor Alice Faber, University of Florida.

Mr Elliot Hersch Gertel, Lincoln College, Oxford.

Dr Barbara Gorayska, University College, London.

Mr Dieter Herde, London.

Mr Shumel Hiley, London.

Mr Christopher Hutton, Oxford Centre for Postgraduate Hebrew Studies and Wolfson College, Oxford.

Dr Dovid Katz, Oxford Centre for Postgraduate Hebrew Studies and St Antony's College, Oxford.

Mr Dov-Ber Kerler, Oxford Centre for Postgraduate Hebrew Studies and Lincoln College, Oxford.

Professor Robert D. King, University of Texas, Austin.

Professor F. E. Knowles, Aston University, Birmingham.

Ms Lindsay Levy, Wolfson College, Oxford.

Ms G. L. Lewis, St Antony's College, Oxford.

Professor Jean Lowenstamm, Université du Québec à Montréal.

Professor James W. Marchand, University of Illinois, Urbana.

Professor David Neal Miller, Ohio State University, Columbus.

Professor Wolf Moskovich, Hebrew University, Jerusalem.

Dr David Patterson, Oxford Center for Postgraduate Hebrew Studies and St Cross College, Oxford.

Dr M. N. Rosenfeld, Rose Chemicals Ltd, London.

Dr L. Sieffert, Hertford College, Oxford.

Mr Hermann Süss, German Federal Railways, Munich.

Ms Heather Mary Valencia, University of Stirling.

Professor Paul Wexler, Tel Aviv University.

Professor Frederick A. De Wolff, University of Leiden.

Language & Communication, Vol. 7, Supplement, p. 145, 1987.
Printed in Great Britain.

0271-5309/87 $3.00 + .00
Pergamon Journals Ltd.

ANNOUNCEMENTS

The Oxford Winter Symposium in Yiddish Language and Literature is held each year in mid December on Monday and Tuesday of the last week of Oxford Michaelmas Term.
For further information, please contact:

The Fellow in Yiddish Studies,
Oxford Centre for Postgraduate Hebrew Studies,
45 St. Giles,
Oxford OX1 3LW
U.K.

The Oxford Summer Programme in Yiddish Language and Literature, an intensive four week summer course, is held each year in the month of August at four levels:
Yiddish I (elementary)
Yiddish II (intermediate)
Yiddish III (higher intermediate)
Yiddish IV (advanced).

For more information, please contact:

The Administrative Director,
Oxford Programme in Yiddish,
Oxford Centre for Postgraduate Hebrew Studies,
45 St. Giles,
Oxford OX1 3LW
U.K.